INVENTING THE NATION

General Editor: Keith Robbins

Also in the Inventing the Nation series:

India and Pakistan	Ian Talbot
Russia	Vera Tolz
Italy	Nick Doumanis
China	Henrietta Harrison
Ireland	R.V. Comerford
Germany	Stefan Berger

France

Timothy Baycroft

First published in Great Britain in 2008 by
Hodder Education, part of Hachette Livre UK
338 Euston Road, London NW1 3BH

www.hoddereducation.com

Hachette Livre UK's policy is to use papers that are natural, renewable and recyclable products and made from wood grown in sustainable forests. The logging and manufacturing processes are expected to conform to the environmental regulations of the country of origin.

British Library Cataloguing in Publication Data
A catalogue record for this book is available from the British Library

Library of Congress Cataloging-in-Publication Data
A catalog record for this book is available from the Library of Congress

ISBN 978 0340 705704

1 2 3 4 5 6 7 8 9 10

Typeset in 10/12pt Sabon by Dorchester Typesetting Group Ltd
Printed and bound in Great Britain by CPI Antony Rowe.

Contents

List of illustrations

For Christine

Acknowledgements

No work such as this is ever accomplished on its own, and I have benefited from discussions, debates and suggestions from many colleagues, students, friends and family during its preparation, which helped to clarify my thinking on many points. For their financial support, I would like to thank the Arts and Humanities Research Council, the British Academy and the Department of History at the University of Sheffield. Among those who have given me helpful advice, I would like in particular to thank Máire Cross, Suzannah Rockett, W. Jack Rhoden, Jennifer Farrar, the anonymous readers and the series editor, Keith Robbins, all of whom made numerous helpful suggestions. The team at Hodder Education have also been extremely patient and efficient. Finally I would like to thank my family, who have put up with the quirks and impatience I have often displayed while working on the book, and in particular my wife Christine, whose support, advice and help have been invaluable, and without which I would never have been able to complete this work.

The authors and publishers would like to thank the following for kind permission to reproduce illustrations:

Figure 1: Art Construction
Figure 2: © Francis G. Mayer/CORBIS
Figure 3: Keystone/Hulton Archive/Getty Images
Figure 4: akg-images
Figure 5: © Goldberg Diego/Corbis Sygma
Figure 6: INTERFOTO Pressebildagentur/Alamy
Figure 7: The Art Archive/Musée des 2 Guerres Mondiales Paris/Gianni Dagli Orti
Figure 8: © Jerome Prebois/Kipa/Corbis
Figure 9: © Bettman/CORBIS
Figure 10: Jack Guez/AFP/Getty Images

Introduction

Given the intensity of nationalist wars and conflicts in the past two hundred years, the question of understanding the rise and development of nations and nationalism has perplexed many a scholar, politician or citizen of the globe. Debates have flourished regarding the origin of nations, how they should be defined, understood and classified, and why they appear in some historical circumstances and not in others. Not only does their immense diversity across time and space give rise to significant differences between them, but nations are also extremely difficult to objectify because of their very nature. States have populations, territories and can be quantified in a variety of means, but nations are the emotional, conceptual, imagined entities behind, beyond or within the states, which have a reality primarily through their representations and the understanding of those who consider themselves to be their members. Without denying their reality as a part of the lived experience of their populations, nations are nevertheless fundamentally mythical. Because of their abstract nature, nations are never constant across a particular moment, and they change over time, grow, evolve and, dare one say, 'mature'. Their attributes and characteristics will also vary according to the experience and perception of the individual. Age, gender, socio-economic background, birthplace, religion, education, ethnicity and any number of other factors will alter how an individual understands, defines and represents his or her nation. Their subjective, mythical, even abstract qualities have lead to the interpretation that nations are invented.

What does it mean to invent a nation? Not to conjure it up out of nothing, or to make up something which has no basis in reality, but to endow certain societies, cultures or territories with the 'mythical' qualities that make them nations. Mythical in this sense does not imply false, only that reality becomes charged with meaning such that real events, people or places acquire symbolic significance as 'national'. An individual becomes a national hero, a battle becomes an event during which a nation was born, a region becomes a national homeland, and a cultural practice becomes a national tradition, each of which eventually serves as a source of identification and identity for the members of the nation.[1] In a similar fashion, states themselves, along with their institutions, can also acquire symbolic meaning and take on the mythical qualities which make them 'national'. Even such a banal thing as a dish of food becomes mythical, and thus 'national', when those who sit down to eat it believe or imagine themselves to be in communion with the rest of their nation while they do so.[2] One can also, of course, attribute national meaning to things which in and of themselves have no objective content, in which case the inventive dimension of nation building is that much more obvious. The simplest example is a national flag, which by itself is just coloured cloth, but can become infused with national significance under the right circumstances.

It is this process by which history, culture, institutions or territory become charged with mythical significance that is referred to by the phrase 'inventing the nation'. Understanding the origins of nations in this way implies that they do not occur naturally in the world, arising spontaneously and existing objectively with their own personalities or 'spirits' passing unchanged through the ages. Products of human society, nations emerge at certain points in history, endowed with the emotionally charged qualities and characteristics that men and women have conferred upon them. Because of their abstract nature, nations are accessible only indirectly through studies of their representations, symbols or myths. Evolving over time, they are subject to a wide variety of influences as they are invented and re-invented across many generations.

This long, slow process by which nations acquire their mythical qualities is extremely complex. The historical, political, social and economic contexts will all have an impact, and determine the character of the nations which will emerge. Though some individuals can influence this creative process through conscious and deliberate attempts at 'nation-building', the thesis that nations are invented does not mean that they can be created *ex nihilo* in any circumstances, take on any characteristics or even necessarily follow the routes that the nation-builders intend. While the limits of conscious human control over the creation and evolution of nations are almost impossible to define, the best that can be said is that because nations are invented, they are subject to manipulation up to a certain point. Much of their evolution and development may be outside the control of nation-builders, influenced by the circumstances, coming from below and limited by what the wider population is prepared to accept, their responses, beliefs, experiences and memories.

Given the variety of characteristics which can become charged with mythical significance as national, no two nations are ever completely alike, or even possess parallel types of myths. Many scholars have attempted to classify nations according to type, period or phase, but no single scheme has yet been found which can cover all of the permutations and combinations. The classical explanations include the division of nations into civic – defined according to citizenship and voluntarism within a political community in a unified state structure – and ethnic, where it is the perception of common ancestry and culture which binds the national community together.[3] Other authors, such as Benedict Anderson, who defined nations as 'imagined communities', stress the element of perception rather than the objective content of the characteristics of the nation.[4] Others have concentrated on nationalism, a term describing a host of different political movements which have used the rhetoric of nations to gain power either within a state or in the international community.[5] Finally, given the inability of theoretical studies to answer all of the questions, a vast number of case studies have also been produced, held by many as the most appropriate manner to approach the study of nations and to understand the processes of how they are invented and what their role is in modern society.

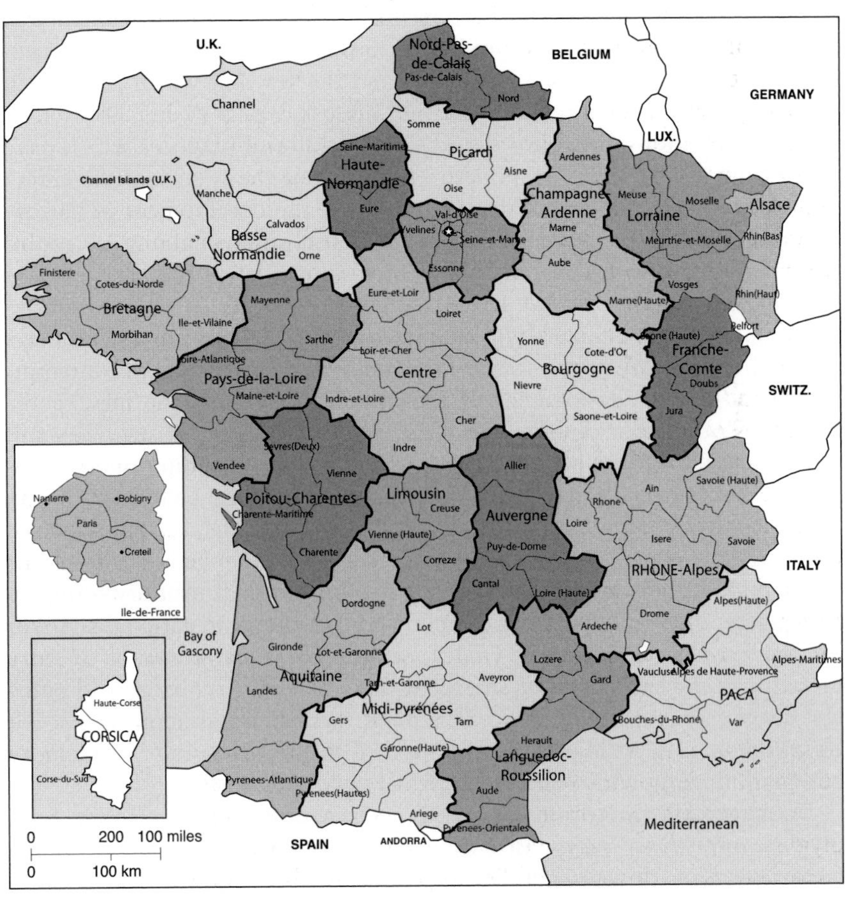

Figure 1 The regions and departments of France

France is among the most well-studied nations and has often been used as an example in the development of models and against which theories of nationalism have been tested and refined. Among European states, France is one of the oldest, with relatively stable borders for several centuries, and is at the same time a 'northern' and a Mediterranean country. Home of the French Revolution, considered the most significant turning point in the history and development of nations, France is also generally considered one of the archetypes of the 'civic' model of a nation built through the extension of citizenship and the highly successful cultural and political assimilation of immigrants. Since the nineteenth century, French nation-builders, whether politicians or scholars, have also been particularly preoccupied with their nation's historical roots, leading to a vast quantity of writings about the history of France. Published histories of France, such as the *History of France* written by the republican historian Michelet in 1869, are themselves a part of the nation-building process, helping to create and establish a meaningful history for the nation.[6]

From that perspective, what follows here is not a traditional 'history of France', but an essay on the process of nation-building over the two centuries since the Revolution. To understand the ways in which the French nation was invented, it will identify and discuss critical events, characters, symbols, traditions, historical narratives and cultural practices which have acquired mythical status in modern France. Since the process of inventing nations is closely tied to political rivalries and the development of nationalist discourses to promote particular political positions fighting for power within the State structure (and sometimes against it), it will also explore the political conflicts which have formed the context of French nation-building. Different chapters will examine the conscious attempts and overt political enterprises of the (often faceless) French political elites attempting to shape the development of the nation, as well as the inescapable influences of popular opinion and resistance to these enterprises. They will also analyse other influential factors such as war, economic modernisation, technological changes and easier communication. This study builds upon the work of historians such as Pierre Nora, whose monumental three-volume work *Les Lieux de Mémoire* brought together a range of chapters describing a vast number of 'sites' of national memory – important places, objects, events and people who have become national symbols for the French,[7] and Robert Gildea, whose *The Past in French History* investigates the links between interpretations of national history and political discourses and expediency.[8] This book seeks to build upon their work by combining, in a single volume, political history, the study of memory and myth making with other recent work in cultural history.

To cover the invention of the French nation, this book has been divided into three parts: Inventing French History, Inventing French Experience, and Inventing French Identity. While it is true that history, experience and identity overlap in several ways, considering them separately allows for different perspectives upon the inventing process. The first section on the invention of French history covers the ways in which various national storylines gradually developed over two hundred years to become the widely recognised classical national 'history of France'. It examines the historical record and the process whereby certain events came to be viewed as central to the nation's past, and interpreted in particular ways, while others have been ignored and forgotten. In this section, the chapters are divided chronologically, with each one looking not only at how national history was experienced or understood at that moment, but also how, at various points in time, each period was interpreted and entered into the historical record as a part of the national story.

The second section on the invention of a national experience examines several recurring themes throughout national mythology, and their place in the self-definition of the French nation, both in terms of itself and its limits. The first chapter describes French society as it sees itself, analysing social structures and the 'typical' French men or women who are said to comprise it. The next three chapters examine defining or formative events and experiences which have come to shape popular attitudes towards the nation, in part through an identification and conception of national enemies. These chapters cover war, revolution and colonialism respectively. Each seeks to make sense of frameworks within which the boundaries of the national population came to be defined, against those held to be outside the nation, as enemies, traitors or subject.

The final section, Inventing French Identity, looks more closely at specific cultural characteristics which have come to embody Frenchness, and the ways in which individuals identify themselves with the nation. The first, on cultural representations, examines a variety of objects, images and practices which have been mythologised as symbols of French national culture in such a way as to define the nature of Frenchness. The next chapter examines the complex relationship between religion and French identity. It includes an analysis of the official position of national secularism, as well as the ways in which different religions negotiated their own ways of belonging to the French nation without compromising religious integrity. The final chapter on identity and difference contrasts the official French discourse of universality as a key element of French identity with real differences in French society. It will cover gender, ethnic and regional differences, and the ways in which these differences have been (or have not been) reconciled with the concept of 'universalism' as an emblematic French value and essential national characteristic.

It is true of course that there is not only 'one' French nation. Different perspectives across time, space, age and education will mean that the nation never means exactly the same thing to any two individuals. This does not mean however, that the possibilities are infinite, nor that common threads and pervasive national characteristics from culture to religion, history and social values cannot be identified and analysed. The modern France which is presented here is the mainstream republican, universalist vision of the nation in which most French men, women and children in the early twenty-first century have been taught to recognise themselves. It is hoped that as the complex process through which this particular idea of France has grown is described, alternative ideas of Frenchness with origins on the political margins will also emerge. Although a case study of one particular way to understanding a nation, its history, culture and defining characteristics, it is hoped that this study will nevertheless also lead to greater understanding of the process of inventing nations more generally.

Notes

1 See Eric Hobsbawm and Terence Ranger, eds, *The Invention of Tradition* (Cambridge: CUP, 1983).
2 For further examples of this type, see Michael Billig, *Banal Nationalism* (London: Sage Publications, 1995).
3 For a full critical discussion of this model, see Timothy Baycroft and Mark Hewitson, 'Introduction: What was a Nation in Nineteenth-Century Europe', in Baycroft and Hewitson, eds, *What is a Nation? Europe 1789–1914* (Oxford: OUP, 2006), pp. 1–13.
4 Benedict Anderson, *Imagined Communities*, 2nd edn (London: Verso, 1991).
5 See, for example, John Breuilly, *Nationalism and the State* (Manchester: Manchester University Press, 1982), Ernest Gellner, *Nations and Nationalism* (Oxford: Basil Blackwell, 1983), Baycroft and Hewitson, *What is a Nation?* Or, for a critical view of the modernist view of nationalism, see Anthony D. Smith, *Nationalism and Modernism: A critical survey of recent theories of nations and nationalism* (London: Routledge, 1998).
6 This does not, of course, make them less scholarly. In addition to Michelet, some of the most famous examples are the 27 volume *Histoire de France* by Ernest Lavisse (written between 1900 and 1922), the famous patriotic schoolbook *L'Histoire de France* by Mallet and Isaac, or more recently the Annales historian Fernand Braudel's *L'identité de la France* (1986).
7 Pierre Nora, ed., *Les Lieux de Mémoire* (Paris: Gallimard Quarto, 1997), 3 volumes.
8 Robert Gildea, *The Past in French History* (New Haven and London: Yale University Press, 1994).

Chronology of Regimes

1789–1792 Transition from absolute to constitutional monarchy

1789 French Revolution begins
Calling of the Estates General (5 May)
Storming of the Bastille (14 July)
Declaration of the Rights of Man and the Citizen
1790 Civil constitution of the clergy
1791 Louis XVI swears loyalty to the constitution
1792 Battle of Valmy (20 September)

1792–1804 The (First) Republic

1792–1795 The Convention
1793 Execution of Louis XVI (21 January)
1793–1794 The Terror
1795–1799 The Directory
1799–1804 The Consulate (Napoleon Bonaparte First Consul)
1801 The Concordat
1804 The Civil Code

1804–1814 The (First) Empire (Napoleon I)

1814–1830 The Restoration (1815–1824 Louis XVIII, 1824–1830 Charles X)

1815 The 100 Days (20 March–22 June)
1830 Capture of Algiers
July Revolution

1830–1848 July Monarchy (Louis-Philippe)

1848 The 1848 Revolution (February)

1848–1852 Second Republic

1848 Manhood Suffrage
Abolition of slavery
Louis-Napoleon Bonaparte elected President of the Republic (20 December)

1851 *Coup d'état* (2 December)

1852–1870 Second Empire (Napoleon III)

1870–1871 Franco-Prussian war

1870 Battle of Sedan, Napoleon III captured

1870–1940 Third Republic

1871 Paris Commune (March–May)

1905 Separation of church and state

1914–1918 First World War

1919 Treaty of Versailles (Alsace Lorraine returns to France)

1939–1945 Second World War

1940 Defeat of France (armistice June 17)

1940–1944 The French State (Vichy Regime)

1940 The National Assembly gives full powers to Marshal Pétain (10 July)

1944–1946 Provisional Government (from September)

Universal Suffrage
Brazzaville conference

1946–1958 Fourth Republic

1950 Schuman Declaration (9 May)

1955–62 Algerian War

1957 Treaty of Rome (creation of the European Economic Community)

1958–present Fifth Republic

1962 Algerian independence

1966 France leaves NATO's command structure

1968 Student and worker protests (May)

1986 Creation of the European Union

PART I

INVENTING FRENCH HISTORY

One of the key elements in a national mythology is a national history: a narrative to which citizens can relate, recounting the story of how the nation passed through the centuries. It will include the glorious deeds in the nation's past, the periods of oppression by tyrants, the defining moments or events which made the nation into what it is, and provide the background for national heroes and martyrs who are later venerated. Such national histories do not merely exist, but are slowly constructed, continually evolving and adapted to circumstances, new perspectives or events, and perpetually subjected to debates of interpretation or content. Given the central place of such national histories in all examples of European nation-building since the late eighteenth century, these debates have often been hotly contested, and means that much historical writing and especially any 'national history' has an unmistakably political dimension.[1] Rival interpretations of national histories fight it out for wider acceptance, may coexist for a period, before the victory of one interpretation or consensus gradually emerges, sometimes taking many generations.

History is one of the most significant elements of French national mythology and a key component French identity.[2] Widely known among the general public, national history has been given a large place in the French primary and secondary school curriculum, and references to the national history can not only be found throughout French culture, but are imbedded in the landscape through monuments, statues, street names and commemorative plaques. Historical debates occupy a prominent place in the public sphere, both in political discourses and the media, and history books have a wide popular reading public. The French are also acutely aware of their past in such a way as to regularly interpret contemporary events (at all periods) in terms of how they relate to national history. This section will examine the historical process of the birth and development of the French national historical narrative. It will examine a selection of meaningful events and people from the French past, as well as the rival interpretations to which they were subjected and political implications of the choices made. For the most part, it will be centred on the dominant 'Republican' narrative interpretation of the nation's history. Nonetheless, it will also analyse the conflicting versions that this narrative did sometimes oppose and sometimes assimilate. The first chapter will concentrate on the Revolutionary and Napoleonic period, viewed as central in every narrative of the French nation, and the subject of the most vehemently contested interpretations over the two centuries that followed. The second chapter, entitled The Battle for the French Nation, covers the period in which the republican interpretation of French history slowly became the dominant one, in particular with reference to the French Revolution of 1789, but also for the events of the nineteenth century. The third chapter concentrates on the Second World War, an historical event which has not yet achieved a consensus of interpretation in France, and which replaced the Revolution as the central contested event of the national past during the remainder of the twentieth century. The final chapter of Part I explores the post-war period, covering the ways in which later events have been interpreted and understood in terms of the remoter national past. This division necessarily gives a great deal more prominence to two major turning points – the Revolution and the Second World War – which is not intended to argue that an objective historical analysis might not conclude that other events should also be given weight, but to suggest that in the popular imagination, these are the events which are the most debated, the most mythologised and the most central in the invented history of the French nation.

1

The French Revolution and the Nation 1789–1815

Central to any understanding of modern France, French identity or the process of nation building in France lies the French Revolution. A defining moment in which the nation was born, a key turning point in the long history of the French people, the interpretations of the place of the French Revolution are plentiful and varied. While recent scholarship has identified numerous elements of continuity across the revolutionary period, the perception of the Revolution as a great rupture or watershed in French history is central to the image of France which has been developed in the two centuries which have followed it. Whether it is held to be the birth of the nation, or as a great 'awakening' into consciousness of the French people, the centrality of the Revolution in the national myths and symbols of France is undeniable.

Likewise the process of the invention of the French nation, if it did not begin with the French Revolution, was greatly accelerated during the years of upheaval which followed and heavily influenced by revolutionary imagery and interpretation. The revolutionaries and republicans who sought to articulate the historical dimension of their visions of France placed the Revolution at the origin of the nation and the heart of the French national identity, and popularised a language of the nation and nationalism throughout France. Nonetheless, these same republicans also looked back into France's pre-revolutionary past, to inscribe its national myth in a far longer national history, equally mythical. The legacy of the years before the Revolution, in terms of their contribution to French identity, has largely been filtered through post-revolutionary republican interpretations of the nation, and needs to be examined before turning to the Revolution itself.

The Pre-Revolutionary Legacy

The period which pre-dates the French Revolution has become known in subsequent years as the *ancien régime*, the 'old regime', the very name of which helps to emphasise the newness and the difference of everything which came after the Revolution, to alienate the past and to cut it off sharply from the present. In this way, it is suggested that the France which existed before 1789, 'old France', was 'another France' which had disappeared with the Revolution (thankfully, according to the republican interpretation), and which, it is hinted, was backward or *passé*. The new France which emerged in the post-revolutionary period, transformed through the adoption of revolutionary values, could be differentiated from the *ancien régime* by its very modernity. The *ancien régime* was nevertheless still France, and the republican nation-builders of the post-revolutionary period did look back to the past for several elements or characteristics of the nation. These include territory and the State itself, structures of governing, religion, patriotism, some facets of culture and the tradition of 'Enlightenment' thinking and writing. Each of these was in some way integrated by the republicans into the national historical myth of France, although not with an equal degree of consciousness or deliberateness.

The most important elements of the French historical myth drawn from before the Revolution were the territory of France and the State itself. Claims to a lengthy history, stretching back before the Roman Empire to ancient Gaul, helped to create a certain sacredness about the territory and the physical extent of France, as well as increasing its legitimacy and prestige. French school textbooks from the late nineteenth century onwards famously refer to 'our ancestors the Gauls' as the origins of the modern French nation and people.[3] They thus not only present the French as the legitimate heirs to the land and territory of ancient Gaul, but furthermore distinguish their most ancient traditions from both the Roman as well as the Germanic ones, adding to their prestige by greater uniqueness and longevity.[4] Vercingetorix, the last of the Gaullish chieftains whose defeat by Julius Caesar brought Gaul under the authority of Rome, occupies a vague position among the lists of great French leaders or heroes. Such links have been reinforced by the references in the Asterix comic book series, most particularly in *Asterix and Cleopatra*, where 'Gaul' is sighted by an Egyptian sailor and represented in a hieroglyphic pictogram with a map of modern France.

With the Frankish invasions and the fall of the western Roman Empire, the territory which is now modern France was divided among several Frankish leaders, much of which was eventually united under a single rule by the Merovingian dynasty in the fifth century AD. The great king to emerge at the end of that century was Clovis, whose kingdom covered much of what is now modern France. According to the republican interpretation of French history, although the regimes have changed, the

French State has existed in an unbroken, continuous line from the fifth century until the twenty-first. Clovis's conversion to Christianity and his baptism in the year 496 by St Rémi in Reims has been entered into the historical record as the birth of France, and the origin of the solid and important links between the Catholic church and the French State.[5] While this particular event in French history has been stressed by the Catholic, rather than the republican historical myth-makers, both groups agreed on the longevity of the contemporary French State, and its origins with Clovis and the Merovingians in the fifth century.[6] The 1500th anniversary of his baptism was commemorated as a great event of French history in 1996.

Neither the variable size of the kingdom, the regular shifts in the boundaries, nor the changes of ruling dynasty over the thirteen centuries between Clovis and the French Revolution altered the perception of the republican nation-builders of the uninterrupted existence of the French State or of its claims on French territory. The age and continuity of the French State became one of the great themes among French nation-builders, and each of the numerous styles of regime during the two hundred years which followed the French Revolution sought to associate itself more or less closely with this uninterrupted history of the French State. Nor did these variables in size and shape alter the claim to the territorial integrity of France which was asserted with greater or lesser intensity throughout the nineteenth and twentieth centuries. One of the most powerful myths surrounding France is its territory, for which the shorthand reference 'the hexagon' refers to the perceived 'natural frontiers': the Alps, the Mediterranean, the Pyrenees, the Atlantic, the English Channel and the Rhine River.[7] The fact that the last of these was at no point in history the border in its entirety between the Alps and the Channel has never reduced the force of the belief that France's six-sided borders are 'natural', and this territory is the right of the State to which has been ascribed such a long, unbroken history. The asserted rights to the land even pre-date the existence of the French State, as mentioned above, since they also rest upon the French claims to be the descendants and heirs of the pre-Roman Gauls.

The benefits of inherent claims on French territory and the continuity from an ancient State include the prestige which comes from longevity and an association with any glory achieved throughout the long period, the legitimacy which they confer upon later regimes, and the ability to forge stronger links between the population and the land of the hexagon. The greatest kings or heroes who could be associated with French history were claimed, with different force by rival groups, but always with the goal of increasing the prestige of the French past. In addition to Clovis, later kings such as Saint Louis, Henri IV or Louis XIV were much lauded, and even Charlemagne, who ruled much more of Europe than what is now France, has been considered a great 'French' statesman and ruler, whose glory confers greater credit upon France.[8] In addition to ascribing continuity and glory to the French past, and the reinforcing of claims on the territory, much effort from the Revolutionary period onwards went into strengthening the land as a central element in French identity. The view that to be French was linked to living in French territory, part of the 'natural' domain of the French State, was a common view of republican nation-builders and of their opponents. By building up loyalty to the land itself, which could then be seamlessly associated with the State, and hopefully with the particular regime, the nation-builders hoped to strengthen their claims for legitimacy and loyalty. Such a tradition is characterised by the chapter 'A Portrait of France' in Michelet's nineteenth-century *History of France*, in which the expression of his enthusiasm for the process of national unification goes hand in hand with an equally enthusiastic description of the wealth and diversity of the French regions.[9] The links between the territory and the history of the nation can also be seen in the organisation of the school curriculum up to the end of the twentieth century, in which history and geography are always studied together, and cannot be taken separately until well past the end of secondary school.

Along with the French State itself, post-revolutionary France inherited from the *ancien régime* a structure and tradition of administrative and government centralisation which would leave its mark upon all of the post-revolutionary regimes. Although in later years this tradition of a strong, centralised State has been most closely identified with the revolutionary Jacobins, the numerous regimes which would follow the overthrow of the *ancien régime* were building upon the legacy of a centralised State-structure which pre-dates the Revolution. From at least the time of Louis XIV, when much of the power of the nobility was reduced after their defeats in the Fronde of the mid-seventeenth century, power in the French State was highly centralised.[10] The growth and development of administrative bureaucracy within this structure served to increase the centralised nature of governing. Looking even further back in time, medieval French kings such as Philippe-Auguste could be praised in republican history books for their contribution to the centralisation of the French State. Further evidence for the links between a powerful state and French identity can be found in the success of popular historical novels such as *Les Rois Maudits*, in which King Philippe le Long is described as 'an evil man, with the qualities of a great king', and whose behaviour is justified by his goal of creating a strong, centralised State.[11] Into the second half of the twentieth century, Gaullists as well as socialists continued to justify French specificity 'historically' in State-dominated, centralised social and economic policies, presenting themselves as heirs to this great French tradition.

Another primary characteristic of France which has its roots in the *ancien régime* is its Catholicism. France has often been described as the 'eldest daughter' of the church, an expression which symbolises the close ties which bound the French State to the Catholic church, beginning with the baptism of Clovis in 496 already alluded to, and lasting beyond the Revolution.[12] The links between the church and the French State were numerous during the *ancien régime*, and the population largely practising Catholics throughout the period. Kings were crowned by the bishops and, in the system of parliament by Estates, the First Estate was that of the clergy, thereby securing institutionalised power for the church. Unofficially, many church leaders held positions of power and influence at the royal court, including regencies in times of underage monarchs. At a more local level, villages were dominated by the parish churches, and priests were among the most influential of the local leaders. The calendar was organised around religious festivals, and the significant markers in each individual's life were marked out by religious ceremonies – baptism, first communion, marriage and death.[13] For Catholic nation-builders in post-revolutionary France, the long tradition of French Catholicism was of great credit to the nation, and they attempted to preserve it as a fundamental element of French identity throughout the period which followed.

The Republican vision of France did not deny or attempt to reduce the importance of the historically close association of France with Catholicism and the church during the *ancien régime*. They linked the Catholicism of pre-revolutionary France to the Royal institution as well as to the former social hierarchy, to help accentuate the dividing line which was the Revolution, after which France was to become the great secular Republic which the republicans envisaged. There was agreement that the pre-revolutionary legacy was one of solid ties with the Catholic church. But the religious nature (or not) of post-revolutionary France and the place of Catholicism in French national identity was to become a great battleground for the competing visions of the inventors of France. During the Revolution itself, the names of Saints and other religious references were officially forbidden as street or city names, and while never going so far in later years, when the Republicans returned to power during the Third Republic, signs of the traditional links between the French nation and its religion were significantly downplayed.[14] In contrast to the state-sponsored republican national memory (or lack of it), ultra-Catholic circles constructed a 'counter-memory' which gave pride of place to the Catholic connections, celebrating Saint Louis, Joan of Arc, the Crusades and the Vendée wars. Its defenders pushed towards the beatification of the Catholic priests who refused to ratify the revolutionary 'Civil Constitution of the Clergy', many of whom were killed in prison during the dramatic massacres of September 1792. Both memories began slowly to converge in the early twentieth century, especially during the First World War, when religious historical allusions began to creep back into the republican discourse. By the late twentieth century, the image of the 'eldest daughter', although more central for Catholics, was sufficiently integrated into mainstream French historical identity for Republican

Presidents to make allusions to the image during official visits with the Pope.[15] Furthermore, on 20 June 1989, in his speech on the anniversary of the 'Tennis Court Oath', socialist President François Mitterrand officially reintegrated those royalist priests killed in September 1792 into the national memory by publicly referring to their tragic fate.

The question of religious tolerance has been an even more complicated issue in French historical memory. Since the Reformation, France has been the home to a significant Protestant community, with several Protestant traditions concentrated in different regions, from the Cévennes to Alsace. It is possible to point to such moments in French history as the Edict of Nantes in 1598, which secured legal recognition of Protestants and freedom of conscience within France, as evidence of a national tradition of religious freedom and tolerance. Pointing strongly in the other direction, one can also find events such as the revocation of that same Edict of Nantes in 1685 which removed the rights that had previously been guaranteed to Protestants, or to the religious wars or the Saint Bartholomew's Day massacre on 23–24 August 1572, in which thousands of Protestants were murdered, as evidence of a tradition of intolerance in the Catholic France of the *ancien régime*. Both of these traditions have been used to justify the republican policy of secularism.

Similar to the case of religious tolerance, the tradition of Enlightenment thinking and writing has greater prominence in some visions of French history than in others. The Republican image of France places great weight upon the 'century of Enlightenment' which preceded the French Revolution as evidence of the avant-garde thinking which helped to bring about the Revolution in the first place, and of the greatness of the French nation as the origin of such ideas. The writings of Voltaire, Jean-Jacques Rousseau (respectively commemorated by the transferral of their ashes to the Pantheon in 1791 and 1794) and others could be held up as a part of a French national tradition of opposing the prevailing established canon in the name of the search for truth, justice and freedom via reason, of which the republican leaders could claim to be the heirs. In the conclusion of his speech on Voltaire on 30 May 1878, Victor Hugo told his listeners to turn for advice to Voltaire, Rousseau, Diderot and Montesquieu, the great voices of the past, and suggested that 'Enlightenment would emerge from the tombs.' His words illustrate eloquently this permanent republican reference to the Enlightenment thinkers as moral guides. The popular impact of Gavroche's song in the musical adaptation of Hugo's *Les Misérables*, which parodies right-wing Catholic discourses and pamphlets about the negative impact of Voltaire and Rousseau, shows how much this question of the role of the *ancien régime* philosophers was, and remained, not purely theoretical but also a concrete political issue in France well into the twentieth century.[16]

A belief that France and Frenchness were inseparably linked to this use of reason formed a key part of French identity in the two centuries following the Revolution. Presenting Descartes as the father of all rationalism, A. Glucksmann did not hesitate in 1987 to entitle a book *Descartes is France*.[17] While for the more hard-line anticlerical republicans, the tradition of reason and Enlightenment was directly opposed to faith and religion, others could find in French history simply a tradition of constructive dissent which was not necessarily opposed to religion, and could be found even further back than the eighteenth century, for example in Jansenist ideas and writings.[18] In both cases, French identity was linked to an historical tradition of creative or progressive philosophical thinking, leading to an image of France as a home for creative thought, progress, Enlightenment and reason throughout the course of its history. As with the earlier cases of Catholicism, the two historical interpretations began to converge in the twentieth century, as space was made for both reason and faith in French history.

One of the most significant elements of French history drawn from the *ancien régime* is French 'culture'. A source of tremendous pride and evidence of the superiority of the French nation, the history of French culture as the centre of European high culture can be traced back well beyond the Revolution. An important centre of art, literature, philosophy and science, France was also held to be the origin of fashionable trends in cuisine, dress and general sophistication. Perhaps most importantly of all, France also gave birth to the French language, that which replaced Latin as the lingua franca of Europe, which was used at all of the European courts and among the educated and upper-classes throughout the continent. From at least as early as the founding of the Académie Française by Cardinal Richelieu in 1635, the history of the French language has long been paralleled with the history of France itself, equally revered across the political spectrum from republicans to ultra-Catholics.[19] The quality and 'richness' of the language itself, as well as the significance and quality of all that has been written in it, from the 'greats' of the *ancien régime* to the post-revolutionary period, formed an essential part of French identity, and conferred glory upon the nation. National literature was taught thoroughly in schools and its wealth and history became an essential part of French identity, even for the general public. In the 'resistance novel' published in 1942, *The Silence of the Sea* by Vercors, it is the enemy, the German officer, who acknowledges French absolute superiority on the literary scene.[20] For many republicans, French, 'the language of Molière', was also 'the language of Enlightenment,' and the links were not merely coincidence, but causal. French was a kind of ideal language of freedom necessary to express the new ideas. Without it, therefore, progress and indeed the Revolution itself could not have taken place. In all of the French histories, language and culture have pride of place at the centre.

High culture is not the only element of French culture which can be traced back to the pre-Revolutionary years. In many cases without any concrete examples, the inventors of French history also pointed simply to numerous traditions which can be traced far back across the centuries, especially those which are linked to the farming of the land, or what might be called 'folk culture': local dances, costumes, tools, techniques of harvesting, festivals and the ways in which they were celebrated, songs or expressions, or indeed the way buildings were laid out and organised.[21] Many of these traditions are of course local or regional, and at no time were they practised in the whole of France, which presents a difficulty to those who wish to invent a 'national' French history based upon such cultural traditions. The link is made through the land, however, such that any local or regional folk traditions tie a locality or group more closely to their specific fields and villages. This can be presented as a part of a larger French national tradition of close association with the land, the territory of which, as discussed already, is historic and natural. Even if such a cultural tradition is in fact relatively recent, its perceived significance is historical, and a long history may be invented for it through an association with the historic territory of France going back to the *ancien régime*.

The longevity of the State itself, its territory, selected episodes from its history, institutions and the structure of government, Catholicism, language, culture and the tradition of Enlightenment are the principal elements drawn from the *ancien régime* which were used by a variety of nation-builders in the invention of France and as a basis for modern French identity. But as Pierre Nora points out in his study of the classic *History of France* by Ernest Lavisse, what was striking was the reconstruction of the *ancien régime* in terms of the principal themes of republican identity at the time of the writing, such as the emphasis on boundaries at a time of obsession with Alsace-Lorraine.[22] Thus from the time it was labelled 'old', the *ancien régime* has been understood primarily in terms of the preoccupations or conflicts which have arisen since the Revolution and the inception of the Republic, as nation-builders sought to construct a national history which was compatible with their evolving conception and vision of France. In this way the national characteristics with origins attributed to the *ancien régime* are those which were of interest to later French men and women, and not necessarily reflective of what would have been considered the most important characteristics of France during the *ancien régime*.

It would be most presumptuous, however, to presume that since the main invention of French identity and history has come about since the Revolution, that no sense of Frenchness or national representation existed during the *ancien régime* itself. With reference to public opinion, it is clear that a sense of patriotism did precede the French Revolution. Although it is difficult to distinguish them from dynastic loyalty either to the monarchy directly or to a particular local noble representing the king, feelings of affection and support for 'France' among the general population did surface on numerous occasions throughout the centuries. It would be a mistake to assume that this patriotism of the *ancien régime* increased continually and steadily throughout the centuries, for although evidence can be found of a deep sense of patriotism on numerous occasions, it came in waves or irregular leaps, and could disappear as quickly as it had appeared. At such times as the Wars of Religion or moments of dynastic instability or rivalry with England, greater patriotism along with a heightened sense of Frenchness were displayed by the people of France than at other moments.[23]

Likewise, such patriotism or Frenchness also varied from place to place, with some regions or communities having a greater awareness of or identification with these ties to the larger national community than others.[24] In unstable regions which were under threat, such as border areas, and where 'France' was looked to for support or aid against the perceived enemy, consciousness of Frenchness was stronger than in settled, unthreatened areas in times of peace. The nature of Frenchness felt in a given situation and its relationships to other identities also varied, depending upon the particular context. Thus, while patriotism and an awareness of attachment to the larger community translating into a sense of Frenchness could be found, they varied a great deal in strength and nature according to the circumstances of both time and place throughout the many centuries of the *ancien régime*.

By the same respect one can find images and representations of France which are distinct from those of the king or the monarchy, and which also appeared in greater or lesser quantities over the centuries. Numerous examples can be found from the Middle Ages, but these declined after the sixteenth century when the monarchy was strong.[25] However much it may have been in the interests of the kings to promote feelings of adoration and loyalty among the populace, especially in times of threat, it was certainly never in their interest to encourage this loyalty towards any collective entity other than the monarch himself, such as became the wider 'nation' of the post-revolutionary period.[26] To credit the monarchy with having built up a sense of nationalism as it came to be understood in the post-revolutionary period would therefore not be accurate, only a kind of patriotic loyalty which could alternately grow strong and then disappear again, and which was always associated as closely as possible to the person of the king.

The French elites during the early modern period, unlike their later counterparts, did not have a *project* of nation-building; they did not think in terms of inventing a nation, developing it, liberating it or even representing it. References to and representations of the French 'nation' which had been present in earlier writings were restricted to opposition to the monarch. Ideas of a national body distinct from the king were preserved within Protestant circles, and later through Jansenist writings followed by the Enlightenment tradition.[27] By the eighteenth century, such opposition, however influential it might be in the intellectual Salons or the Parliament, still remained outside the circles of power and had little influence on the political destiny of France. According to some scholars, this type of opposition, expanding during the conflicts between the monarchy and the Parliament of Paris from 1750 onwards, eventually grew enough to be considered a kind of counter society based on reason, which could use the image of a nation based on popular sovereignty as a way of opposing the monarchy.[28] The doctrines articulated by this form of 'public opinion' were built upon in the Revolutionary years as a foundation for national identity by those who, unlike their predecessors, did have a conscious policy of nation-building.[29]

Thus, by the year 1789, France was a unified State with several institutional, cultural and historical ties, and a population which had on numerous occasions displayed a potentially powerful sense of patriotism. This patriotism and loyalty which could be found among the wider population during the *ancien régime*, surfacing periodically in times of crisis or conflict, does not imply the presence of a 'national identity' such as that term was understood after the Revolution: an identification with any of the objective cultural or ethnic characteristics which were called 'French', beyond the State and the king (with only a blurred distinction between them). It was certainly a foundation of loyalty upon which national identity could be developed and constructed during the years after the Revolution, and successfully harnessed during the Revolutionary Wars. An opposition had also developed which had begun to articulate the idea of the nation as an alternative to monarchy, using the discourse of individual liberties and the rights of peoples, ready to invent a nation to go with the French people. While the *ancien régime* would contribute numerous elements to the identity of France, it is the French Revolution which would be the key episode in the invented history of the French nation.

The Early Revolution (1789–1798)

As described at the beginning of the chapter, the French Revolution of 1789 is the most important historical period for the development of French identity and has a central place in the development of every historical narrative of France. Details vary from one interpretation to another, in terms of which events and characters within the period are highlighted, the relative weight accorded to different causal factors, and the particular models of analysis used. While the general conclusions were hotly contested in the years immediately following the Revolution, the next two hundred years saw a general consensus gradually emerge not only over the Revolution's centrality, but also over its interpretation. This section will begin with an examination of the place of the early Revolution within French history, including the events and symbols drawn from the Revolutionary years. The dominant Republican interpretation will be followed by the counter-revolutionary legitimist interpretation, before turning to the elements of consensus which emerged many decades later. The final section will treat the way historians' work has influenced popular perceptions of the Revolution, as well as the differences between the mythical place of the Revolution within French history and the actual achievements during the Revolutionary years themselves.

The place of the Revolution within French history has primarily been determined by Republicans, both during the period and afterwards, who sought to create a popular myth whereby a positive vision of events would link republicanism with France and the French people, creating a French identity with republicanism as a central value. Myth is used here as it has been defined by Robert Gildea: a 'construction of the past by a political community for its own ends'.[30] Unlike the elites of the *ancien régime*, the Revolutionaries had a clear project of nation building, and saw themselves as consciously creating their own myth as the Revolution progressed.[31] The abbé Grégoire, one of the leading revolutionary theorists in 1789, identified their task as myth builders from the outset, arguing that to completely rebuild a government, 'you have to republicanise everything.'[32] The republican myth they set out to create can be broken down into several dimensions, each symbolising a part of how the republicans hoped that the Revolution would be seen within the context of longer term French history, and which will be examined in turn. We will look first at the causes which republicans felt sparked the revolution, and then turn to some of the new institutions which they created, the ideas, theories and values which lay behind the revolutionary activity, the language and symbolism they used, and finally the relationship of the French population as a whole to the Revolution and revolutionary activity.

The first step in placing the Revolution within the larger sweep of French history, portraying it as the birth of the French nation, its awakening, coming into consciousness, and entering onto the political stage as a serious player, was to establish a sharp contrast with that which came before.[33] The monarchy and the aristocratic elite of the *ancien régime* were portrayed as decrepit, self-absorbed, loaded down with privileges and so oppressive that the French population was bound to revolt in protest. The problems of the old system, according to the republican interpretation, were so acute, so entwined with the basic structure of a regime of privilege, that nothing short of Revolution could help the French people out of the terrible situation in which they found themselves. They repeatedly asserted that their task was to work from a *tabula rasa*, a blank slate, and to begin everything anew.[34] This involved the renaming of streets and public squares, the removal of old statues commemorating the monarchy and their replacement with republican ones, paralleling the execution of the king in the remainder of public space.[35]

Thus the causes of the Revolution lay in the very structure of the *ancien régime* itself. The differences were perceived as so great that the revolutionaries were constantly in the process of declaring a new beginning for France via the creation of a new calendar. In 1789 many of the Revolutionaries began spontaneously to write the date as Year I of liberty. After the execution of Louis XVI in 1792, Year IV of liberty was still used, but also Year I of equality, before the Convention set up an official act declaring it, on 25 September, to be Year I of the French Republic, with a whole new structure of months linked to the seasons.[36] While this can also be partly attributed to a desire to refuse the Christian calendar in the name of reason, it was even more strongly motivated by this simple desire to demarcate the Revolution from everything that came before, and the continual perception that they had taken yet another step which required a full-scale declaration of novelty and profound significance.

In the revolutionary and republican myth of 1789 as a great watershed in the history of France, the most significant transformation could be found in the new representative political institutions which emerged from it. Louis XVI, faced with mounting economic difficulties, was forced to call a meeting of an ancient representative political body – the Estates General – for 5 May 1789. The Estates General was a form of legislature divided into three parts, or Estates: the First Estate comprised the Catholic clergy, the Second Estate represented the nobility, and the Third Estate represented the rest of the population (which made up 96% of the total). Almost immediately, reforms were proposed by the members of the Third Estate, who called themselves 'nationals' and 'patriots', and who were joined by several members of the lower clergy and a few nobles. They wanted to double the representation of the Third Estate, to have the three Estates meet together as one single body, and to change the voting pattern so that each representative had one vote, replacing the existing pattern of one vote per Estate, under which the Third Estate could be outvoted by the other two.

The patriots of 1789 justified their demands for institutional reform in the name of Reason and the philosophy of the Enlightenment, most directly formulated at the time in the book *What is the Third Estate?* by the abbé Emmanuel Joseph Sieyès, which appeared just a few months before the opening of the Estates General.[37] In this work, Sieyès argued that the Third Estate and those it represented should be considered as the whole of the nation (going so far as to exclude the other two Estates altogether), and that it was from this nation or 'the people' so defined that true legitimacy should be derived. The assertive group of patriots, inspired by Sieyès' and others' work, gradually gained power, and their demands were met. The three Estates met together as the National Constituent Assembly, and set themselves the task of drawing up a new constitution for France based upon the principle of national sovereignty, with an accompanying document entitled the Declaration of the Rights of Man and the Citizen, which would guarantee equal rights for all individuals, and declare the rights of all nations to determine their own fate. Within these texts the place of the nation is always central. Marxists such as Brian Jenkins acknowledge the significant role of the Revolution in advancing the political concept of the nation in both theory and popular consciousness, as one of the elements of bourgeois interest.[38] This consciousness of the nation went so far as to penetrate the vocabulary of the everyday within popular Parisian circles, where for example the watchword of the National Guard had become 'Are you of the nation?' as early as the autumn of 1789.[39]

The transformation of France into a constitutional monarchy in a few short months in 1789 held profound significance for the long term history of France and the French people. The Revolutionaries themselves already asserted this point clearly, and it was never later called into question within the republican vision of French history. The term Revolution was employed for precisely that reason, and a number of symbols and specific vocabulary were employed to accentuate the magnitude of the event in the minds of the French people, and to make it easy to identify with. The vocabulary included catchphrases and slogans such as 'Liberty, Equality, Fraternity',[40] the terminology of rights from the Declaration and elsewhere, notions such as 'popular sovereignty', and popular songs such as the Marseillaise. The symbolism was even more widespread, with the tricolour flag, the Phrygian cap and Marianne, the female incarnation of the Republic as the most popular symbols.[41] The church of St Geneviève in Paris was deconsecrated and transformed into the Pantheon, a way of doing honour explicitly to the 'Great Men' of the Republic, instigating a cult of heroism and in some cases also martyrdom, associated explicitly with the Revolution, the Republic and the transformation of France in the short time following 1789.

The widespread promotion of this symbolism and vocabulary, along with a selection of the events of the Revolution as evidence for the importance of the Revolution within French history, were used as a way to solidify the values of later republicans within French society. Whether simple republicanism as a political creed, or other associated values such as reason or secularism, the creation of a glorious history of republican values associated with 'progress' for France and the French nation was an important step within a society particularly preoccupied with its history.

The final element of the republican vision of French history ascribed to the Revolution was the entry of the masses as an important participant in the political future of the nation, held at the same time to be a 'good' thing as well as a fact of the nation's history. The will of the nation was considered to be the foundation for political legitimacy throughout the revolutionary years, and the participation of the crowds during the Revolution itself an important element in its progress, whether in the march to Versailles or the storming of the Bastille. The willingness of the population to risk their lives in the Revolutionary wars or in defence of their perceived freedoms symbolised by the 'nation in arms' was a key component of the myth of the Revolution. In reality the participation of the masses was always problematic: within Paris they were always difficult to control and outside of Paris the Revolution barely touched the population, where actual participation rates were low. Some feared that this was due to low levels of knowledge of the French language (which in many regions was only spoken by the elites), and others that the rural population was too much under the thumb of the clergy. At the time and later, these facts were either ignored or simply used as a reason to promote education, since, the story went, once the people were educated they would see the rightness of everything that the Revolution and the Republic stood for.[42] Hence the programme of the abbé Grégoire that argued that the French language needed imperatively to be taught to everyone throughout France in order to ensure that all could read the language of Enlightenment, and to aid and encourage their political participation in the nation. Grégoire and others hoped to build upon the Greek and Roman notion of the citizen-soldier, further elaborated by Jean-Jacques Rousseau in his *Social Contract*, who should be both a full political participant as well as a defender of the nation.

While the republican interpretation of French history regularly portrayed the French Revolution as the great turning point in French history, marking the first step towards the triumph of Reason and the freedom of the French nation and people from tyranny, a counter myth with a different interpretation did emerge in the years that followed the Revolution. Put forward by those who hoped that France would once again become and remain a monarchy, this reactionary counter-myth for a time challenged the republican interpretation.[43] In supporting the legitimist claims of the monarchy, the Revolution and the republican ideology which supported it were thus portrayed in terms of violence and illegitimacy which brought only destruction, disorder, death and misery to the French people.

Developed directly in opposition to the republican myth, this counter myth is very much symmetrical in its contents. It too had its symbols drawn from the events of the Revolutionary years, in the martyrdom of the king and many of his loyal subjects on the scaffold or in the prison massacres of September 1792, as well as in loyalty to the Catholic church. The biggest symbol for the counter-myth is that of the Vendée region in the west of France, which remained loyal to the church and the crown and was the centre of a counter-revolutionary uprising which threatened the Republic until it was suppressed by the Revolutionary troops.[44] Overall, the myth portrayed the majority of the French population, the clergy, the nobility and the provinces as suffering through the Revolution at the expense of the narrow interests of a handful of fanatical, bloodthirsty, bourgeois Parisians. It also tried to focus attention on the reign of Terror in 1793–4 as the logical and indeed the only possible outcome of the Revolution and republican thinking from the beginning. In this vision, the Revolution was not the great positive turning point, but the point at which France went wrong, and from which appropriate lessons needed to be learned.

During the nineteenth century, as long as monarchism remained a viable alternative political system within France, this counter-myth of the Revolution was taken seriously, both by its makers and its opponents. The most significant historical debate centred on the question of Terror and its place within the Revolution, which remained hotly contested within all political circles throughout the nineteenth century. The republican interpretation of the Revolution attempted to focus upon the events of 1789, while the critics of the Revolution continually recalled 1793. In response to the criticism from the reactionary interpretation of the Revolution, many republicans were forced to recall the events of the Terror more often than they probably would have chosen. Some reacted by placing the blame for the Terror with Robespierre and a few of his close associates, thereby separating out a 'good' revolution from the 'bad' revolution. In this case the latter was not a result of the structural, and much less the theoretical base of the Revolution, but only the circumstances and individuals. Other republicans claimed that the Terror was a necessary result, not of Revolution and the values which supported it, but of the need to deal with the counter-revolution and the foreign wars simultaneously, which pushed the revolutionaries to this extremity. By late in the century, others were pushed so far as to claim that the Terror was by no means a terrible thing, and that it had been necessary to purge the new French nation of the old ways of thinking. Georges Clemenceau famously claimed that the Revolution 'was a block', by which he meant that it was not enough to accept the values of 1789, but to be a proper Republican one needed to acknowledge the necessity of 1793 as well.[45]

Once the real threat of a restoration disappeared however, the dominant and victorious republican interpretation gradually absorbed the reactionary one, and they grew together into a romanticist view of the place of the Revolution within French history. By the closing years of the nineteenth century, and increasingly throughout the twentieth, it was recognised that valiant individuals died for causes they believed in, but the deaths of the Revolutionary years came to be seen as tragic rather than as a sign that the Revolution was other than a great turning point for France, which had as its cause the values which the republican interpretation ascribed to it. Examples of this portrayal can be found from as early as Balzac's novel *Les Chouans* (1834), or Victor Hugo's *Quatre-vingt treize* (*Ninety-three*, 1874) right through to popular history films and documentaries in the second half of the twentieth century.

The position of the French Revolution as the great turning point of French history has for the most part been sustained and supported, if not positively encouraged by the work of professional historians. As discussed in the previous section on the *ancien régime,* the most well-known historians were themselves republicans, and developed and enhanced the republican myth of the birth of the French nation via revolution. It was not until the second half of the twentieth century that historians such as François Furet began to develop theories of late eighteenth-century French history in which continuity rather than change was stressed across the Revolutionary period. Such work has suggested that most of the major reforms were begun during the *ancien régime*, and leads to the conclusion that the Revolution itself was much more a symbol than the substance of change. This symbolic role is significant, and the French Revolution retained its central place within French history in the popular imagination through to the end of the twentieth century and beyond. While much of the detail in terms of events and names of many of the minor figures became forgotten by the wider public, the Revolution and its major events remain one of the most powerful elements of the national identity such as it is experienced through the history of the nation. As has been discussed already, the main events which have been debated and considered important for French history from the revolutionary period concern the early years 1789–93, and there is widespread popular ignorance of everything which happened in the years between the end of the Terror and the advent of Bonaparte at the close of the decade, at least insofar as the long-term history of the nation is concerned. It is for that reason that we can skip over the years of the Directory and the early years of the Consulate, which have such a small place in the mythical history of the French nation.

The Triumph of Napoleon 1798–1815

The seizure of power by Napoleon Bonaparte, a young general of the revolutionary armies, marked the beginning of what has come to be viewed alternatively as a new phase in French history or as the completion of the Revolution. The myths surrounding Napoleon are substantial, and the place of his regime in the history of the French nation, while large, is also somewhat ambiguous. On the one hand, he set out deliberately to create an image of himself which was larger than life, filled with historical resonance, positive and glorious, and the fulfilment of the Revolution. Yet on the other hand, he has also been represented as the tyrant responsible for war all around Europe, and as the man who put a definitive end to the Revolution when he overthrew it. This section will examine Napoleon's place in French history through the myth which he and his followers hoped to create, as well as the counter-myth, before turning to examine the contribution to the development of the French nation which occurred during his reign.

Like the Revolutionaries before him, Napoleon was fully conscious of the importance of myth surrounding his rule in order both to confer legitimacy as well as to reinforce his own power. He used numerous means to develop and enhance his image, which subsequent events have tended to magnify further. The two primary images which he sought to project were grandeur and unity, whereby the success of himself and his regime was also conferred by extension to the whole of France and the French nation. The image of greatness was founded first of all upon his military campaigns, where he had an extremely effective propaganda machine that was able to portray glorious victories even out of such disasters as the Egyptian campaign of 1798–9. Napoleon had already begun to produce such material indicative of his own greatness long before he came to political power, for during his rise through the officer ranks during the Italian campaign, he produced a newspaper for distribution back in France which presented the French with a glorious image of the brilliant soldier on campaign.[46] Once in power, greater resources could be put into the production of such paintings as Jacques-Louis David's *Napoleon Crossing the Alps* (Figure 2). This image of the glorious military leader was complemented throughout his reign, not only with full-scale paintings of himself and his armies, but also with much smaller prints which could be produced cheaply and distributed widely. In promoting his military glory, Napoleon also intended to reflect glory upon his soldiers, and upon the French nation which could boast such splendid and victorious troops.[47]

Figure 2 *Napoleon Crossing the Alps* by Jacques-Louis David

The portrayal of Napoleon's greatness was not restricted to the military domain, but extended to himself as political leader as well. The French Revolution had been in a large part dominated by debates about legitimacy, and Napoleon worked hard to ensure that his image of greatness helped to solidify his claims to power. Allusions to ancient Rome which had been common during the Revolution increased during the Napoleonic period. Napoleon himself was portrayed as Emperor in Roman dress, linking himself with the glory of Rome and its historical tradition. Such a parallel conferred legitimacy upon himself and upon the future hereditary dynasty he hoped to found. Much of the Napoleonic legend was built upon this theme. Describing the year 1802, Victor Hugo (himself the son of a general in Napoleon's army) wrote: 'this century was two years old, Rome replaced Sparta; Napoleon was already in hiding behind Bonaparte.'[48]

Like the links to Rome, Napoleon also had himself paralleled with Charlemagne, the Carolingian king who had also conquered much of Europe and then had himself crowned as Emperor in Rome in 800 AD. This was particularly true in Napoleon's relationship with the church, but it can also be seen in the fact that his crown was called the crown of Charlemagne, as was his imperial sceptre. Such links to the Carolingians were made essentially during his reign; after his exile to St Helena, where he spent most of his time trying to craft his image for posterity, the image of Napoleon as Charlemagne was far less prominent. Perhaps because it broke too strongly with the revolutionary tradition, it did not survive as an image of Napoleon in the same way that Napoleon as Roman Emperor did. Both at the time and later, such images inscribed his regime solidly within a lengthy historical tradition of past great Empires, and served the multiple function of solidifying his own legitimacy, glorifying himself and France, and creating a place for the French nation at the centre of Europe.

The second dimension to the Napoleonic myth was that of unity, reconciling the two warring factions within France, the Revolutionary and Counter-Revolutionary or traditionalist forces, both ideologically and in the sense of stopping civil war. In this sense he was portrayed as the man who was able to complete the Revolution, gain the support of the masses and of republicans without at the same time alienating the old elites. As an illustration, at the highest rank within his government he was able to incorporate both Tallyrand, an *ancien régime* noble and bishop in the Catholic church, and Fouchet, a regicide who was directly involved in the violence of the Revolution, as his ministers of foreign and domestic affairs. Napoleon also brought reconciliation with the Catholic church, signing a Concordat with the papacy in 1802 officially linking the church and State in France. He reinstated nobility, albeit without the same privileges as the *ancien régime*, and created a new nobility of the Empire. At the same time he claimed to preserve the meritocracy desired by the Revolution via the civil service and military promotion schemes. His consolidation of the legal and administrative structure of France, via first and foremost the Napoleonic Civil Code of 1804, was praised as the necessary middle way between the muddle of the *ancien régime* and the excesses of the Revolution. He thus presented himself as a kind of moderate, above all political factions, who could get all parties to agree, and behind whose reformed system the French nation rallied.

Viewed as the man behind whom all of France could be unified, Napoleon was nevertheless in practice much more interested in reconciling the elites than in reconciling the people with these new elites. In spite of his recourse to plebiscites, and the highlighting of his popularity among the common people, he was in fact much less interested in democratic support than his propaganda suggested. Unlike his revolutionary predecessors he had little interest in mass primary education or with the teaching of the French language to the people, but focused instead on secondary education and the preparation of a qualified and capable class of administrators to run the civil service, via the State-controlled Baccalaureate examination. As evidence of his sentiment, he later declared to Benjamin Constant that he was not interested in simply being brought to power at the head of the mob, and thus merely the 'king of a jacquerie'.[49]

This Napoleonic myth of grandeur and unity was promoted overtly by Napoleon himself, but it was also recovered, perpetuated and accentuated by various political heirs in the hundred years which followed. During the Restoration and July Monarchy, Napoleon was held as a model by the Republicans in opposition. Once his nephew, Louis Napoleon, staged his coup d'état in 1852 and became himself Emperor Napoleon III, there was a full-scale cult of historical reference to the greatness of the uncle. Republicans seeking to discredit Napoleon III often did so not by decrying the Bonapartes altogether, but by stressing the differences between the 'great' Napoleon I and his nephew, who was but a 'weak imitation'.[50] Even though less was officially made of Napoleon during the Republics, many French military figures and politicians, most notably Marshal Pétain and Charles de Gaulle, made references to Napoleon, attempting to build at least upon his military reputation and to preserve French greatness. A spontaneous popular fascination with Napoleon also developed, with many more works of art, music, literature and cinema devoted to him than to any other figure, building upon and magnifying the myth in the popular imagination.[51]

A negative myth of Napoleon did exist throughout the nineteenth century, of the ogre, the despot, the bloody tyrant who preserved Europe in war and was insatiable in his appetite for conquest. Preserved at times by elements of both the extreme right and left, this myth saw Napoleon presented as the usurper both of the Revolution and of the monarchy, betraying any trust of the French people and illegitimate on all counts. Such a vision was also perpetuated abroad throughout Europe, by the peoples and other elites with whom Napoleon had fought. He has also been negatively represented by feminists as a misogynist, given his complete lack of recognition for women or women's rights within the Napoleonic Code and elsewhere. For each of these negative myths and images, though consistent and enduring, the political position of those who supported them were often on the political margins of France, and each group always had higher priorities than the perpetuation of this negative view of Napoleon, which therefore remained relatively peripheral compared to those of glory and achievement.

Napoleon was also to contribute to the development of the French nation, in the sense that his European legacy was to have spread nationalism throughout the regions penetrated by the French armies. This was also true for France itself, both within the climate of developing nationalism for the following decades, as well as the fact that in France the Napoleonic period was looked back to with nostalgia by old soldiers and by later regimes seeking to increase the glory of France and their own past therein. In this sense Napoleon's place within French history was to symbolise the ideals of French grandeur and unity, as well as the incarnation of the man of the people. The Empire forms that part of French history which was looked back to with nostalgia, and claimed in part at one time or another by all parts of the French political spectrum. The Empire, in closing the revolutionary period, rounded out the significant transformation of the French nation, and the century and a half which followed would be viewed as the attempt to come to terms with the legacy of Revolution and Empire.

Notes

1 On the centrality of history writing in nation-building, see Stefan Berger, Mark Donovan and Kevin Passmore, eds, *Writing National Histories: Western Europe since 1800* (Routledge, 1999), especially Stefan Berger with Mark Donovan and Kevin Passmore, 'Apologias for the nation-state in Western Europe since 1800', pp. 3–14.
2 See Robert Gildea, *The Past in French History* (New Haven and London: Yale University Press, 1994).
3 See Paul Viallaneix and Jean Ehrard, eds, *Nos ancêtres les gaulois* (Clermont-Ferrand, 1982).
4 On the subject of this Gaullish position (neither Roman nor Germanic) in the French memory, see Krzysztof Pomian, 'Francs et Gaulois,' in Pierre Nora ed., *Les Lieux de Mémoire* 2 (Paris: Quarto-Gallimard, 1997), pp. 2245–2300.
5 See Jacques Le Goff, 'Reims, ville du Sacre,' in Nora, *Les Lieux de Mémoire* 1, pp. 649–733. The place of Catholicism in the French nation will be treated at greater length in Chapter 10.
6 The publication by Jean Lacouture of the book, *L'histoire de France en 100 tableaux* (Italie: Hazon, 1996), raised a significant debate by beginning with Henri de Vulcoq's painting of Clovis's baptism, thereby adding strength to the idea of a fundamental link between Frenchness and Catholicism.
7 See Eugene Weber, 'L'hexagone,' in Nora, *Les Lieux de Mémoire* 1, pp. 1171–90.

8 See Robert Morrissey, 'Charlemagne,' in Nora, *Les Lieux de Mémoire* 3, pp. 4389–4425.
9 Michelet, *Histoire de France*, Book III (Edition Robert Laffont, 1981), pp. 185–227. Originally published 1869. Ernest Lavisse, in his *Histoire de France* also begins with such a description.
10 For more on the structure of the French State, see Roland Mousnier, *The Institutions of France under the Absolute Monarchy 1598–1789*, 2 vols, Brian Pearce, trans. (Chicago: University of Chicago Press, 1979 and 1984), and Franklin L. Ford, *Robe and Sword, The Regrouping of the French Aristocracy after Louis XIV* (Cambridge, Mass.: Harvard University Press, 1962).
11 Maurice Druon, *Les Rois Maudits*, 7 volumes (Livres de poches, 1970–77), quotation from vol. 4, p. 334. In this series, Druon, famous Gaullist and author of the resistance hymn the 'chant du partisan', presents Philippe le Bel and his son Philippe le Long in a positive political light throughout their terrible struggles for power and against the curse put upon them by the Templars whom they had condemned.
12 René Rémond 'La fille ainée de l'Eglise', *Lieux de Mémoire* 3, p. 4321.
13 For more on the history of the Catholic church and its relationship to France, see Chapter 10 and Gérard Cholvy and Yves-Marie Hilaire, eds, *Histoire Religieuse de la France Contemporaine,* 3 vols (Paris: Privat, 1985–88).
14 Republican school manuals tended to call St Louis simply 'Louis IX'. After 1900, *Le tour de France par deux enfants* no longer included any references to a Cathedral or a national Catholic hero. See R. Rémond 'La fille ainée de l' Eglise', *Lieux de Mémoire* 3, p. 4345.
15 Both Charles De Gaulle, when received by Paul VI in Rome in May 1967, and Valery Giscard d'Estaing, when receiving John-Paul II in Paris, made reference to this expression.
16 The song, entitled 'Je suis tombé par terre c'est la faute à Voltaire, le nez dans le ruisseau c'est la faute à Rousseau', had a level of popularity which surpassed that of the musical itself, and yet was so particular to France that it was dropped altogether from the English version.
17 André Glucksmann, *Descartes c'est la France* (Paris: Flammarion, 1987).
18 The Jansenists were involved in a series of religious debates in the seventeenth and eighteenth centuries, and among other things opposed the absolutism of Louis XIV. On the Jansenist movement in France, see Catherine Maire, 'Port Royal: La fracture janséniste,' in Nora, *Les Lieux de Mémoire* 2, pp. 2605–52.
19 See Alain Rey, 'Les trésors de la langues', and Jean-Claude Chevalier, 'L'"Histoire de la langue française" de Ferdinand Brunot', in Nora, *Les Lieux de Mémoire* 2 and 3, pp. 2189–2205, 3385–3419.
20 Vercors, *The Silence of the Sea/Le Silence de la mer,* James W. Brown and Lawrence D. Stokes, ed., (New York and Oxford: Berg, 1991), pp. 49, 78–9.
21 See Daniel Fabre, 'Proverbes, contes et chansons', in Nora, *Les Lieux de Mémoire* 3, pp. 3555–81.
22 Pierre Nora, 'L'"Histoire de France" de Lavisse', in Nora, *Les Lieux de Mémoire* 1, p. 885.
23 For more information on pre-Revolutionary Frenchness, see Liah Greenfeld, *Nationalism: Five Roads to Modernity* (Cambridge, Mass.: Harvard University Press, 1992), pp. 89–188.
24 Such as the community studied by Peter Sahlins, *Boundaries: The Making of France and Spain in the Pyrenees* (Berkeley: University of California Press, 1989).
25 For descriptions of the representations of France during the Middle Ages, see Colette Beaune, *The Birth of an Ideology: Myths and Symbols of Nation in*

Late-Medieval France. Trans. Susan Ross Huston (Berkeley: University of California Press, 1991). For more on the relationships between representations and power structures, see Christopher Allmand, ed., *War, Government and Power in Late Medieval France* (Liverpool: Liverpool University Press, 2000), and for the transitions during the Early Modern period, see David Bell, 'Recent Works on Early Modern French National Identity', *JMH* 68 (March 1996), pp. 101–2.

26 In this way the 'patrie' of the *ancien régime* can be distinguished from a 'French' ethnic or cultural community not synonymous with the person of the King. See David Bell, 'Recent Works', p. 99.
27 See Ibid and David A. Bell, 'Lingua Populi, Lingua Dei: Language, Religion and the Origins of French Revolutionary Nationalism', *AHR* 100, 5 (December 1995), pp. 1403–37.
28 Keith Michael Baker, *Inventing the French Revolution: Essays on French Political Culture in the Eighteenth Century* (Cambridge: CUP, 1990), pp. 167–72 and Lynn Hunt, 'The French Revolution in Culture: new approaches and perspectives', *Eighteenth-Century Studies*, 22 (1989), pp. 293–301.
29 For more details on these questions, see the introduction and section II of Peter Jones ed., *The French Revolution in Social and Political Perspective* (Arnold, 1996).
30 Gildea, *The Past in French History*, p. 12.
31 See François Furet, 'L'Ancien Régime et la Révolution', in Nora, *Les Lieux de Mémoire* 2, p. 2301.
32 The abbé Grégoire, quoted in Gildea, *The Past in French History*, p. 21.
33 See Mona Ozouf, 'La Révolution Française et l'idée de l'homme nouveau', in Colin Lucas, ed., *The Political Culture of the French Revolution* (Oxford: Pergammon, 1988), pp. 213–32.
34 See Furet, 'L'Ancien Régime et la Révolution', pp. 2301–25.
35 See Gildea, *The Past in French History*, p. 21.
36 Furet, 'L'Ancien Régime et la Révolution', pp. 2307–11.
37 E. J. Sieyès, *Qu'est-ce que le Tiers Etat?* (Paris, 1982). Originally published January 1789.
38 Brian Jenkins, *Nationalism in France: Class and Nation since 1789* (London and New York: Routledge, 1990), p. 13.
39 Lynn Hunt, *Politics, Culture and Class in the French Revolution* (London: Methuen, 1986), p. 20, quoted in ibid, p. 20.
40 See Mona Ozouf, 'Liberté, égalité, fraternité', in Nora, ed., *Les Lieux de Mémoire* 3, pp. 4353–88.
41 For more on Marianne see the three books by Maurice Agulhon, *Marianne au combat. L'imagerie et la symbolique républicaines de 1789 à 1880; Marianne au pouvoir. L'imagerie et la symbolique républicaines de 1880 à 1914,* and *Les Métamorphoses de Marianne. L'imagerie et la symbolique républicaines de 1914 à nos jours* (Paris: Flammarion, 2001).
42 See Jenkins, *Nationalism in France,* p. 25.
43 For the origins of the counter-myth, see Gildea, *The Past in French History*, pp. 21–2.
44 See Jean-Clément Martin, 'La Vendée, région-mémoire', in Nora ed., *Les Lieux de Mémoire* 1, pp. 519–34.
45 Such a position can be found throughout republican writing, and is for example the basis of a scene in Victor Hugo's *Les Misérables*, in which one of those who voted for the execution of the King was pardoned, acknowledging that there was no other choice at the time.
46 On the question of Napoleon's early myth building, see Jean Tulard, *Napoléon, le mythe du Sauveur* (Paris: Fayard, 1977).

47 For a full discussion, see Sudhir Hazareesingh, *The Legend of Napoleon* (Granta, 2004).
48 Hugo refers to the Empire which took over from the Greek democracy, as exemplified here by Sparta.
49 Quoted in Gildea, *The Past in French History*, p. 66.
50 See for example Victor Hugo's poetry collection, *Les Chatiments.*
51 See Maurice Descotes, *La Légende de Napoléon et les Ecrivains français* (Paris: Minard, 1967) as well as the dossier 'Napoléon et son mythe', *Notre Histoire* 218 (February, 2004), pp. 16–41.

2

The Battle for the French Nation 1815–1940

Maurice Agulhon entitled the first of his three-volume history of republican symbolism *Marianne into Combat*, a representative interpretation in which it is the female incarnation of the Republic who is fighting for survival.[1] In many ways, it is the whole period that can be described as the battle for the French nation. This is certainly the image that has been retained of these years within the mainstream republican vision of French history, as well as within the more fragile and less well-remembered alternative national myths. In terms of French historical identity, this was the period in which the battles of the French Revolution were fought again and again, sometimes hotly and sometimes slowly, until such a time as France's future as a Republic was secured and consolidated. One of the key weapons in the struggle was the ability to have a particular interpretation of the Revolution and the First Empire gain wide acceptance, since rival political positions were each closely associated with one of several conflicting historical interpretations. The stakes in the political battle were the nature of the French regime, which changed at least once in every generation throughout the nineteenth century. While this chapter will focus on the national political struggles about the regime, the period as a whole is seen, with hindsight, as one of perpetual and manifold conflict, both concrete and ideological, internal and external. Disputes about class and social mobility, gender and the rights of women, regional culture and decentralisation, colonialism, race, as well as wars between France and its numerous European enemies permeate these years which also saw the first wave of economic modernisation of France, with ensuing social upheaval.[2] In spite of these conflicts, the retrospective attitude has been generally to remember it as a time of the gradual triumph of reason and of the values of the Revolution, both politically in the sense of France becoming a Republic for good, but also the gradual acceptance of republicanism, including its associated values and principles, within French society. This chapter will be divided into three sections, the first covering the period leading up to the Third Republic, founded in 1870, in which numerous regimes came and went in the quest to hold power and secure a lasting constitutional arrangement for the country. The second section will cover the Third Republic up to the First World War, a period in which Republican attitudes towards the nation and national history, thus far referred to as the republican myth, became solidified. The final section will examine the years between the First and Second World Wars, before examining the political legacy which the entire period has left and its place within the larger scheme of French history.

The Struggle for the Republic 1815–1870

The decades which followed the defeat of Napoleon at Waterloo in 1815 saw France change constitution and regime numerous times. Three dynasties put themselves forward for the throne – the Bourbons, the Orleans and the Bonapartes – battling it out with those who wanted to have a Republic.[3] The struggles for power were ideological as well as political and military. Each regime sought to legitimise itself in terms of its relationship to the French people, as well as through the elaboration of a vision of the history of the French nation which would strengthen its claim. The legacy of the period as well as its place within French identity, however, given the eventual victory of the Republican system, is that of the gradual domination of republicanism, both as a regime and as an increasingly popular ideology. Thus the way that the numerous regimes between 1815 and 1870 have primarily been remembered is less in terms of their actual contribution to the history of the French nation, but primarily with respect to the lessons which republicans were able to learn from each regime.

The restoration of the Bourbon family to the throne of France, for a short time in 1814 and then solidly in 1815, was achieved primarily through the European coalition against Napoleonic France. The new king, the younger brother of Louis XVI, took the name of Louis XVIII with the aim of constructing a history of France in which the reign of his family had been unbroken. He presented the past as if his nephew (the Dauphin during the Revolution) had become Louis XVII after his father's death, and claimed that he had begun to rule, not in 1815, but at the time of the presumed death of his nephew. This interpretation of the past, if it did not contend that the Revolution had never taken place, presented the entire episode and all the revolutionary governments as entirely without legitimacy, and not really influencing the 'unbroken' reign of the Bourbon dynasty. Louis XVIII sought to portray himself as the 'tender and indulgent father', whose subjects had been misguided by fanatics during the years of upheaval, and upon whom he would not seek revenge, but on the contrary whom he would be quick to pardon since they had now seen the error of their ways, returning to the bosom of the traditional, legitimate rulers of France.[4] After years of war and upheaval, which had resulted in as many as one and a half million deaths, the French greeted the restoration with a sense of relief in that at least it meant that peace would return.[5]

Surrounding and supporting the Bourbon restoration was a certain degree of romantic literature, which linked the royal family and their period in exile followed by a return to power with a kind of romantic heroism which was quite effective in symbolic terms, and resonated well. Such writers as Chateaubriand or the young Victor Hugo were able to link legitimism with romanticism as a historical interpretation of the fortunes of the dynasty. The publication of *La Génie du Christianisme* by Chateaubriand also marked the return of the Catholic Church not only to French society but also as a key inspiration of political thought and action. The contrast between the image of the Empire dominated by the army and that of the Restoration dominated by the church also runs through Stendhal's *Le Rouge et le Noir* and Musset's *La Confession d'un enfant du Siècle*.

While granting a constitution to the French people, the theory which underpinned Louis XVIII's reign was nevertheless one of absolutism. He was the king of France by divine right rather than by the will of the nation. After a few short years, the political entourage of the king became dominated by the ultra-monarchist group who were hostile to the Revolution and keen to re-establish the influence of the church and the landed nobility of the *ancien régime*. Led by the Comte de Villèle, they ran the government from 1821–27, into the reign of Charles X, the younger brother of Louis XVIII who succeeded him in 1825. The perpetual threat to all of those who had gained during the Revolutionary years meant that opposition to the regime gradually increased. This was particularly true among the new class of administrators, soldiers and particularly those who had been able to purchase the former church lands when they had been seized and sold in 1789 and who feared a return of their property to the church.[6]

When the second restoration king, Charles X, was overthrown in the July Revolution in 1830, the interpretation which has stuck is that the Bourbon family was too absolutist, not listening to the people or according them the proper amount of respect in political decision making. Charles X himself was unpopular, and with his attitude of hauteur denying any personal accountability to the French nation, it was only a matter of time (so the interpretation goes) before he was overthrown. The reinstated Catholic church, with its insistence that French society needed to repent the sinfulness of the Revolutionary years, was also credited with contributing to the dissatisfaction within French society which led to the ultimate failure of the Restoration. Even many from among the elites joined with the Revolution, but preferred to replace the monarch with another one who would be more in tune with the French nation, and inspire less fear among those who had been sympathetic to, or who had at least made gains during the Revolution.

After the July Revolution, it was a cousin of the king, the Duc d'Orléans who became the new constitutional monarch Louis-Philippe I. He was the son of 'Philippe Egalité', one of the nobles who had participated in the French Revolution, famously voting in favour of the execution of his cousin, Louis XVI, and later executed himself. Styling himself King of the French, rather than King of France, Louis-Philippe I cultivated an image as the 'citizen-king'. He reinstated the tricolour flag, swore loyalty to the constitution, and portrayed himself as respecting the values of the early phase of the Revolution – representational democracy and individual liberty – creating what would be remembered as the 'bourgeois monarchy'. His legacy within French history has been that his regime failed to deliver on social issues. The July Monarchy was felt to be too interested in keeping the franchise restricted to the wealthy and thereby guarding power within a very limited circle, paying only lip-service to the people he was supposed to represent. The words of his prime minister Guizot, 'enrich yourselves through hard work and savings', came to symbolise the regime's supposed desire to please only the economic and business elites, devoid of the romanticism associated with the Bourbon family. Orleanism and its representatives came to be characterised as the heartless elite of money and capital, whether in or out of power.[7] Overthrown in its turn during the Revolution of 1848, the July Monarchy was replaced by the Second Republic, which set out to give power back to the people in practice, not just in rhetoric, and incorporate the 'true' values of the Revolution into their constitution.

The Second Republic has an ambiguous place in the republican vision of French history. While in many ways representative of the values which republicans hoped to spread, the nature of its failure and downfall has meant that both the 1848 Revolution and the republic which emerged from it have in many ways been forgotten in French history. If one looks at monuments, celebrations, famous events, heroes and martyrs among the French historical canon, very few are drawn from this period. It is not that the Revolution and Second Republic lacked candidates, but when Napoleon's nephew, Louis-Napoleon Bonaparte was elected as the first president and went on to suppress the Republic and declare himself Emperor with the support of the population expressed in a democratic plebiscite, the Republic as a whole could not even be seen in the glorious light of sacrifice and defeat.[8] Since it was via the popular will expressed in voting with universal male suffrage that the Republic disappeared, the unhappy but inevitable conclusion was that it was defeated by its own democratic principles. This shameful failure was thus not much of a recommendation for democracy, hence the 1848 Revolution and Second Republic's conspicuous absence from the official republican as well as the popular myth of French history.[9]

Louis-Napoleon, in founding the Second Empire, took the name of Napoleon III, following in the footsteps of Louis XVIII in trying to establish dynastic legitimacy as if there had been an unbroken chain between Napoleon I, his son (the Duc de Reichstett, held to have been Napoleon II) and then himself. Napoleon's son became a romantic figure, referred to as the 'Eaglet', making reference to the Imperial Eagle which had symbolised his father, and he appeared in numerous works of literature at the time.[10] Much use was made of the imagery of the (First) Empire, and great Napoleonic victories were celebrated nationally. In a similar way to Louis-Philippe, Napoleon III claimed to be ruling by the democratic will of the French nation, in his case justified firstly by his electoral victory to the presidency of the Second Republic (by universal male suffrage), and later confirmed on several occasions by victorious plebiscites. Napoleon III also sought an image as a moderniser, as the leader who brought peace and economic progress to the French nation, preferring economic to military conquests.[11] During the Second Empire, modernising programmes were implemented, such as the construction of new railway lines and the rebuilding of Paris by Baron Haussmann, replacing the small streets with great avenues and creating the architectural face of Paris which has lasted to the present day. Napoleon III also sought to have himself portrayed as the one who was able to reconcile the Catholic church with the French State, as his uncle had done before him, thus drawing together the two sides of at least one of the profound cleavages through French society left by the Revolution. Republican opponents of Napoleon III, unable to criticise his democratic support, portrayed him as weak and ineffectual, a poor imitation of his uncle,[12] and had to wait until external military defeat in the Franco-Prussian War brought an end to Napoleon III's reign, before the return of the Republic could be envisaged.[13]

Although it lasted for only a few short months, a full consideration of the failed nineteenth-century regimes would not be complete without a brief discussion of the Paris Commune. When Napoleon III was captured during the French defeat in the battle of Sedan in September 1870, the Third Republic was created to fill the power vacuum, but in spite of continuing the war effort, they were unable to turn the tables on the Prussians and were forced to concede defeat in January 1871. The Parisian population, refusing to accept the French defeat, set up a provisional municipal government in the capital, which seized power in opposition to the national authorities and sought to put in practice a series of radical republican and socialist measures. The French government retreated to Versailles, and after a few weeks of waiting, sent the army in to Paris to subdue the insurgents, ending in 'the bloody week' of May 1871 in which the working-class population of Paris was decimated. Like the regimes before it, the Commune also tried to inscribe itself in the French historical Revolutionary tradition, picking up on the symbolism of the barricades and the image of the people in arms against tyranny. Later, its successors hoped to commemorate the martyrdom of those who sacrificed themselves for the cause, as well as the great inspirational leaders, such as Louise Michel. While in this way the extreme left attempted to keep the memory of the Commune alive as a tragic reminder of the excesses of 'bourgeois' republican governments, and to perpetuate the tradition via street protests and the construction of barricades well into the twentieth century, the Commune has instead entered mainstream historical memory as a tragic attempt to impose change too quickly, as well as an example of the dangers of revolutionary excesses.[14]

Each of the regimes during this period inspired a political ideology to support its claims for legitimacy, which was also used to describe the political parties that supported it. There were the monarchists, divided into the legitimists supporting the heirs of Charles X, and the orleanists who favoured the claims of the descendants of Louis-Philippe, the bonapartists who supported the claims of the Bonaparte family, as well as the republicans. The political ideologies – legitimism, orleanism, bonapartism and republicanism – had fully worked out claims to defend their system, and the debates occurred not only within the political arena, but also in the literature of the period. Superimposed upon these ideologies, other discourses gradually appeared, such as that of the socialists who argued for a new Revolution in the name of the working classes, sometimes allied with, but often in opposition to the republicans.[15]

The efforts by each of the regimes between 1815 and 1870 to inscribe itself positively within the long term history of the French nation show the extent to which links to the past were also important within the French political scheme. Such associations were as much a part of their claims to legitimacy as their ideological position. Each regime sought to present itself as the inevitable, natural heir to the complicated history of France since the Revolution, be it for the return to stability or the ability to integrate the values of the Revolution. Each regime was also faced with the inevitable problem of reconciling the 'two Frances' which emerged from the Revolutionary years, and, in particular, of integrating both the Catholic church as well as at least some of the democratic, revolutionary values within their regime. In this way, each regime drew not only from its own antecedents, but also from the other political traditions in order to cover the entire political territory. In this way, Louis-Philippe brought back the body of Napoleon in great ceremony to rest in the Hotel des Invalides in Paris. A final dimension to the presentation of each regime with respect to France's past was to show that it was the regime of progress and modernity, setting itself apart from the other regimes in the past as the one which was best able to modernise the country. Overall, links to the past were a way to ensure that French greatness, glory and prestige, even if achieved in fact before the start of the regime in question, were magnified and, as much as possible, directly linked in the minds of the people with that particular regime. Thus each regime sought, within the bounds of its own ideological framework, to legitimise itself through a demonstration that it was an inevitable, logical and positive conclusion to the history of the French nation.

The details of the political debates of the nineteenth century, as well as many of the events and the main protagonists have not been retained within the popular perceptions of the history of the French nation. Much emphasis was placed upon social problems associated with the development of industry and urbanisation, which were in turn used to support the republican vision of French history. Insofar as advancement for common French men and women was achieved, it was only thanks either directly to the action of the various Republics or at least due to republican pressure from opposition. The conclusions which emerged were that France was a great nation, gradually coming to terms with its revolutionary legacy in the decades which followed, up to the time when France would become a republic for good.

The period was not without its historical lessons, but these were drawn primarily in terms of how to secure a lasting republican constitution for France. In this way the fall of the Second Republic showed that universal suffrage was something to be treated with caution, and the repeated changes of monarch showed that the various houses were continually waiting in the wings to step back into power, making constant vigilance necessary to keep them at bay. The importance of popular literature for the historical legacy of the period also contributed to the lack of memory of historical detail, even in the places where it was not in overt support of the republican position. Numerous writers gave romanticised accounts of the different regimes, from the orleanist heroes in Balzac through the republican heroes of Victor Hugo and the description of the human cost of modernisation during the Second Empire found in Emile Zola, to the characters in Eugène Sue's *Mystères de Paris*. A synthesis of the literature of the period converges with the republican myth of the history of the French nation, in that many of the writers themselves began as or were gradually converted to republicanism, and other myths (legitimist or bonapartist) were either forgotten or marginalised. Much of this interpretation of French history, including the memory of the Revolution itself, was to a large extent popularised during the 'victorious' Third Republic, which also clearly aimed to place itself both as the historical heir and the interpreter of French history, the ultimate conclusions of which remained primarily unchallenged throughout the twentieth century.

The Triumph of the Republic 1870–1914

With retrospect it is easy to assume that the Third Republic declared in 1870 seemed as secure as we now know that it became, lasting for 70 years and brought down only following a serious external defeat. For almost a decade, however, the Chamber of Deputies was dominated by monarchists who hoped to bring about a restoration as soon as possible. Division over which of the rival royal houses to choose, as well as personality conflicts and the refusal of the Comte de Chambord, the legitimist heir, to recognise the tricolour flag meant that the Republic remained the regime by default until such a time as the quarrelling royalist parties could agree. Before this ever happened, however, the republicans had turned the tables on the monarchists in several elections, finally achieving a majority position in both of the legislative houses, the Senate and the Chamber, as well as in the municipalities across the country, in 1879. The precariousness of each of the previous regimes taught the republicans to take nothing for granted. Behaving from the outset with the understanding that the Republic was completely insecure, with enemies on all sides such that it could be toppled at any time, successive republican governments sought to solidify their hold on power through a variety of means, one of the most important of which was to perpetuate the republican vision of French history. The various actions they took became the great legacy of the Third Republic, presented as a kind of 'golden age' for the French nation and for republicanism. The remainder of the chapter will examine the various events, images and principles drawn from the period which have come to symbolise the Third Republic and its place in French history, before turning to its legacy in terms of cultural practices.

One of the earliest images of the Third Republic is that of the domination of the moderates. Within the first few months of its existence, the Third Republic had to deal with the large scale revolt of the Parisian population during the Paris Commune. After the bloody suppression of this extremist left-wing revolt, the remaining republicans used their success to prove their own moderation and their ability to preserve order. The episode of the Commune demonstrated that a Republic was not bound to degenerate into an extremist-dominated popular terror and chaos reminiscent of the 1789 Revolution. The Republic claimed that its historical roots were in Revolution, but tried hard to downplay the excesses of revolutionary violence, centring the historical legacy of the Revolution on revolutionary values. The historical legacy of the period which followed is that of the crystallisation of a moderate form of republicanism, presented as the inevitable historical conclusion to the turbulent years of French history which had preceded it, and which gave rise to a golden age in French history.[16]

The golden age of the French nation and republicanism during the early decades of the Third Republic is conceived in terms of a variety of republican and national historical images, the most prominent of which is the mythical ideal of the birth of mass education. Already clearly identified as central to the republican project during the Revolution, when national sovereignty implied an educated citizenry capable of engaging with national debates. The Third Republic has been credited as the first regime to put into practice a concrete and effective policy of the integration of the French population more closely into the national culture through the development of primary schools, thereby 'creating the nation' from below. One of the first acts of the republicans after they came to power was to make primary education free, compulsory and secular with the Ferry laws of 1881–2. The corps of primary school teachers became known as the 'black hussars of the Republic' for their black dress and for the secular republicanism which they taught alongside the French language in the schools of rural France.[17] The reputation of the period is that the population came to see the benefits of republicanism and were able to become full participants in the politics of the nation as they learned to read and write the French language and became aware of their national history. To teach French national history required the development of textbooks, as well as the enhancement of research into French history, promoted increasingly in France's universities. An example is the government's establishment of the chair for the History of the French Revolution at the Sorbonne, a clear indicator that the Republic wanted French national history to be developed and enhanced at every level, from the elite to the popular.

One of the most enduring images of change among the population which emerged from the period is what Eugen Weber has called the transformation of 'Peasants into Frenchmen'.[18] While the term does not come from a French historian, it nevertheless encapsulates well an important image which the French themselves have of the period, that of the modernisation of the country which included the integration of the population into national citizenship and mainstream republicanism. Weber himself argued that via the construction of transportation networks increasing contact between the various regions of France, alongside the work of the primary schoolteachers and compulsory military service, the population was integrated into the French nation. This position is completely consistent with the republican image of the period: that the conscious efforts of the republican nation builders, by developing the transportation network, increasing schools and creating compulsory military service, were directly responsible for the victory of republicanism. This victory was the result of over one hundred years of struggle and came to symbolise the period in French history.

In addition to popular education, the Third Republic also entered into history as the regime which affirmed France's nationalism through the symbolism of the French Revolution. It was the Third Republic which declared the 14th of July a national holiday, which had statues of Marianne, the female incarnation of the Republic, erected in the village hall in every village in France, and which organised an international exhibition in Paris in 1889 to commemorate the centenary of the French Revolution. This direct link to the past, accompanied by the showcasing of French industry and science, symbolised by the Eiffel Tower which was built for the exhibition, was overtly intended to demonstrate the potential greatness of republicanism to the world. France as a world leader, showcasing its own democracy and republican constitution, and particularly proud of its history and revolutionary heritage, is exactly the image which has been retained of the early years of the Third Republic, of a republican France with the nation behind it.

A key dimension to the historical image of the Third Republic is that of secularism.[19] Not only were the schools secularised, but the republican leaders fought what they portrayed as a desperate fight against the forces of reaction within the church hierarchy. They sought to limit the church's impact within French education, as we have seen, but also in the domain of French politics, restricting the rights of priests to preach political sermons, and in French society as a whole. One of the explanations for the prolonged exclusion of women from the vote in France throughout the Third Republic was the fear of the church's influence on women in French society. The culmination of an active campaign of anticlericalism in the years around the turn of the century was the separation of the church and State in 1905, the ending of the concordat which had been signed between Napoleon and the Catholic church just over one hundred years earlier. While the conflict with the church has been portrayed in some ways as the triumph of reason over superstition, in order to avoid alienating much of the Catholic population, the historic position targeted the institution of the church. Anticlericals argued that it was the institution and hierarchy which schemed to keep the population in ignorance in order to dominate them, meanwhile hoping to overthrow the Republic. A serious attempt was made to suggest that the anticlericalism of the Third Republic was primarily a kind of secularism which was combined with a firm belief in freedom of religion for all. The support of the Republic by Protestants and Jews has been held as confirmation of this interpretation. To increase this image further, the role of the Catholic church as a reactionary force was brought to the fore in the historical memory of the *ancien régime*, the revolutionary period and the remainder of the nineteenth century.

Outside the political sphere, the period has been remembered as a time of progress and cultural greatness for France. The final decades of the nineteenth century and the pre-war years in the twentieth became known in retrospect as the 'Belle Epoque', the glorious years, in which France and particularly Paris were the centre of the world for art, fashion, theatre, music and high society.[20] This was the time of the Impressionists and the Moulin Rouge, of café society and intellectual activity. It was also a time of technological progress, when science and industry developed rapidly in France and wealth increased. Even though there was much social unrest, and any social progress was hard won via conflicts and strikes, the period has nevertheless been remembered as a time when concessions were slowly wrung from industrialists and the State, and things did get better for workers. The literary images of the period which portray the misery and perpetual struggles of the workers, even if at the time they were written were considered supportive of the extreme left and critical of the republican government and elites, came to be romanticised into an overall picture of struggle for improvement which was not in fact contradictory with the Republic and the republican view of French national history.

It was also a period in which France's international and military greatness were rebuilt. Although recovering from military defeat in 1871, the French army and its prestige were gradually reconstructed. The evidence of the successful recovery was that, like its European neighbours, France possessed and was extending its colonial Empire.[21] It was also rebuilding its diplomatic position within Europe, and gradually increasing the size of its army and forging alliances such that when the call to war came in 1914, the French nation answered the call with renewed confidence. Although the period before the First World War was often viewed as one of perpetual crisis, particularly by the republicans who lived through it, and saw a conspiracy to overthrow the Republic behind every bush, in retrospect it has been reconstructed into French history as this golden age in which republicanism triumphed, monarchism declined, the church was de-throned, socialism kept at bay and the economy modernised. At the same time, the efforts of the republican governments to integrate the population of France into national culture and politics through the free compulsory school system were credited as the accomplishment of the revolutionary project. Looking back from after the war, the pre-war crises seemed minor squabbles in a period when in fact the republic was finally secure. The Great War, the war to end all wars, would bring the golden age to an end, marking a major turning point in every version of French history.

The Republic in Crisis 1914–1940

As the golden age before the war was golden only in retrospect, in many ways the same can be said for the crisis of the interwar period, at least in terms of the fragility of the Republic. To examine these years, we need to look at the question of French greatness and France's relationship with other countries, the conclusions which were drawn from the First World War and the ways the war was perceived to have altered French society, both demographically and in its attitudes, and more particularly its place as a great but in many ways hollow victory within the history of the nation. It will also require an examination of the 1930s and the challenges to republicanism, the relationship of the different political parties to the Republic, most particularly the Popular Front government of 1936, as well as the ways in which the knowledge of the subsequent war and defeat coloured the interpretations of the interwar crises.[22]

Any analysis of the French victory in 1918 can be viewed with a certain sense of irony.[23] The victory could have been remembered in similar ways to those French victories under Napoleon, primarily as a great heroic moment for the French nation in arms. After all, the victory showed that Republican France was now strong enough not only to defeat its internal enemies (for good) but even to defeat its great external enemy, take revenge for the defeat of 1870–71 and recover the lost territories of Alsace and Lorraine. The presence of war memorials to the dead in each and every village of France commemorated the patriotic sacrifice for the nation and can be seen as symbolising the true nationalisation of the masses, who at the very least were made brutally aware of the nation. In the national memory, however, the victory did not usher in a period of simple triumphalism and stability based upon the most solid position that France had been in for generations. Instead the war has been a symbol of victory, but at the same time of sacrifice and loss in the name of the nation. It is furthermore considered as the cause of great fragility for the French nation, such that between 1918 and 1939, the Republic was weakened, and in even greater crisis than before. In part this is again the retrospective reconstruction, knowing that the two decades which followed the victory were going to lead France to the greatest military defeat it had ever suffered, and to the fall of the Republic in 1940.

The position of France in 1918 led to very high expectations among the French people for the years that followed. In many ways, the perception of the interwar period as fraught with crisis and lack of success for France is not only coloured by hindsight, but at the time it was also coloured by frustration in the face of these high expectations. A republican France had proved that it could be unified and victorious and among the great powers of the world, yet in order to do so it had suffered greatly, and the victory ought to have ensured increased greatness and prolonged security during the years of peace which followed. Instead, the years which followed the victory were extremely difficult, as the country tried to rebuild and re-gain economic and financial stability, social cohesion and international security. One minor crisis followed another in such a way as the hoped for peace and stability were never achieved to the level expected following the victory, and frustration and deception rapidly replaced joy and celebration.

France's inability to recover completely at a time when Germany was able to re-build and ultimately defeat France in 1940 has alternatively been explained as a betrayal in the peace by France's wartime allies or by structural problems within French society. The war had left France weakened and ultimately unable to resist a renewed Germany on its own, and the French continued to feel some resentment towards her former allies for their perceived lack of support for French interests in peacetime. Since France had suffered so much material damage as a result of the war taking place on French soil, the French government had hoped that the allies would help with the rebuilding both through credits and the forgiveness of its war debts, freeing up resources for reconstruction, and also by continuing into peacetime the centralised and coordinated economic planning which had been put into practice in the closing years of the war in order to encourage the war economy, particularly in the coal and steel sectors. The United States was unwilling to forgive France its war debt and both the US and Great Britain rejected such suggestions of economic cooperation or planning to help France out of depression or inflationary periods. So, when the kind of support hoped for from the allies was not forthcoming, France was forced to rely solely on reparations payments to come from Germany under the Treaty of Versailles. Even in this area, France often felt undermined by its allies, who it felt were trying to restrain French recovery by going too easy on Germany. The 1920s were years of monetary difficulties for France, and the tight money policy insisted on by Britain and the United States, aiming for a strict return to the pre-war gold standard, meant that the French government was continually under pressure, and economic recovery much slower in coming.[24] In terms of finding a lasting military peace arrangement, the United States refused to support the collective security initiatives of the League of Nations, and the British championing of the policy of appeasement towards Hitler during the 1930s was also seen as a willingness to allow France's former enemy to rearm and gain the strength needed to invade France once again.

In addition to a perceived betrayal by France's allies, the second major difficulty for the French during the years which followed the First World War stemmed from the changes the war brought to French society. In addition to the material damage which needed to be repaired and the land which needed to be recovered, the loss of young men was held to be a fundamental problem for the recovery of French society. With 1,358,000 dead and over 1 million permanent invalids, a generation was missing, both to help with the work of rebuilding, and to become fathers and provide the next generation of Frenchmen. Absence of labour in certain sectors and regions caused friction within society and meant that France had to recruit immigrant labour, which contributed to the social unrest. In addition, as the wounded and veterans who had lived through the carnage of the Western Front returned to French society, civilians gradually became aware of what the costs had been and how high a price had been paid; the glory and honour of the victory became hollow in many ways.[25] The result was increased pacifism and a reinforced belief that France occupied the moral high ground, certainly with respect to Germany, but also with respect to France's wartime allies. While these problems were real, they entered the French historical myth as primary causes for the perceived weaknesses in French society which led to the subsequent defeat in 1940, not just as a means to understand the period.

The positive image of a period in which France remained a great nation and in which republicanism triumphed over its numerous adversaries, internal and external, was not completely without negative counterparts. Negative historical interpretations of the Third Republic underline the perpetual conflict, the instability and weakness inherent in the republican constitutional system, and the hypocrisy of a supposedly democratic system oriented towards helping the population, while at the same time the working-class masses were suffering under unbridled capitalism, repeatedly ignored and repressed by the political elites claiming to represent them. While the Third Republic was never overthrown, endless quarrels erupted between the various parties, between the State, the church, trade unions and numerous other groups. Strikes were regular and often violent, and all political debates took on a character of urgency. Because of the fear of a Bonapartist-style coup d'état, the executive power had been kept perpetually subservient to the legislature within the constitution of the Third Republic, with the result that individual governments were often short-lived, lasting only a few weeks or months. As such, many governments had so little time in office, or were so vulnerable to being thrown out, that they were unable to implement any new programme or significant change. Nevertheless, for the first decades of the Republic the domination of the legislature was perceived as a triumphant characteristic of republicanism, since it had guaranteed the survival of the Republic and prevented any seizure of power by strong-minded individuals who might have been enemies of republicanism.[26]

The constitutional arrangement came to be viewed differently during the interwar years, however. In this climate of perpetual menace of renewed war with Germany, the perception of the Third Republic as weak and ineffective came to be seen as more serious a problem for France. Furthermore, the ability of the French governments to take action in the face of the numerous economic and political crises of the 1920s and the 1930s appeared particularly limited, especially when contrasted with the reactions in many of France's neighbouring States, who were all turning towards more centralised, executive-dominated if not completely authoritarian systems. It was felt in France by many that the authoritarian regimes found in Mussolini's Italy, Franco's Spain and Hitler's Germany were better able to respond to the Great Depression, using their executive authority to direct the economy in ways which the republican government in France, handicapped as it was by the domination of the legislature, was unable to do. Although the Depression began later and was not as severe in France as in other nations, it lasted longer, and criticism of the republican constitution was tied to the perceived inability of the French governments to pull France out of economic depression. Criticism of the weakness of the republican system, already rife during the interwar years, grew even more swiftly following the defeat in 1940, when the army leaders (and then the Vichy government) refused to interpret the defeat as a purely military one and read into it deep political and moral meanings. Although it has been shown that there are solid military explanations for the defeat and is possible to argue that the longevity of the Third Republic compared to any other regime since 1789 showed that it had the necessary flexibility to survive internal political crises (but not external defeat), nevertheless the image of social and institutional weakness would endure in French national collective memory.[27]

The perception of the interwar years, and especially the 1930s, as characterised by weak, ineffective French governments is dominated by the perception of the Popular Front government of 1936.[28] The Popular Front was a left-wing coalition formed by the Radical party in the centre, the Socialist party and the Communist party on the extreme left. The Communists had only begun to cooperate with the other parties after being encouraged to abandon their revolutionary doctrine and participate in mainstream politics by the Soviet Communist Party, which feared a swing towards the extreme right if they did not help out. These parties had been driven to cooperate after a large demonstration of 'the leagues' in February 1934, which indicated that the threat from the extreme right was real. They entered the elections as allies and emerged with a majority of the deputies. The socialists, as the largest party within the coalition, led the new government, with their leader, Léon Blum, as the new prime minister. The first weeks of the Popular Front were characterised both by legislation in favour of the workers, such as the first paid holidays and a shortening of the work week, but also by widespread strikes, as the labour movement found the position of the Popular Front government did not live up to their expectations. High hopes had been held that the first socialist-dominated government would change the situation much more in favour of the workers than was in fact the case. Criticised from both left and right, Blum's ministry lasted only just over a year, but served as a symbol for both the right and the left. For the right, it was the worst of the weak, concessionary-style politics of the republic, unable to stand up either to the labour movement when times were tough internally, nor for France's interests when faced with a re-arming Germany. For the left, it symbolised hope and promise, the possible achievements of socialists when in government, and when supported by a unified left. It was criticism of the Popular Front which would signal the eventual comeback of a Republican right, finally free of royalist commitments and able to integrate the republican mainstream, since the image of weakness charged to the Third Republic as a whole would cling to the Popular Front and its heirs even into the post-war years. The fact that Léon Blum was Jewish was used by the antisemitic right as one more negative image of the Popular Front, and one which would be widely discussed during the aftermath of the defeat in 1940.

Each of these negative images of the republic has nevertheless been subsumed into the overall republican-dominated history of France as a part

Figure 3 The Popular Front

of the unfortunate process of republican consolidation and advancement of French society, often painful, but nevertheless in the right direction in the long run. French greatness was not questioned, and economic difficulties and military defeat were at least in part explained by external betrayal by former allies and the unfortunate effects of the sacrifice needed to win the First World War on French society. Regarding the negative image of a weak constitutional system, most often used to criticise the left, the mainstream reaction has been to underline the repeated and constant threats to the Republic of a Bonapartist-style coup d'état, and to look at the overall record of the Third Republic across the whole of its seventy-year history. During that time, much progress was made for the French population in terms of material well-being, social mobility and education, as well as integration into the national culture, and any excess time that such reforms may have taken being laid at the feet of the perpetual opposition, rather than any weakness or problem inherent in the system. Thus one can think of the crises of the 1930s, as real as they were for those at the time, as simply the latest episode of the crisis-filled, unstable political agitation which had characterised the whole of the Third Republic.

The Third Republic therefore retains an important place within the constructed popular narrative of French history, in which the values of the Revolution were finally put triumphantly into practice, and (in spite of the reality of political exclusion for women and racial minorities in the colonies) the period when the French population was held to have become fully integrated into the nation. It included the golden age of republican nationalism, the definitive demise of monarchism and bonapartism, as well as the integration of revolutionary socialism within mainstream parliamentary republicanism as consenting participants, as well as the greatest military victory France had ever achieved. French society became modernised, the population educated, and an enduring republican political culture was created to serve as a legacy for later republics. This culture included a sense of political urgency about all disagreements and a tendency to see enemies everywhere, traditions of popular protest in the streets, anticlericalism, republican triumphalism, and a belief in 'state-centred' solutions to problems. The overall political climate was shaped by the interpretation of the French Revolution which left France divided into two great halves, alternatively labelled left and right, republican and reactionary, change and order, which left an interpretation of French history which was one of perpetual civil conflict, the 'Franco-French war' which would continue beyond the Third Republic. This history of the French nation in this period was also understood primarily in terms of the internal dynamics of the country, rather than as a part of the wider process of European development, in which industrialisation, democratisation and the transformation of society were also taking place. It is also the history of white, educated males which has become the national history, and that of other groups consigned to parentheses. While during the years of the Third Republic the interpretation of French history and especially the French Revolution raised serious conflicts within French society and its elites, the period of occupation which followed the defeat of France and the replacement of the Third Republic with the authoritarian regime of Marshal Philippe Pétain would bring a new conflict to France, and in its aftermath the conflicts of the period discussed so far became consigned to historians.

Notes

1 Maurice Agulhon, *Marianne au Combat: L'imagerie et la symbolique républicaines de 1789 à 1880* (Paris: Flammarion, 1979). See also his *Marianne au Pouvoir: L'imagerie et la symbolique républicaines de 1880 à 1914* (Paris: Flammarion, 1989), which describes how the republicans used imagery and symbolism to consolidate their position in power.

2 These other conflicts will be discussed in later chapters, while this chapter will focus upon high politics and the choice of regime.

3 For a complete discussion of the influence of these dynasties on the evolution of the right in France, see René Rémond, *The Right Wing in France From 1815 to de Gaulle*, 2nd Ed., J. M. Laux trans. (Philadelphia: University of

Pennsylvania Press, 1969).

4 See the Proclamation of Louis XVIII, quoted in Robert Gildea, *The Past in French History* (New Haven and London: Yale University Press, 1994), p. 22, and also the preamble to the 1814 charter, quoted in Robert Tombs, *France 1814–1914.* (Harlow: Longman, 1996), p. 329.

5 See Tombs, *France*, p. 330.

6 See Tombs, *France*, pp. 339–44.

7 See Rémond, *The Right Wing in France*. For a study of the July Monarchy, see H. A. C. Collingham with R. S. Alexander, *The July Monarchy: a Political History of France 1830–1848* (London and New York: Longman, 1988).

8 For more detail, see Timothy Baycroft, 'Commemorations of the Revolution of 1848 and the Second Republic', *Modern & Contemporary France* 6, 2 (1998), pp. 155–68, and also Chapter 7.

9 See also Maurice Agulhon, *Les Quarante-Huitards* (Paris: Gallimard, 1992), pp. 9–15.

10 See, for example, the play by Edmond Rostand, *L'Aiglon* (The Eaglet).

11 See Tombs, *France*, pp. 399–403.

12 See, for example, Victor Hugo. Even Karl Marx, in his *Eighteenth Brumaire of Louis Napoleon*, took up the theme of the weak imitation of the uncle.

13 For a study of the Second Empire, see Alain Plessis, *The Rise and Fall of the Second Empire 1852–1871* (Cambridge: CUP, 1985); Roger Price, *Napoleon III and the Second Empire* (London: Routledge, 1997); W. H. C. Smith, *Second Empire and Commune: France 1848–71* (Harlow: Longman, 1996); and Sudhir Hazareesingh, *From Subject to Citizen: The Second Empire and the Emergence of Modern French Democracy* (Princeton: Princeton University Press, 1998).

14 For a general history of the Commune, see: Robert Tombs, *The Paris Commune, 1871* (London: Longman, 1999), Donny Gluckstein, *The Paris Commune: A Revolution in Democracy* (London: Bookmarks, 2006) and David A Shafer, *The Paris Commune* (Basingstoke: Palgrave, 2005).

15 Other types of political debates, such as colonialism or women's rights, cross-cut these political groupings which were primarily defined in terms of their choice of regime.

16 For a general history of the period, see Charles Sowerwine, *France since 1870: Culture, Politics and Society* (Basingstoke: Palgrave, 2001), J-M. Mayeur and M. Rebérioux, *The Third Republic from its Origins to the Great War 1871–1914* (Cambridge: CUP, 1984), and R. Gildea, *France 1870–1914.* 2nd Ed. (Longman, 1996).

17 The term was coined by Charles Péguy, *L'Argent* in volume 8 of complete works in prose (Paris: Pleiade), p. 799.

18 Eugen Weber, *Peasants into Frenchmen: The Modernisation of Rural France, 1870–1914* (Stanford: Stanford University Press, 1976).

19 For further developments see Chapter 10.

20 See Charles Rearick, *Pleasures of the Belle Epoque: Entertainment and festivity in turn of the century France* (London: Yale, 1985) and Eugen Weber, *France: Fin-de-siècle* (Cambridge, Mass.: Belknap Press, 1986) for more on the period and its image.

21 For more on this, see Chapter 8.

22 For further general reading on the period, see Philippe Bernard and Henri Dubief, *The Decline of the Third Republic* (Cambridge: CUP, 1985), James F. Macmillan, *Twentieth-Century France: Politics and Society 1898–1991* (London: Arnold, 1992), Maurice Agulhon, *The French Republic 1879–1992* (Oxford: Basil Blackwell, 1993), Rod Kedward, *La Vie en Bleu: France and the French since 1900* (London: Allen Lane, 2005) and J. V. F. Keiger, *Raymond Poincaré* (Cambridge: CUP, 1997).

23 Note that a study of the war itself will be undertaken in Chapter 6.
24 See Stephen D. Carls, *Louis Loucheur and the Shaping of Modern France 1916–1931* (Baton Rouge: Louisiana State University Press, 1993) on the transition between wartime and post-war economic planning.
25 Hence the title of Eugen Weber's *The Hollow Years.*
26 The most obvious example being General Boulanger in the 1880s.
27 For more on the 1930s and the attraction of authoritarianism, see Eugen Weber, *The Hollow Years: France in the 1930s* (Sinclair-Stevenson, 1995), as well as the debate over French fascism: Zeev Sternhall, *Neither Right nor Left: Fascist Ideology in France* (Princeton: Princeton University Press, 1996), Robert Soucy, *French Fascism: The First Wave* (New Haven and London: Yale University Press, 1986), idem, *French Fascism: The Second Wave* (New Haven and London: Yale University Press, 1995).
28 On the Popular Front, see Julian Jackson, *The Popular Front in France: Defending Democracy 1934–38* (Cambridge: CUP, 1985) and Maurice Larkin, *France since the Popular Front: Government and People 1936–1996* (Oxford: Clarendon: 1997).

3

Defeat and its Aftermath 1940–1944

The overwhelming defeat of the French army in 1940 and the period of occupation by Nazi Germany which followed have become known as 'the dark years' in French history.[1] They brought not only national shame and humiliation, but also created and intensified profound internal divisions within French society such that the ensuing debates would make these years not only an historical turning point, but also provoke a profound crisis of national identity. The years of war and occupation touched the French nation so profoundly that they even took over from the French Revolution as the most hotly contested period in French history for the remainder of the twentieth century and beyond. One of the primary controversies has been simply how to integrate these years within the historical narrative of the French nation, and indeed the French State. The search for the most appropriate historical interpretations went well beyond the circle of professional historians and permeated French society. While many sections of French society hoped simply to pretend that they did not occur, placing them as years of parenthesis in the history of the nation, others fought over ways to integrate them, with conflicts over historical interpretation entering the political realm in much the same way as those of the Revolution had done in the previous century. Indeed, French preoccupation with these years became so extensive as to have led one historian, Henry Rousso, to characterise it in terms of a mental illness for post-war French society – the Vichy Syndrome.[2] He likened the war and occupation to a past trauma, which is first covered up and suppressed, only to later emerge from the subconscious to a place of active unease and disquiet. The profundity and significance of the period's history for the French nation is revealed by the scale of public and private attention it has received and continues to receive, as well as the scope of the debates surrounding it.

There is not one single debate for the years of occupation, but several, intertwined debates, each of which had its origin in the period itself. For simplification, therefore, this chapter will be divided according to the areas of controversy in historical interpretation, treating each of the following debates in turn: the causes of the defeat and the decision to accept an armistice, the fall of the Republic, the behaviour of 'France' and whose actions in the name of France were 'legitimate', the question of what the French 'nation' did during that period, and most conspicuously of all, the French role in the deportation of Jews to Germany. Once each debate has been examined, we will return to the larger problem of the place of 'the dark years' in the larger narrative history of the French nation.

Defeat and the Armistice

For the first few months of the Second World War, known as the 'phoney war', the French and their British allies organised their defensive lines through France, Belgium and Holland, and awaited the German attack. The Germans were preoccupied in Poland and it was almost a year before the awaited attack came, rapidly cutting through the allied lines, encircling and capturing many troops and material, and forcing a hasty retreat out of the port of Dunkirk before turning southward through France. As the German tanks raced through northern France in May and June of 1940, the French government itself retreated in some confusion and haste out of Paris along the road to Bordeaux, where they met to discuss the catastrophe. With the army scattered and the roads blocked by millions of refugees fleeing the oncoming onslaught, the government and military leaders were faced with two choices: ask the Germans for an armistice, thereby breaking their agreement with the British government not to accept a separate peace with Germany, or to flee, as had other continental governments, either to London or to the French colonies in North Africa and continue the war from there. The cabinet split over the decision. The president of the council, Paul Reynaud, favoured exile and a continuation of the war, and found himself opposed by those who favoured an armistice. Lacking the conviction to push the issue to a vote, he instead resigned, and a new government was formed under the leadership of Marshal Philippe Pétain with the goal of asking for an armistice, duly requested on 17 June 1940. These events led to two significant questions regarding the long-term history of the French nation: how could such a huge military defeat be explained, and was asking for an armistice the appropriate response? Both questions have engendered lengthy debates, and although they can be treated separately, they have nevertheless come to be conflated in enough accounts of the period to suggest that it is appropriate to take them together here.

Even before the chaos left by the war had begun to subside, the first question of responsibility for what was France's greatest military defeat of all time was at the forefront of French consciousness. The magnitude of the defeat, in addition to the speed with which it had been achieved, left France with communications networks broken down, millions of refugees on the roads, the army scattered, the government on the run and the population in a state of shock and confusion. The firm belief in the strength and greatness of their nation and its armed forces, which had emerged victorious from the Great War only a short time before, and the deep confidence in a French victory merely increased the bewilderment at the humiliating defeat. How was it possible that so great a nation could have been overcome so quickly and so thoroughly? Answers to this question need to be differentiated between those provided in the immediate aftermath of the defeat and those arrived at years later with hindsight and greater availability of sources of information.

A straightforward explanation of poor performance by French soldiers or strategic error by their commanders was initially inconceivable, since it clashed so violently with the deeply held belief in French military greatness, following its long and glorious history. The most prominent early explanation was that the French were greatly outnumbered, facing such superior firepower that there was little they could have done. Even that, of course, also required an explanation, for how did France arrive at a position of being outnumbered and overpowered? While perhaps the most reassuring type of answer for the defeat would have been through betrayal by France's allies or a hidden conspiracy against France, it was quickly felt that the answer would also be found deep within French society and its institutions, responsible for the inadequate preparation and then prosecution of the war. The next years would see a profound internal examination of the French State and society, in which not only the army, but the political leadership, the State institutions, and the prewar behaviour and attitudes of the French population would all be called into question. While it is easy to suggest that a complete overhaul of the French State and society was an overreaction, it does nevertheless demonstrate the extent to which the defeat shocked and undermined the French nation's perception of itself, as well as the depth of need for an explanation which might restore a comforting, or at least acceptable vision of the nation. It also goes part of the way to explaining the extremity of some of the policies which would follow in the next few years, and the desire on the part of the Vichy leadership to pursue major social change even in the midst of occupation, when one might have thought it not the most opportune moment.

With hindsight, reasons for the French defeat put forward by historians of the war and which became current among the French population can be grouped into four categories: the purely military, the breakdown of alliances, the political structures of France, and French morale.[3] Under the military dimensions of the defeat, explanations have included numerical advantages of men and material, the superiority of German arms, tactics, the overall ability of officers and the high command, in particular the use of outdated military strategy, the poor use of intelligence and overall lack of communications between different units and especially between the allies. While the nature of the conflict and the number of imponderables render a definitive explanation impossible, military historians have come a long way in presenting a detailed account of the battle and the errors committed, and have certainly been able to demonstrate that some of the earliest military explanations cannot be sustained against the evidence. It is relatively clear, for example, that in spite of numerous assertions of German technical and numeric superiority, especially in the immediate aftermath of the war by the military leadership, the French were not in fact outnumbered in men or tanks, and had themselves superior, or at the very least equivalent equipment in several respects.[4] While it is true that the Germans had a clear superiority in the air, and that the French did not make the best strategic use of the planes which they had, it is nevertheless difficult to conclude that this difference alone can account for the speed and thoroughness of the defeat, such as it unrolled in practice. The explanations that emphasised the numeric superiority of the German forces, therefore, can by and large be explained as easing the blow to French egos, and in particular to the military's prestige, but are inadequate as genuine historical explanations.

Alternatively, if not in relative strength and numbers, then the explanation of the defeat has been identified as the inadequate preparation for and the poor conduct of the war by the French military elite. Such an interpretation could be partly found already during wartime in the short memoir *Strange Defeat* by the Annales historian and French officer Marc Bloch, written shortly after the defeat but not published until after his death at the hands of the Gestapo in 1944.[5] He suggested in several ways that the trouble in the French army came at the level of the conduct of the war, and the overall atmosphere. Later historians have echoed Bloch's early analysis that the fault lay primarily with the French military elite, drawing upon a much wider range of evidence to conclude that the French suffered from 'chronic unpreparedness, muddle and demoralisation, and an outdated concept of war.'[6] While it is clear that mistakes were made by the French high command and its front line officers, it is once again difficult to conclude definitively that the French leaders suffered so greatly from outdated use of machines or from an overall strategy which was blatantly lacking in flexibility or good planning that one need look no further for causes of the defeat. Several individual battles saw the French using their tanks effectively to counter the oncoming attacks, but it was the surprise of the main thrust of the German attack through the Ardennes forest which caught the French off their guard. The main French preparations for defence had been through the Maginot line in the south, and at advanced posts in Belgium and the Netherlands in the north, where the presumed German attack would fall.[7] When the attack came through the centre, held by some of the weakest French troops, they were indeed caught off guard, but if one examines the doubts and hesitancy in the German High Command about their own strategy, and their assessment of its very high risk, it is more difficult to condemn the French leadership out of hand for having failed to plan for such an unlikely attack.[8] More recent analysis, such as that of Julian Jackson and Ernest R. May, each of whom has given lengthy and detailed accounts of the battle itself including the strategic and leadership dimensions, provide much more balanced assessments of the French High Command. While not pretending that the defeat was anything other than a case of military outmanoeuvring on the part of the Germans, or presenting an apologia for the French military leadership, each gives a greater place to contingency or luck, and suggests that a simple condemnation of the High Command is also not fully satisfactory as an explanation for the French defeat.[9]

Similar conclusions emerge when examining the other causes. At the lower level militarily, errors of judgement with respect to the handling of intelligence, poor internal communications and individual commanding officers who were unable to respond quickly can certainly be found. However, given the level of similar difficulties on the German side, as well as the counter examples of heroic leadership and appropriate military responses under fire, one wonders whether such evidence can fully explain the defeat either. Likewise, problems of communication and understanding between the allies existed, the fault for which must be shared, but which are also insufficient to explain the magnitude of the defeat. While the French political structures had been under a lot of criticism during the 1930s, they had successfully prosecuted the First World War and had succeeded, if barely, to rearm France by 1939. Most of the criticism of the republican institutions and constitution have been clouded by the immediate reactions, as well as the fact that we know that the constitution was about to fall (see below). Finally, the defeat had also been explained (by Bloch and others) by the supposedly low morale of the French soldiers, civilian population and even the government, resulting from overconfidence, too much pacifism or a general moral decline in the population, depending upon the point of view. While it is true that some eyewitness accounts tell of low morale affecting the troops and their fighting quality, other accounts present a contrasting picture in which the atmosphere among the troops was positive, and the civilians at least resigned and determined to make a good job of it, leaving the question open. Even in the oft-made comparison with 1914, it is difficult to conclude with certainty that morale was significantly lower in 1939–40. This is partly due to the overrating of war enthusiasm in 1914, but also to a retrospective belief that morale was lower than some evidence suggests just prior to the French defeat.[10]

When seeking an overall explanation for the crushing, speedy defeat of the French army, the most convincing arguments have been put forward by Julian Jackson, who argues that while many errors or weaknesses can be detected, the French High Command was taken by surprise by a risky and improbable German strategy. Insofar as there was reasonable fault, it lay with the belief that the war would be of long duration. Preparations for a full mobilisation within the context of a longer war prevented adequate attention from being given to the short-term, resulting in a failure to react quickly enough in response to the surprise attack.[11]

Such an historical conclusion, however, leaves the place of the defeat and the way it has been understood within the longer-term history of the French nation still to be explained. With hindsight, of course, it became much easier to downplay the defeat as simply a setback within the longer struggle with Germany, either from 1939–45, or indeed 1914–45, from which the French nation emerged victorious. Such a reassuring interpretation was not available in 1940, however, and even in the midst of defeat the question of its meaning and interpretation within French history preoccupied the French leadership. How to find a way both to comprehend and accept the defeat, while at the same time preserving the vision of the greatness and continuity of the French nation? The imperativeness of this question increased the importance of identifying responsibility for the defeat, be it military, social, political, moral, or as a result of a conspiracy or betrayal. French leadership thus turned rapidly towards large scale changes, and their sweeping programmes of reform during the occupation need at least in part to be understood against this backdrop of the tremendous French need to rationalise the defeat within the framework of French history in a manner which could lead beyond the conclusion of a general weakness in the French nation. Their reforms pointed towards social and political explanations for the defeat and showed them to be putting the nation back on track along the lines traced by its glorious history. New beginnings for the French nation would become a recurrent theme in all of the various conflicting political discourses over the following years.

Once the French army had been defeated, it still remained to the government to decide what to do immediately: go into exile or ask for an armistice. The decision to ask for an armistice was closely linked to the interpretation of the defeat held by Marshal Pétain and his entourage, and is visible in three ways. Firstly, that decision indicated an inability or an unwillingness to view the defeat in terms of a setback in a longer war, in which there was still a hope of victory, but rather as definitive in terms of that conflict. Part of making the defeat acceptable was the belief that it was only possible because Germany had overwhelmingly superior forces, and thus it could never be turned into victory. And however much they may have desired a defeat of Germany, French pride was unwilling to base policy upon a hope that Great Britain could do alone what France and Britain together had failed to do. Secondly, the decision to ask for an armistice and to remain on French soil was based upon the importance of the continuity of the French State. It has already been shown how important the long tradition of national history was to French identity, and to end it by going into exile was unthinkable. In spite of the rhetoric that the colonies were a part of France, the emotional attachment to the hexagon, to metropolitan France, was such that to have no government there on French soil was viewed by those among the leadership as even greater national dishonour than the defeat. Pétain's personal presence at the head of the government was of course designed to reassure the population, and serve as a reminder of the days of victory and glory, and of the ongoing continuity of French history.

The third link between the perceived causes of the defeat and the decision to ask for an armistice, was to ensure that it would not be understood in purely military terms, but seen also as a political defeat. It was of course a military defeat, but the French army, in particular its leadership, was not at all willing to take the blame single-handedly. Actively encouraged by the military leaders therefore, the capitulation of the government tacitly acknowledged that the political leadership of the Third Republic was also directly responsible. Answers to the questions regarding responsibility went on to determine many other choices made by the French and their leaders in the years which followed. Other decisions and positions were also predicated upon conclusions regarding the reasons behind the defeat. In this sense, both for the decisions to ask for an armistice and later political choices, the 'real' reasons for the defeat are of secondary importance to the perceived causes.

Blame for the political leadership of the day has also become a part of the longer-term perspective of how these events fit into the greater history of the French nation. It is clear that the defeat has been dwelt upon as little as possible and always interpreted within the context of the later victory. The armistice, however, was later portrayed as a bad choice, a betrayal of the nation, made by a government which would go on to demonstrate its inability to act appropriately in the name of France. Firstly taking blame upon themselves rather than having it fall upon the army, the government could then also be singled out as having taken the bad decision to request an armistice. In some ways, later attacks upon this choice has allowed criticism and national embarrassment to be deflected away from the defeat itself, somewhat blurring its negative implications for national pride, and making it easier to gloss over the problems of disunity and low morale in the population which immediately followed the defeat.

A final longer-term consequence of the episode of the defeat and the armistice was to increase anglophobia within France. The initial criticism of Britain's lack of adequate help and support, while not repeated officially after the war, nevertheless had some resonance in the long term. Negative feelings towards the former ally were not helped by the British decision to attack the French fleet in the Algerian port of Mers-el-Kébir on 3 July 1940 in order to prevent it from falling into German hands, or by the RAF bombing raids of much of northern France, which no matter how necessary militarily, did nevertheless result in French civilian casualties. Thus even in the post-war period, the relationship with Britain continued to be strained, due in a large part to the memories of discord during the war. The difficulties of integrating the defeat and the armistice into the history of the French nation were less difficult in comparison to the interpretation and integration of the next few years, given that the defeat led to the almost complete collapse of the French political system and social structures, and the adoption of various embarrassing policies by the new French regime.

The Fall of the Republic

The conditions of the armistice which France signed with Germany on 22 June 1940 stipulated that France would be divided into several zones, leaving most of the north and the west coast occupied, with a 'Free Zone' in the south. The French government was permitted to establish itself in either zone, but preferred not to return to Paris in the occupied territory. Even so, rather than going to Lyon, the largest city in the Free Zone, they opted to go to the small spa town of Vichy, which was close to the demarcation line between the two main zones and had one of the most modern telephone exchanges in France, as well as ample hotels to accommodate the various ministries. Barely installed in Vichy, a motion was placed before the National Assembly (the united Chamber of Deputies and the Senate) to throw out the constitution and hand over full powers to Marshal Pétain. The vote was held on 10 July 1940 and, by a margin of 569 to 80 (with 17 abstentions), Pétain was given the right to draw up a new constitution. Theoretically he was to submit it to the French nation for ratification, although this was not accomplished during his years of power which lasted until 1944. The short-term legal constitutional arrangement was that the houses of parliament were dissolved until further notice, and that all executive and legislative power was in the hands of Pétain: the Republic had ceased to exist. The newly created authoritarian regime called itself simply the French State, and was referred to at the time and in later years as the Vichy government, due to its location.

The overthrow of the republican constitution can be understood in terms of an enhancement of the idea that the responsibility for the defeat lay with the political elite and the constitutional structure, furthering its interpretation as a political defeat, not just a military one. With such a move, it was the Third Republic and its institutions that were seen to have brought about the great catastrophe, rather than the nation, its army or people. Handing over to Pétain the task of rewriting the constitution showed rather an incredible confidence in the Marshal himself at a time of severe crisis and an inability to come up with a better solution, than a desire on the part of the politicians for the kind of authoritarian regime which he in fact created, or indeed any genuine dissatisfaction with republicanism as a whole.

The regime change had significant consequences for the overall place of the Vichy years within the long-term myth of French history, however. It has already been suggested that one of the primary reasons for the government remaining in France in the first place, and asking for an armistice rather than fleeing to the colonies to continue the war, was to permit the continuity of the French State. Yet ironically the demise of the Republic almost immediately allowed for a reinterpretation of the actions of Pétain's government, and indeed of the years of war and occupation, as a complete rupture with the French past. By signing the armistice or by overthrowing the Republic (or both), Pétain could be portrayed as having betrayed the French nation, thereby forfeiting all legitimacy and claims that he and his government represented France. In this way, the dark years could be presented as a kind of parenthesis, justifying their reinterpretation and the exclusion of the actions of Pétain and his government from the overall history of the French nation.[12]

An ability to put the Vichy years to one side, however, did not meet the still very real need for the perceived continuity of the French nation through these years. Into this space stepped Charles de Gaulle. Promoted to General in the field during the battle of France, and having been a junior minister in Reynaud's government, de Gaulle had flown to London, refusing to entertain the idea of an armistice, and announced on the BBC on 18 June 1940 that the French resistance to Nazi Germany would continue under his leadership with all true Frenchmen who loved their country. His unceasing efforts and eventual success meant that French pride in their war record could be salvaged, and in terms of continuity, 'true France' could be seen to have been with de Gaulle in London all along, where other occupied countries also had governments in exile. This position, denying the legitimacy and responsibility of the whole nation for the actions of the Vichy government, meanwhile still preserving the long-term continuity of the French State, can be cynically viewed as the French nation trying to have its cake and eat it too. While undoubtedly an overstatement, such a position was only necessary because of the profound importance of the continuity of national history for French identity. It is worth noting that while an acceptable version of national history through the war years is thus possible, it has not prevented significant unease and embarrassment about the behaviour of the French nation, and not just the Vichy government, which gave rise to the Vichy syndrome already referred to. It was ironically not the catastrophic military defeat which was to preoccupy and trouble the French nation when examining its history, but the perceived actions of the nation insofar as it did follow Pétain's government, and the fact that a simple and easy dismissal of the Vichy period as 'not really France' was not really adequate given the magnitude of the crimes committed during those years.[13] It is to this which we will turn now, examining the actions of both the Vichy government, and in particular the French nation, throughout the years of occupation.

The Behaviour of 'France'

Marshal Pétain's Vichy government was not content to overturn the constitution and then patiently await the outcome of the war. Within months of the defeat, he had already embarked upon an ambitious programme of national reform, and initiated several policies which have become symbols of occupied France, most notably the National Revolution and Collaboration. The National Revolution was the name given to a wide-ranging series of reforms aimed at transforming French society by re-orienting it towards its roots and rebuilding a French nation cured of the ills which had led to its defeat in 1940. It grew out of the belief that the defeat was not only military and political, but social and cultural as well, caused by structural and moral problems within French society. The main elements of the programme were drawn primarily from the discourses of the traditional French right, with their vision of the French nation, combined with some elements of what could be recognised as European fascism. Thus the National Revolution prescribed a return to traditional family values such as the land, hard work, motherhood, loyalty to others and unity within the nation, in order to overcome the perceived decadence, laziness and divisiveness which had supposedly weakened France. It advocated a renewal of family values and an increase in the birth rate to overcome the deficit of young men, both necessary for the strength of the nation. A key element of the National Revolution was the concept of national purity, which when combined with the discourse of internal decay, allowed for the invention of enemies or conspiracies against the nation. Jews, Freemasons, communists, trade unionists, homosexuals and foreign immigrants were all identified as enemies who had infiltrated the nation, thereby contributing to (if not directly causing) France's recent downfall.

A concerted effort was put into propaganda promoting the National Revolution, including posters, leaflets, newsreels and radio broadcasts. A key part of the propaganda was a devoted cult of the person of Marshal Pétain via the publication of his speeches, the distribution of photographs, the singing of hymns of praise to him and his public acclamation both regularly in the town of Vichy, and via tours of the Free Zone, all of which was reminiscent of Bonapartism. Figure 4 shows an example of the presentation of Pétain as a solid father figure, leading the nation towards reform and recovery through the National Revolution. Other activities included the creation of special youth training camps to form young men, known as the *Chantiers de Jeunesse*, and the creation of an elite training school, each of which emphasised physical training alongside education.

Figure 4 National Revolution poster

Trade unions were suppressed and replaced with a 'corporatist' structure involving both employers and workers in the same organisations.[14] The church was allowed greater flexibility and given state funding for its schools. The sum of the policies came with the rejection of the revolutionary and republican slogan 'Liberty, Equality, Fraternity', and its replacement in state propaganda with 'Work, Family, Fatherland' (Travail, Famille, Patrie).

None of these positions of the National Revolution was new to France in the 1940s, but drew upon existing French positions from before the war, many of which had been articulated vociferously in the 1930s alongside anti-parliamentarism. Closer links to the Catholic church and anti-communisim had long been strongly promoted by the French right, and it played upon pre-existing feelings of antisemitism and xenophobia in large segments of French society. Conspiracy theories were also already abundant even before the German victory was completed, and were merely extended and promoted further by the Vichy authorities. Legislation such as the Jewish Statutes, passed within months of the defeat, which restricted the civil rights of naturalised Jews within France and barred them from public service, amongst other measures, was the implementation of ideas which had been present in France for many years.

Although the thinking and the attitudes behind the National Revolution had roots within France which by far pre-dated the war, it was the conclusions drawn about responsibility for the defeat which gave the impetus allowing them to be put into practice. The diagnosis that French society was at fault, which was by no means restricted to the ultra-right, had a wide resonance within French society. Such a conclusion can even be found in the highly respected work of Marc Bloch.[15] While it was not published during the war, Bloch's work nevertheless demonstrates how far such thinking could be found within republican intellectual circles, in addition to those on the right. Therefore since the belief that France's ills had deep roots in national society came from profound feelings and discourses within the French nation, it was much less easy in fact to dismiss criticisms of Vichy and its National Revolution as unrepresentative and illegitimate or as simply imposed from without by the Nazi occupiers, and thus to put a parenthesis around it as not a part of mainstream national history. The painful process of re-examining wartime activity, in particular by those who wanted to expose and to think about this dimension of France and to face up to this reality of French history rather than sweep it under the carpet, in the face of a mainstream desire to forget is one key dimension of the Vichy syndrome which has already been alluded to.

The second major policy of Pétain's Vichy government which has brought down the condemnation of later generations is Collaboration. In the official policy unveiled after a meeting with Hitler at Montoire on 24 October 1940, Pétain envisaged a 'sincere' collaboration with Germany which would be an overall constructive process of mutual benefit to both parties. He and his prime minister, Pierre Laval, came under severe criticism for having met with Hitler at all, dubbed 'intelligence with the enemy', and in the long run collaboration was seen as treason to the nation (independent of the legality issue), earning both of them a death sentence after the liberation, although Pétain's was commuted.

At a more detailed level, collaboration meant working with the occupiers in order to ease the occupation conditions through regular negotiations and deals. Although what Hitler would have most liked was for France to join with Germany in the war effort against Great Britain, he was content to arrange commercial and industrial benefits for Germany in exchange for the (promise of the) release of French prisoners of war, or other such gestures. Three obvious objectives existed for Pétain's government to engage in collaboration: trying to gain any improvement they could in the material conditions for the French population, attempting to gain better eventual peace conditions through the demonstration of some goodwill towards the victors, and preserving French sovereignty by ensuring that it was their own officials and orders who continued to govern France, thereby also assuring the important continuity of the French State. At a simple level, the policy of collaboration can be seen as perfectly reasonable, a logical conclusion to the decision to accept an armistice in the first place. After all, why should the legal government of an occupied country not negotiate regularly with the leaders of the occupying country in order to make life better for all concerned, and to enter into agreements where any common ground of mutual benefit could be found? Once it became clear that the occupation was going to be long, it becomes even more obvious that such a government would seek to negotiate with the occupiers. It was also largely based, at least in the initial stages, in a firm belief that Germany was going to win the war, and that the only thing France could really do to salvage what it could from the wreckage was to cooperate as much as possible and secure the best possible peace terms once the conflict was finished. By the time it became clear that Germany was unlikely to win the war, the policy was already too entrenched for any realistic changes at such a late stage.

Even if one were to give the Vichy government the benefit of the doubt with regards to entering into negotiations with the Germans, many of the individual agreements were nevertheless subject to question in terms of their appropriateness and compatibility with the dignity and pride of the history of the French nation. For, whilst resisting overtures to join in the war effort against Britain, France nevertheless contributed to the German war effort. Sometimes this was direct – in letting the Germans have access to air bases in North Africa or allowing the production of engines for military vehicles by the Renault factory – but more often it was indirect – by providing Germany with commercial non-military goods, thereby freeing up German labour and other resources which could be channelled into the war. One of the most notable was the scheme known as the *Relève*, where the Vichy government secured the release of one French prisoner of war for every three volunteers it could persuade to go and work in Germany. Not enough volunteers were forthcoming to satisfy the German demands for labour, and in February 1943 it was transformed into a compulsory work scheme (the STO) where young Frenchmen were conscripted to go and work in Germany. Such direct support for the German war economy on the part of the legal representatives of the French nation, even if it was clearly intended to help France as well (which in fairness it did), clearly does not sit well with the vision of the history of a great nation, loyal to itself and to its own principles.

Far more negative yet is the role of the French in the deportation of Jews from France to the death camps in Germany and Poland in the latter years of the war. As has already been discussed, the Vichy government passed several antisemitic laws restricting the rights of Jews in France, set up the Institute for the Study of the Jewish Question which encouraged and promoted antisemitism, and had several notorious antisemites in office. All this was home-grown French antisemitism, not at all a result of pressure from the Nazi occupiers. In 1942, however, things were to change. Partly as a result of the absence of a quick victory in the Soviet

Union, and partly because they had decided on the Final Solution as a new strategy against the Jews of occupied Europe, the Nazis began to make much more stringent demands upon the French. In addition to labour for German factories, requests were made for the deportation to Germany of Jews from both the Occupied and the Unoccupied zones. At this point, Laval was interested in advancing any negotiations with the Germans that he could, and although not an antisemite himself, he was perfectly willing to bargain with the Jews in France if that was what the Germans wanted. This was particularly true for the Jewish refugees that had poured into France from Germany and Eastern Europe in the years immediately prior to the war. France was having enough trouble feeding its own population, and anything that would help them deal with the refugee crisis was also welcome to the government facing increasing pressure from all sides, even if that meant sending them back to Germany.[16]

The result of the demands therefore was that the French government, using the French police force, civil administration and French transportation, began to round up Jews in both zones, taking them first to Drancy, a French holding camp on the outskirts of Paris, before deporting them to Auschwitz. The first objects of persecution were foreign Jews who were refugees in France, although many arrests were also made of naturalised French Jews and there was much more willingness to protect the latter than there had been for the former, both within the administrative, police and government hierarchies, as well as among the general population. The most notorious of the round-ups occurred in Paris in July 1942, when the French police rounded up thousands of Jews in the capital, and took them to the Vélodrome d'Hiver (the winter velodrome) where, in overcrowded conditions, they awaited deportation in confusion and humiliation. Although well short of the 28,000 that the Germans had wanted, almost 13,000 Jews, including several thousand children, were arrested in that particular operation, which has become a symbol of the Jewish deportation and the date chosen for commemoration in 1995. In total, over 75,000 Jews were deported between 1942 and 1944, and several thousand more had already died in French camps, which represents a quarter of France's Jewish population in 1940. Of these, approximately 2500 survived, under 4 per cent of the total.[17]

The level of French participation in the arrests and deportations has become a significant source of embarrassment and one of the primary difficulties in coming to terms with the dark years for their integration into the history of the French nation. The first wave of arrests were undertaken almost entirely by French officials, and it is clear that without French cooperation, the Germans would never have been able to arrest and deport even close to that number of Jews, especially in the southern zone, from which the French government had actually volunteered to arrest foreign Jews, much to the surprise of the Germans. Even if the actions of the government are seen as primarily trying to assert and defend French sovereignty by reducing the German police presence and activity in France, or in the context of the collaboration negotiations where they sought at least to gain concessions for France, nothing can alter the fact that French leaders and many individual French people contributed actively in the deportation, while most others did nothing to stop it (at least at first). On the other hand, the initial requests for the deportation did come from outside, and the first wave of arrests in the summer of 1942 provoked a widespread negative reaction among the French population, such that after that many individuals and even organisations began to help hide the French Jews in their area to prevent their arrest. Government and official cooperation in the actual carrying out of the arrests also diminished significantly after 1942, and while not going so far as actively defending the French Jews, they were nowhere near as cooperative as they had been when it was the foreign Jews who were being arrested.[18] It took several years and the work of foreign historians before the full extent of these shameful truths became widely known, forcing the French nation to come to terms with them and to ask the question of their appropriate place within the national story.

Understanding the motivations and ideological stance of the collaborationist government and its range of supporters is important for placing wartime activity into the longer invented history of the French nation. A key distinction to be made first of all is the difference between the policy of collaboration – pragmatically accepting the defeat and negotiating with the Germans to secure benefits for France – and what has come to be called 'collaborationism' – an ideological sympathy with Nazism leading to genuine support for Germany, its antisemitic and especially anticommunist ideology, its fascist vision for a new Europe, and a sincere hope that Germany would win the war. While advocates of collaborationism could be found in the Vichy government, they were far less significant than those who collaborated pragmatically as a solution to the immediate problems facing France. One needs also to differentiate the elites from the population as a whole who, although they supported Pétain wholeheartedly and saw him as the national hero who would help them out of their immediate difficulties, by and large could not be said to have been ideological collaborators. Even when rejecting de Gaulle's widely popularised myth that the entire population were resisters, the automatic conclusion was not that France was therefore a nation of collaborators. Post-war interpretations of French behaviour have swung from an initial belief in the nation of resisters, through the discovery of the active French participation in the deportation of Jews and the Holocaust and a subsequent conclusion that France was a nation of collaborators, to end with the notion that the majority of the French population was simply trying to get on as best as it could in what were difficult circumstances, neither actively resisting nor actively collaborating. Numerous studies of institutions such as the church or the army, individual towns or regions, and groups within

French society such as artists or workers present popular reactions to the occupation in a much more balanced light. For the most part guilty of indifference and turning a blind eye to the fate of the Jews, loyal to Pétain as the great French hero who was saving the nation, but not ideologically sympathetic towards Nazism or even much of the National Revolution, unwilling or unable to fight, but nevertheless hoping for a German defeat and sympathetic to de Gaulle, the activity of the population can be largely understood as survival tactics, or 'accommodation' to the circumstances of occupation.[19]

While such a conclusion may appear satisfactory and reasonable, it is the result of decades of national soul-searching and frustration expressed in countless works of history, published memoirs, films, documentaries, newspaper articles and talk shows, and is by no means a calmly accepted commonplace, but conceals a profound discord among the French population and its leaders. Far from diminishing, interest in the dark years has increased with every decade that has passed since the end of the war. So much has been produced, that in addition to *The Vichy Syndrome*, a significant body of literature has developed, analysing the phenomenon of fascination and debate surrounding the war and occupation, the way in which collective memory has been constructed and debated, and its importance for the French nation.[20] Much of French society, long after the war years, continues to believe in the historical interpretation of France as a nation of resisters, the Vichy government as an illegal government of traitors to the nation, and the continuity of the nation to be understood as having followed de Gaulle and the Free French. Others have repeatedly questioned that position, on the grounds that the memory of the dark years ought to continue to cause pain and embarrassment for the French nation. Calling this conflict the Vichy Syndrome is a good response, given the profundity of frustration and nature of the struggles for interpretation.

Conclusion

The problem of how to face up to and integrate the numerous 'shameful' events of the dark years into an acceptable vision of French history has thus been a major preoccupation of the post-war French down to the present day. The Gaullist consensus that the Vichy government was illegitimate and illegal, that the French Republic was kept alive in the person of de Gaulle and his followers in London and the French Empire, and that the French people had been a highly unified nation of resisters to Nazi Germany, with only a handful of collaborators who were justly punished, did not last more than a couple of decades. Seriously questioned towards the end of de Gaulle's presidency in the late 1960s and afterwards, the debates have run deep and been significant. The problems with the Gaullist consensus in the post-war period came essentially from the unwillingness of elements of

French society to simply allow the past to be forgotten, and who wanted to keep alive the memory of 'victims', as well as to come to terms with their own past, which did not sit easily with many of the war generation, and even more from among the generations which followed. Denying the legitimacy of Vichy's activities as truly representative of France and the French nation was just not good enough any longer, and the unease was so deep that it appeared in the eyes of one historian as a mental disease of the nation. Many have felt that the French must accept responsibility for the actions of the Vichy government in the name of the nation, and to recognise that the history of the French nation between 1939 and 1945 was not merely one of a temporary military setback followed by years of heroic resistance to occupation followed by liberation and victory.

To recognise the Vichy government's activities as a legitimate part of French national history (which by no means everyone does in France), includes not only accepting collective responsibility for the embarrassing policies of collaboration and deportation, but also a recognition of the depth of the resonance of Vichy policy and thinking within France, and the extent of its genuine impact on post-war French society. The oft-articulated criticisms of parliamentary republicanism, the assertion of back-to-the-land conservatism and widespread fear of communism did not just disappear in 1944. In spite of the prominence of former resisters in high profile political positions, many of the key figures in important public administrative and journalistic circles in post-war France had received part of their training directly under Vichy.[21] The numerous debates are linked to wider questions about the nature of French society (whether it is fundamentally open, antisemitic, heroic, etc.), as well as about France's legitimate place within Europe and the wider world. They draw together and concentrate the various dilemmas of a coherent national narrative, which includes all of the characteristics of the supposed nation. Perhaps the best example is the myth of French national unity, found in both Vichy and Gaullist discourse, in spite of the presence of recognised internal 'enemies' to the nation, and the fact that for much of the period, the French were fighting each other in what is sometimes called the Franco-French war.[22]

In the second half of the twentieth century, how to interpret and integrate the dark years into the national story became the new central historical debate within French politics and wider society, having taken over from the Revolution as the hotly contested episode in French history. Such a transition included the formation of a general consensus on the interpretation of national history for all that went before, including the Revolution.[23] The perpetual re-examination and discussion of the dark years is still capable of creating profound division among the French population, although it does not map as neatly onto French politics as the Revolutionary divide had done throughout the nineteenth century. Nevertheless, it is a powerful political motive, with 'resistance credentials' being very important in elite circles and for upward mobility in post-war France. A good answer to the question 'What did you do during the occupation?' was crucial for success in public life (local and national) throughout the 1950s, 1960s and even into the 1970s. In the next chapter we will examine the post-war years, beginning with the 'purge' of French society which followed the liberation.

Notes

1 See Julian Jackson *France: The Dark Years 1940–1944* (Oxford: OUP, 2001) and Claire Andrieu, Jean-Pierre Azema and François Bédarida, *La France des années noirs*, 2 vols (Paris: Broché, 1999).
2 Henry Rousso, *The Vichy Syndrome: History and Memory in France since 1944*. Arthur Goldhammer, trans. (Cambridge, Mass.: Harvard University Press, 1991).
3 For a thorough discussion of the military, social and political explanations of the French defeat within these categories, see Julian Jackson, *The Fall of France: The Nazi Invasion of 1940* (Oxford: OUP, 2003).
4 See, for example, Jackson, *The Fall of France*, pp. 12–21, for a breakdown of material.
5 Marc Bloch, *Strange Defeat: A Statement of Evidence Written in 1940*. Gerard Hopkins, trans. (London: W. W. Norton & Company, 1999).
6 Alistair Horne, *To Lose a Battle: France 1940* (London: Papermac, 1990) [1969]. See also Nicole Jordan, 'Strategy and Scapegoatism: Reflections on the French National Catastrophe, 1940', in Joel Blatt, ed., *The French Defeat of 1940: Reassessments*. (Oxford: Berghahn, 1998), pp. 13–38.
7 For a full description of French strategy in the north, see D. W. Alexander, 'Repercussions of the Breda Variant,' *French Historical Studies* 8 (1974), pp. 459–88.
8 Jackson, *The Fall of France*, p. 32.
9 See Ibid and Ernest R. May, *Strange Victory: Hitler's Conquest of France* (London: I. B. Tauris, 2000).
10 For a nuanced view expressing doubts about the standard vision of war enthusiasm in 1914, see Regina M. Sweeney, *Singing Our Way to Victory: French Cultural Politics and Music during the Great War* (Middletown, Conn.: Wesleyan University Press, 2001). See also Jackson, *The Fall of France*, for more on French public and military opinion.
11 Jackson, *The Fall of France*.
12 The case was also made by Pétain's opponents that his regime was downright illegal, although the case is in fact extremely weak. For more on the discussion of the legitimacy and legality of the Vichy regime, see Jackson, *France: The Dark Years*, pp. 133–5.
13 Stanley Hoffmann pointed out that there is no 1940 syndrome, only a Vichy syndrome, see Stanley Hoffmann, 'The Trauma of 1940: A Disaster and its Traces', in Blatt, ed., *The French Defeat of 1940*, pp. 354–70.
14 The new organisations were quite complicated, with many layers, and never popular or even properly understood by the workforce.
15 Bloch, *Strange Defeat*.
16 For a full description of the context and evolution of the deportation negotiations, see Michael R. Marrus and Robert O. Paxton, *Vichy France and the Jews* (Stanford: Stanford University Press, 1981), pp. 228–34.

17 Marrus and Paxton, *Vichy France and the Jews*, p. 343.
18 See Jackson, *France: The Dark Years*, pp. 360–81.
19 See Philippe Burrin, *Living with Defeat: France under the German Occupation 1940–1944*. Janet Lloyd, trans. (London: Arnold, 1996).
20 Some of the more prominent examples are: Richard J. Golsan, *Vichy's Afterlife: History and Counterhistory in Postwar France* (Lincoln & London: University of Nebraska Press, 2000); Sarah Fishman, Laura Lee Downs, Ioannis Sinanoglou, Leonard V. Smith and Robert Zaretsky, eds, *France at War: Vichy and the Historians* (Oxford: Berg, 2000); Adam Nossiter, *The Algeria Hotel: France, Memory and the Second World War* (London: Methuen, 2001), Pieter Lagrou, *Mémoires Patriotiques et Occupation Nazie: Résistants, requis et déportés en Europe occidentale 1945–1965* (Paris: Editions Complexe, 2003); Henry Rousso, *The Haunting Past: History Memory and Justice in Contemporary France*. Ralph Schoolcraft, trans. (Philadelphia: University of Pennsylvania Press, 2002); and John Keegan, *The Battle for History: Re-Fighting World War Two* (London: Hutchinson, 1995).
21 See John Hellman, *The Knight-Monks of Vichy France: Uriage 1940–1945*. 2nd Ed. (McGill-Queen's University Press, 1997).
22 For more on the Franco-French war, see Chapter 7 on Revolution and Civil War.
23 While professional historians and some political activists still studied and disagreed about the Revolution, among the general public such controversy no longer had the capacity to galvanise or mobilise genuine political activity, as it had done up to the Second World War.

4

Modern France 1944–2000

To write of the invention of the history of the post-war French nation is in some ways a contradiction, in that it is a period which is viewed to a large extent as the present, rather than history. Much of the population remembers a great deal about it, and if unable to remember all of the events personally, has at least heard about most of them first-hand. Nevertheless, the period has been significantly understood, interpreted and mythologised in terms of its place within the long and glorious history of the French nation. Interpretations of recent or contemporary actions and developments have often been conceived in order to enhance existing historical visions of the nation, as a continuation of the historical legacies and traditions of the French nation's past, and in some ways as a confirmation of existing interpretations of the more remote past. In addition to continuity, claims for pride based on the longevity of the French nation and simple assertions of French national greatness, one phrase emerges more than others to categorise the interpretation of the history of post-war France: 'French exceptionalism'. Found in the political, economic and cultural spheres, this is a phrase which has been used repeatedly to justify French policies and to explain French actions, and which summarises the interpretation of France's most recent history. No longer preoccupied with the internal disputes surrounding the legacy and interpretation of the French Revolution, concentration on the historical interpretation of the French nation centred around justifying the place of France within the world, and particularly within the contexts of European integration and globalisation.[1]

The approach to the period taken in this chapter will not be strictly chronological, but will explore several dimensions of the history of the nation and the contexts in which it has been placed when thinking about and inventing national history. After examining the first few years of post-war consolidation and return to social, economic and political stability, it will be necessary to examine the history of the French nation in relation to several other factors. Firstly, there will be an analysis of republican interpretations of post-war political history and the economic boom.

Following consideration of decolonisation and the history of the nation with respect to its colonies and the colonial wars, attention will then turn to the period of de Gaulle's presidency, examining the Gaullist vision of France, both historically and through the constitution he drew up for the new Fifth Republic he created. This will be followed by an investigation of the break up of Gaullism, through the protests of May 1968, before proceeding to look at the place of the French nation in European construction and within the global institutional framework of the late twentieth century. The chapter will conclude with a brief examination of Socialist and Communist visions of the history of the French nation, especially in light of the fall of the Berlin wall and the end of the Cold War, and with several examples of how 'contemporary' problems in French society are regularly viewed historically, and how proposed solutions can still be interpreted as inventing history.

The Liberation and the Purge

Spread across several months in 1944 and 1945, the Liberation of France from German occupation has become a symbol of French triumph and unity. It entered into French 'popular imagination as a moment of national regeneration when the French people surmounted extraordinary obstacles to embark on a path of post-war renewal.'[2] Notwithstanding such an image, the Liberation was in fact diversely experienced across France, both in terms of time and the nature of events which local populations witnessed.[3] An image quickly arose that, although the allied armies were of course important, the French nation itself, through the resistance and the Free French armies led by Generals Leclerc and de Lattre de Tassigny, played a significant role in its own liberation. When commenting upon the liberation of Paris on 25 August 1944, Charles de Gaulle congratulated Paris for having liberated itself, with the help of the French armies and 'the whole of France' but without reference to the allies at all.[4] In fact though, as Julian Jackson demonstrates, 'the importance of the Resistance to the Liberation was political and moral, rather than military.'[5] De Gaulle's speech and the subsequent activities of himself and others built up the solid belief in and image of the French nation as victorious in the Second World War. This provided a way to overcome the shame of the defeat in 1940, reinterpreting it as simply a temporary setback, as well as a means to secure a place for France among the victorious nations at the end of the war. To confirm this vision of the nation's history, the French celebrated the anniversary of the final victory over Germany in 1945 (VE day, 8 May) as a public holiday throughout most of the remainder of the twentieth century. The national commemoration of the nation's victory is in addition to local commemorations in towns and villages on the specific anniversaries of their liberation, celebrating the local resistance and its contribution to the national struggle.

While not as important as the 11 November commemoration, such ceremonies contribute to the vision both of a glorious military history and of a nation prepared to make significant sacrifices when threatened.[6]

The Liberation was closely followed by what has become known as 'the purge' (l'épuration), in which those who had collaborated with the Germans in some form during the occupation were punished for their activities. Considered collusion with the enemy and therefore treason to the nation, collaboration was judged in several ways. In the first weeks and months, there were drum trials and summary executions, followed by official court cases, often in a series of courts specially established to try collaborators. Although rumours ran wild about the large numbers executed without a proper trial, historians now agree that the number was around 10,000. Once order had been more solidly established, over 300,000 cases were considered by the courts, of which 171,252 were brought to trial (40%). In three-quarters of these cases a sentence was pronounced, including 6760 death sentences (3910 *in absentia*), of which 767 were actually executed, the remainder being commuted by de Gaulle to prison terms.[7] One of the most common sentences (50,000) was 'national indignity', most often for life, which was handed out for 'unpatriotic behaviour' not technically a crime. An enduring image of the purge was the women whose heads were shaved for having slept with Germans.

These examples show the extent to which the post-liberation purge was as much about French pride and dignity as it was about investigating genuine criminal behaviour. Overall, the objectives were mixed: partly (especially initially) it was revenge or at least reaction to the atrocities committed days or weeks before in the context of the war, and partly it presented a way to set out national traitors as scapegoats in order to preserve national dignity and pride. Identifying a specific and restricted group of traitors thereby maintained and confirmed the French claims to participate as one of the allies in the international negotiations which followed the war. Furthermore, once the traitors had been labelled, the implication was enhanced that the rest of the nation was therefore composed of patriotic, resisting, Frenchmen, who could then proceed with the reconstruction. Former supporters of Vichy suggested that there had been great excesses in the purges, and that they represented a new terror, but by and large the population felt that genuine justice was done to those who had behaved inappropriately during the occupation. The purge was inconsistent in its application across France, both from place to place according to the local individuals and circumstances, as well as in terms of class, where the working classes tended to fare worse than those of the educated or wealthy bourgeois classes.[8]

Although representing only a handful of cases after the initial period, the purge was continued up to the end of the twentieth century. Individuals were brought to trial as late as the 1990s, in this case for crimes against humanity perpetuated during the occupation, rather than simply for 'collaboration'. Here again the question of the pride of the French nation was the main objective, although by the late twentieth century national embarrassment was no longer primarily about having been perceived to have helped the Germans in the war effort, but about the direct French contribution to the deportation and the Holocaust, and their overall treatment of Jews during the dark years. Thus individuals such as Maurice Papon, not identified as a national embarrassment in the immediate post-war era and who went on to have a successful career in the French public service, was brought to trial in 1996 for his complicity in the deportation of Jews from the Gironde, where he had been a civil servant. The presence of historians as witnesses in his trial at least in part demonstrates the extent to which he was on trial as a representative of, or a scapegoat for, the French nation, and that the nation itself was also on trial.

Rebuilding

Between the chaos caused by the purge and civil conflict and the material damage from the fighting, the end of Second World War left France with a great deal of rebuilding to do. To the material damage can be added the poor state of the economy following several years of occupation which had itself come on the heels of a decade of economic depression. The power vacuum and the ambiguous constitutional status of the country after the demise of the Vichy regime added to the obstacles facing the new regime. After social order had been re-established, the infrastructure and the economy needed to be developed, the people put back to work and fed, society re-unified, the wounds of occupation and civil conflict healed, and a new political structure put into place. De Gaulle became the leader of the provisional government, recognised by the French people, the administration and the allies who were still in France. He integrated the fighting units of the resistance into the French army and extended the number of courts to deal with cases of collaboration, thereby halting as quickly as possible the wild purge taking place outside proper legal channels. To smooth over the divisions within French society he encouraged the trials of the leading Vichy authorities and suggested that the best way forward once that had been done was for the entire nation to quickly put that past behind them. Then he turned to the institutions of the French state.

When de Gaulle arrived in Paris immediately following the liberation, he was urged to go straight to the Hôtel de Ville and proclaim the Republic. This would have been an historic gesture, creating the present as a continuation of the past, since several times in French history a republic had been proclaimed from that spot. He refused, however, since according to the Gaullist interpretation, the Republic had never ceased to exist, and the Vichy regime and all of its acts were simply illegal. A simple return to the constitution of the Third Republic, given the depth of shame from its defeat in 1940, was not perceived to be a good solution to the problem, and after more than one draft and several referenda, a new constitution was accepted on 13 October 1946 creating the Fourth Republic. Lacking the strengthened executive and president independent of party politics which de Gaulle wanted, in practice the Fourth Republic largely replicated the Third in its institutional structure, and would be praised and criticised for the same reasons as its predecessor. With such an arrangement, in political terms the French nation was able simultaneously to maintain an unbroken history of French republicanism, while at the same time developing a new constitutional identity freed from any embarrassing associations with specific elements of failure in what could now be identified as a 'past' regime.

France was in quite poor shape economically at the end of the Second World War. Slow to recover after the First World War, the depression lasted longer than elsewhere in Europe, and France had barely emerged before being plunged into war again. The years of occupation had seen overuse of equipment coupled with low investment in infrastructure, and production in many sectors geared to what the Germans had demanded. The first decades which followed the Liberation saw high levels of economic growth in France, accompanied by rises in living standards for average French men and women, and a significant modernisation of the overall French economy. Production increased, incomes rose and consumerism became the order of the day. So positive were the changes viewed that they became known as the '30 glorieuses' or the '30 glorious years' in which France experienced a kind of 'economic miracle' of growth and modernisation. While historians have since pointed out that the growth was not as significant as it appeared, particularly taken in the context of the general economic patterns in the industrialised west, and that the expansion did not really last 30 years, the image of spectacular growth of the nation's economy for three decades has endured, rendering the '30 glorious years' as one of the most significant phases in the constructed history of the French nation during the second half of the twentieth century, attaining the status of a popular historical myth.[9]

The character of the modernisation of the French economy in the decades which followed the end of the war forms a key part of the invented history of the French nation in the period. These include nationalisation of key sectors of the economy (electricity, gas, coal and several banks), planning and government intervention in the economy, all of which can be understood under the term 'dirigisme'. While ideas of government planning in the economy had been around since at least the First World War, it was not until this period that they were ever put into practice on a large scale in peacetime, and have come to be seen as a part of the French way of doing things, held up on occasion as an alternative model to 'Anglo-Saxon' style liberalism.[10] This did not mean a complete rejection of liberalism – far from it. It only meant that the French, through the control of key industries and centralised economic planning were able to rebuild and to modernise not only the infrastructure but the most important areas of the economy as well. This 'dirigiste' (directive) French economic style forms part of 'French exceptionalism', an image of the nation which is used to mark France out both in order to have it appear as more proactive and meritorious, but also to justify any particular French policies which go against dominant world or European thinking. This is particularly true in the cultural sphere, but also in the economic one throughout the second half of the twentieth century. It is a central element in French national identity from the second half of the twentieth century, and one of the most significant images to be invented for the nation for this period.

De Gaulle's Republic

The post-war constitutional arrangement did not last very long before it became destabilised, shaken firstly by the conflict in Indo-China and then more profoundly by the Algerian War. By the late 1950s the institutions of the Republic had been thrown into crisis, with seemingly no way out of the Algerian War; the leading politicians turned to Charles de Gaulle to bring France through. While extracting France from the colonial impasse in Algeria, he also profited from the occasion to revise the constitution, strengthening the presidency and the executive at the expense of the legislature, and becoming the first president directly elected since the Second Republic in 1848.[11] De Gaulle's political position has been described by René Rémond as a part of the Bonapartist tradition of the French Right – populist with an emphasis on the strong executive.[12] Since the coup d'état which brought down the Second Republic in 1851, republican thinking was permeated with great fear of another Bonapartist-style overthrow of the Republic if the executive and president had too much constitutional power. De Gaulle's fervent republicanism allowed him to found a Fifth Republic which did include a strong presidency, without threatening the main republican representative institutions.

The new regime de Gaulle created out of the chaos was a final point in the republican (and Gaullist) vision of the political history of the French nation. The constitution of the Fifth Republic could be seen as bringing about an end to the conflicts over regime in France: a final, appropriate balance between executive and legislative powers, drawing together the French past into a single form which represented all that was best in the French historical tradition. This is a more formal example of the resolution in the second half of the twentieth century of the conflicting interpretations of the French Revolution, and the establishment of a general consensus about the history of the French nation before the Second World War.

Contrary to many of the expectations of him when he was called to the presidency, de Gaulle also extracted France from much of her formal Empire, and brought an end to the Algerian conflict. Although the Algerian War has an important place in the history of the French nation in the twentieth century, and is likely to become more and more contentious in the early decades of the twenty-first century, the resulting dismantling of the French colonial empire brought about a greater reduction of the importance of the colonies for 'French' history. With decolonisation, 'France' became firmly centred in French minds as exclusively the hexagon, and the history of the French colonies and French colonialism increasingly conceived of and treated as peripheral to the history of the French nation: a related story, which had an impact upon the French nation certainly, but which was not thought of as central.[13]

Within the greater history of the French nation, de Gaulle represents the arch-symbol of unity. Unifying the nation in resistance during the Second World War and personally embodying the continuity of the Republic, he also became the great statesman and constitution-builder, above petty party politics, who was able to impose his vision of a strong presidency successfully for the first time within a stable and lasting republican constitution. De Gaulle's vision of the French nation and its history is the dominant vision in the second half of the twentieth century, presenting a French nation characterised by unity, greatness and what came to be called exceptionalism. His vision was the pole which attracted support or criticism, although the Gaullist domination of historical interpretation began to loosen with the student and labour protests in the 1960s.

May 1968 and Post-Modern France

The wave of protests and strikes which swept through France in May 1968 have come to be perceived as an important turning point in the history of the French nation in the second half of the twentieth century.[14] Beginning in the overcrowded universities as a protest against consumerism, inequality and Vietnam, harsh reprisals on the part of the police provoked anger, frustration and the massive escalation in the size of the protest. Students erected barricades in the streets around the Sorbonne in Paris, linking themselves to the great historic revolutions of the nation's past. Although completely unplanned, the workers also joined the protest, leading to the largest general strike in post-war France, extending from the capital throughout the provinces. The strike took place notwithstanding the initial reluctance on the part of the trade union leadership and the leaders of the Communist Party, one of whom, Georges Marchais, had been sceptical towards the emerging leader of the student protest, Daniel Cohn-Bendit. Marchais described him as a 'German anarchist' who had nothing to do with French politics. The union and political leadership did eventually take over the negotiations with prime minister Georges Pompidou, although the results of the hastily concluded Grenelle Accord were not well received among the rank and file.

After some early misjudgement and clumsiness on the part of the government and the police, de Gaulle made a well-calculated intervention on 30 May, in which he refused to resign, threatened to bring in the army, thereby reasserting his authority before then channelling remaining protest into a new election campaign by dissolving the National Assembly. The protest did not last much longer, given that the street level participants were hoping to see a power vacuum emerge which they could fill with their myriad of ideas for reform, but were unwilling to stage a genuine armed revolt against a determined president with the army behind him. On the other hand the main political force on the left – the Communist Party – had kept its distance from the movement right from the start, provoking accusations of Stalinist betrayal of the principles of revolution, and ended up also losing support in the form of votes for themselves and all of the other parties of the left who had hoped to capitalise upon the wave of seeming unhappiness with the status quo. The resounding electoral victory which followed for de Gaulle and the right, coupled with the rapidity (once de Gaulle had intervened) with which the authorities had been able to re-impose order without major concessions to the protesters and strikers in practice, might lead one to conclude that May 1968 showed how solidly 'bourgeois' economic and political power was entrenched in the Fifth Republic.[15] While that is true, and the events of May could therefore be interpreted as a setback for the forces of 'revolutionary progress' in the history of the French nation, a surprising degree of consensus would later emerge for the opposite position.

In spite of the very diverse aims of the original protesters, the memory of the protests of May 1968 and the place they have come to acquire in the longer history of the French nation is relatively uncontroversial and positive. Represented primarily as a conflict of generations, about the cultural and lifestyle changes which accompanied modernisation, the official story is 'stripped of any violence, asperity or overtly political dimensions.'[16] It is from that moment onwards that 'youth' as a category became an autonomous social force in contemporary French society, conscious of the uniqueness of their position and of their potential influence.[17] The story goes that from May 1968 onwards, this youth was ever at the ready to challenge authority in the name of equality or to overcome cultural alienation, just as their '68er' forebears had done, the original protest having set the pattern.[18] Fundamentally symbolising a crisis of values, May 1968 pitted the older generation against the younger over questions of equality and morality.[19] This was also the point at which the Gaullist consensus over the occupation is seen to begin unravelling, as the younger generation who had not lived through the war began to question the true conduct of their parents and grandparents.[20] In the decades which followed, as the '68 generation grew older and entered positions of power, its members identified with the protest as a fundamental formative moment in the formation of their identity (collective and individual), holding the protest as an important shift forward in the history of the French nation.[21]

More important then in memory and in the changes it symbolised, rather than the actual changes which it brought about in the short term, Michael Seidman has called it 'the imaginary revolution'.[22] In her work on its 'afterlife', Kristin Ross shows how the mainstream interpretations and the memory of May 1968 assert that French society by the end of the twentieth century, 'far from representing the derailment or failure of the May movement's aspirations, instead represents the accomplishment of its deepest desires.'[23] This historical interpretation, she argues, is a teleology of the present, considering that the official story has erased the memory of any alternative visions in the protest than the one which in fact happened. The generation of May 1968, who twenty years later had come to have the leading positions in the media and in politics, believed themselves to have remade France through their protest, that following the economic recovery and advances of the 1950s, their efforts had succeeded in modernising the culture and moral structure of the French nation at the end of the 1960s. They also interpreted their actions as having modernised the historical concept of revolution in France, both by having built barricades in the great historical tradition, and having created a new model of mass social protest without excessive violence which could be carried forward throughout the rest of the twentieth century (and beyond). At the same time the events and symbols of May '68 captured the imagination of the younger generation who had not lived through it and whose aspirations towards its ideals made it perhaps an even more important symbol for them than it had been their elders.[24]

Thus while on the one hand May 1968 clearly demonstrated the solidity and unshakeability of the Fifth Republic and its institutions, it has entered into the history of the nation as a great progressive turning point in terms of its social and cultural value structure. It became a great historical moment for the French nation, perceived as the point when a new generation took control of the nation's future while remaining true to France's historical tradition of revolution and progressive thinking. At that moment everything was possible and the nation was on the brink of great changes in the entire structure of modern life;[25] subsequent social, cultural or moral progress has since been read as having had its origins in May 1968, the point when the French nation became truly 'modern'.

The events of May 1968 have also been interpreted as a watershed in the post-war history of the French left. Since the Second World War, the left had been dominated by the Communist Party, both in numbers of political representatives and in terms of its influence among leading intellectuals. Jean-Paul Sartre famously likened 'an anti-communist to a dog.' All of the main national political disputes or negotiations during the Fourth and early Fifth Republic had to contend with the bipolarity between Communism and Gaullism. May 1968 symbolised the change of generation and renewed political positioning on both the left and the right. Once de Gaulle fell from power, the leadership on the right was taken up by Pompidou and later Valéry Giscard d'Estaing. On the far left, there was a rise of those no longer identifying primarily with the Communist Party, but with the Maoists or Trotskyites. Out of power since 1960, the alliance between François Mitterrand and Marchais brought the moderate left back into power in 1981. At first glance it seems to be the old left, the communist apparatchik supporting the former socialist minister from the Fourth Republic into the presidency. However, the attempt to implement a radical left-wing agenda was relatively short-lived, and the younger generation who had accepted the basic economic constraints of power in western Europe in the late twentieth century became the dominant force in the party. While more 'dirigiste' perhaps than the right would have been, the socialist governments such as that of Laurent Fabius did not represent a radical break. The young ministers of the '68 generation such as Jack Lang at the Ministry of Culture and then Education represented the reconciliation between the youth culture of the generation of protest and mainstream socialist politics. Without completely rejecting in principle the radical speech-making which characterised the handful of parties on the extreme left, the socialist party's policies became those of a party of government, fully modernised and oriented towards electoral success and staying in power. This ambiguity between discourse and practice only proved to be fully sustainable as long as the strong personality of Mitterrand was at the helm. Once he had gone, the unity of the socialist party became harder and harder to sustain and their alliances with other parties of the left more fragile. Their version of French exceptionalism also prevented their complete solidarity with other European socialist parties, causing even more division over European questions than elsewhere. Thus ironically May 1968 has become reinvented as a symbol for radical change in the history of the French nation, even though analysis suggests that it was the point when the moderate left began its rise.

France and the Wider World

Defending French greatness and the notion that France is a European and world leader has been an important dimension of the mythical history of the French nation throughout every period. Not only is France represented as a military, economic and diplomatic power, but also in moral terms, as the country originating new ways of thinking and ways of doing things, a model for the rest of the world to follow. Although salvaging a victory in the Second World War thanks to de Gaulle, the second half of the twentieth century nevertheless saw France in a precarious position in terms of its potential self-image in the world. France seemed always to be only catching up in terms of economic modernisation, and the lead in international relations had been taken away from them in the preceding decades. In two areas, however, the French nation would assume a leadership position during this period: European construction and the development of an alternative economic model to that of the free market capitalism of the United States or the communist command economy of the Soviet Union.

The two areas are intricately linked, for a key dimension of France's self-perceived role at the heart of European construction was in fact providing an alternative model on the international scene for what the French saw as 'Anglo-Saxon' free market liberalism.[26] Two elements were crucial in the French perception of their place in the history of European integration – reconciliation with Germany and the marginalisation of Great Britain. Given the levels of carnage in the two world wars, the most important factor was clearly Franco–German reconciliation, to attempt to avert another such major conflict. This required not only French, but also German economic recovery from the war. The Marshall plan, which invested American money into the rebuilding of Western Europe, was of course important, but French thinkers thought that more was necessary, and sought some form of overarching political guarantees of future co-operation such that the French and German economies would be sufficiently linked as to render future conflict 'not only unthinkable, but materially impossible.'[27] This idea was concretely expressed by the French foreign minister Robert Schuman in what became known as the Schuman declaration of 9 May 1950. Initially focussing on the coal and steel industries, Schuman called for the creation of a 'High Authority' which would oversee production and centrally plan and organise the distribution of these key sectors of the economy. His proposals led to the creation of the European Coal and Steel Community in 1950, which grew into the European Economic Community in 1957 with the addition of other economic sectors, and eventually into the European Union in 1986. Thus French centrally planned or 'dirigist' economic strategies became adopted across Europe in spite of British objections.

The centrally planned 'super-national' dimension of the European project meant not only that the economic model would no longer be founded upon British and American ideas of individualism, liberalism and state non-intervention, but also that individual states had to give up some of their sovereignty. The success of European economic co-operation in bringing about peace and prosperity is considered in the history of the French nation as proving the French right and the British and Americans wrong in the inter-war attempts to achieve the same goals by a strict return to pre-war economic liberalism, which had helped to cause the

Great Depression and lead to the Second World War. The French had hoped in vain after the First World War to prolong the inter-allied economic co-operative planning, only to be thwarted by the British and American desire to return to the pre-war economy. After the Second World War, the French were determined not be thwarted a second time. Britain refused to join the ECSC and the EEC initially, and when they sought to join later had their membership application twice vetoed by de Gaulle. These vetoes are as clear and overt an expression as can be found of the French desire to preserve their vision of European integration from British (and by extension also American) influence. Thus partly through genuine British reluctance, but also through French action, the French could build an image of themselves as the key leaders in European construction.

Within wider world politics, from trade negotiations through to international associations like the United Nations and the NATO military alliance, the history of the French nation in the second half of the twentieth century has been conceived in a similar way to its role within Europe – as an important counter-pole to the Americans, and to a lesser extent the British. While perhaps overemphasising the genuine significance of any disagreement with its allies, what in another light might be seen as minor differences were often highlighted in order to create a history of French independence of action. An independent nuclear deterrent, withdrawal from the NATO command structure, nuances in policy in Africa or Palestine, and the French refusal to participate in the Iraq war of 2003 are all examples contributing to such an interpretation. The French were also at the heart of developing an international organisation in the style of the period called the 'francophonie', regrouping all of the world's nations which had French as one of their languages, in which France could play a key role of leadership and consolidate a global sphere of influence outside the influence of the 'Anglo-Saxons'. To take yet another well-known example from de Gaulle, his Montreal speech in which he gave a boost to the Quebec separatist movement when he cried 'Vive le Québec libre' (long live free Quebec) can certainly be seen within the context of a France seeking a global sphere of influence.

The desire to present the course of French history as that of an alternative to the United States is tied up with the phenomenon of anti-Americanism. Difficult to define, changing in nature depending upon circumstances and appearing alongside a fascination and desire to emulate America as a positive model, feelings and expressions of anti-Americanism have been a constant feature of French political and intellectual discourse in the second half of the twentieth century.[28] The diverse French responses to American culture, economic success and political and military power have arisen from a fear that America and things American represent a threat to the French way of life, or indeed to French 'civilisation'.[29] Admiring though they may be of much that comes from America, it became quite common throughout the period to voice opinions of concern that there might be too much American influence. While this phenomenon is found to some degree in all parts of the world, it is particularly acute in France, where the French feel that theirs is a great nation which ought also to be held in high esteem throughout the world, including by Americans. It is for this reason that Theodore Zeldin puts much of French anti-Americanism down to American lack of interest in France, resulting in a 'French sense of being undervalued and, worse, ignored.'[30] Such a view explains the importance in the post-war history of the French nation as providing an alternative model (cultural, political and economic) to America, interpreted this way in order to increase the prestige of France. The fight within Europe to have French thinking accepted and to keep out the 'Anglo-Saxon' or American model is about international standing, with the Americans presented (rightly or wrongly) as the villains.[31] Even the rejection of the European Constitution by referendum in 2005 was partly interpreted by its opponents as opposing the Anglo-Saxon liberalism they thought the Constitution represented.

The history of the French nation in the second half of the twentieth century is thus not only one of French modernisation, but a modernisation according to a specifically French model which can be summarised in the concept of 'French exceptionalism'. Whether the State role in regulating the economy, the placing of workers' concerns ahead of consumers' wishes or in simple protectionism of cultural industries such as cinema, the French think and speak of their own situation as always meritorious of special consideration. An important dimension of French exceptionalism in the twentieth century is its historical roots, from Jacobin centralism to the heritage of the Enlightenment and the revolutionary tradition.[32] France has always been exceptional, the story goes, therefore it is not surprising that in the modern and contemporary periods it should continue to be so, and anyone with an interest in the history of the French nation will search for and highlight examples justifying the interpretation of France as exceptional. In his study of French exceptionalism, Yves Tinard devotes a full third of the work to its historical heritage, with many references to the great length of time that the French nation can be characterised as exceptional.[33] Late twentieth-century reformers, such as Christian Saint-Etienne, seek to encourage change along particular lines through the argument that for France to retain its importance, it must continue to be 'exceptional', and invoke a fear of the 'end of exceptionalism' to promote their ideas.[34] These examples show the depth of resonance in modern France that the history, culture, economy and society of France are exceptional, particularly when held up against the 'Anglo-Saxons'.

Thus in the second half of the twentieth century, while rebuilding and modernising within the context of globalisation and European integration, the history of the French nation has been seen as one of continued greatness and leadership at the international level. France provided an alternative economic model to 'Anglo-Saxon' liberalism, was at the heart of European construction, and could be characterised as justifying exceptional status in its perception by the French people. Although partly originating in anti-American or anti-British sentiment, French exceptionalism is also a very positive feeling that can be derived from a close examination of the history of the nation on its own, without the need of outside references.

At the end of the twentieth century and into the twenty-first, 'contemporary' French problems continued to be significantly understood in historical terms.[35] Since 1989, the many dimensions of the 'foulard affair', in which Muslim girls were prevented from attending French state schools when wearing Islamic headscarves, were coloured by an historical awareness of the anticlerical struggles which had taken place in the late nineteenth and early twentieth centuries with the Catholic church. Hard-line republicans argued that the secular republic was founded upon the separation of church and State, and that as the republic had taken on the Catholic church over the question of religion in public schools one hundred years previously, so it should insist that other religions also remain outside of the schools. The continued electoral success of the extreme right National Front at around 15 per cent also has historical roots, and their opponents repeatedly try to discredit them through association with France's Vichy past. On the other side of the spectrum, parties of the extreme left also look to the past to assert their role as the true heirs to the tradition of protest in the name of the workers which had helped to make France great.

Overall, belief in French exceptionalism in the contemporary world is strong, and principally justified and enhanced through an understanding of the history of the French nation. In the second half of the twentieth century, this history is presented as a continuation of the nation's long and glorious past, with the French nation bursting into modernity: in economic terms (growth), social terms (May 1968), and political terms (the Fifth Republic). France's leadership role in European and world affairs is the natural continuation of the long history of French greatness. Through its strong international position, as well as the alternative models it has presented to the world, and through the example of the protest in May 1968, the French nation confirmed its moral authority, prolonging the historical tradition of the nation that was home to the Declaration of the Rights of Man. The image of Charles de Gaulle looms large throughout this period. From the leader of the Resistance and the provisional government which brought France out of the Second World War with its international position relatively intact, to the architect of the constitution of the Fifth Republic, the one who was able to bring decolonisation and an end to the colonial wars, the champion of France in international relations to the pole against which the 'revolutionaries' of May 1968 took a stand, de Gaulle was at the heart of the major events of the second half of the twentieth century. He was also a visionary in terms of the greatness of the French nation and the central importance of its history for French identity, and the greatest single influence by far upon the course of development of the national historical myths invented and reinvented throughout the century.

Conclusion to Part I

The history of the nation is the most significant component of French national mythology. National political discourses, social conflicts and all manner of contemporary culture and events are understood in terms of their relationship to the grand historical narrative. References to this narrative have been widespread not only among the elite, but also throughout popular cultural and literary output. Much of French pride comes from its belief in the historical achievements of their nation and France's perceived rights, among nations and to territory, respect and honour, are firmly grounded in these historical accomplishments. The national history was developed through the extremely complex process of perpetual interpretation and re-interpretation of both the nation's past and its present, seen routinely in terms of a continuation, affirmation and justification of the past. Individuals and groups consciously tried to influence, fashion and manipulate French national history, with rival visions invented and re-invented across the generations. The gradual acceptance of the republican vision by the wider public as the 'true' history of the nation was crucial in the political battle to ensure that France became and remained a republic.

The development of French national history was fraught with conflict and rival interpretations, particularly surrounding the French Revolution. Throughout the nineteenth century and well into the twentieth, the conflict deeply divided French society, erupting regularly in violence, until the republicans emerged victorious. By the mid-twentieth century, although still subject to the occasional dispute among historians, a consensus had nevertheless been achieved around the national interpretation of the Revolution and its aftermath. This is one of unfortunate violence that nevertheless brought the French nation along the road to progress, enlightenment, republicanism and freedom, leading to the triumph of the republic as the national form of political organisation.

While the interpretation of the nation's history in the post-1930s period is not as controversial as that of the Revolution had been, neither had it become firmly established and agreed upon by the end of the twentieth century. After the breakdown of the Gaullist consensus in the late 1960s, the question of how to interpret Vichy France and the occupation in terms of the longer run of French history remained a hot subject of public and political debate, breaking out in popular film, literature and music, as well as among historians and the political elite. Conflicts regarding the interpretation of decolonisation had also begun to emerge towards the end of the century. Given the currency of the question to other debates such as immigration, conflict seems likely to increase in the twenty-first century before any kind of consensus of interpretation is reached.

The various political conflicts surrounding the interpretation of the nation's history did not prevent a wide range of common themes and reference points in all versions. The most significant is the perception of France as a continued great nation, regularly demonstrating and living up to its glorious history through the series of triumphs in all spheres of political, social and cultural endeavour. Such a belief includes the idea that the French nation is a leading example for the world, either for its avant-garde republicanism and enlightenment, or indeed its model Catholicism, and also the belief in French modernity, economic advancement and 'exceptionalism'. This belief in French exceptionalism, drawn from the national historical narrative, has been used regularly to justify a wide range of other economic and cultural policies, and to reinforce the conviction that history repeatedly demonstrates French greatness. Furthermore, a basic chronology of France, with key turning points at the French Revolution, First and Second World Wars, as well as an extensive canon of national heroes and events to commemorate are all elements which became widely accepted by the end of the twentieth century.

The final conclusion from this section is to confirm that the enduring images of the history of the French nation have been for a large part consciously constructed, manipulated and invented. This is as true of the nineteenth-century republican nation-builders of the nineteenth century as it is of Charles de Gaulle, the arch myth-making nation builder who cemented previous conflicts of interpretation into a much more widely accepted and uncontroversial vision of the glorious history of the French nation. The next section will turn to the lived experience of individuals and the nation throughout that history, to examine the ways that experience also became a part of the national mythology.

Notes

1 For general works on the period, see: Maurice Larkin, *France since the Popular Front: Government and People 1936–1996* (Oxford: Clarendon: 1997); Rod Kedward, *La Vie en Bleu: France and the French since 1900* (London: Allen Lane, 2005); Richard Vinen, *France 1935–1970* (Basingstoke: Macmillan, 1996); James F. Macmillan, *Twentieth-Century France: Politics and Society 1898–1991* (Arnold, 1992); Charles Sowerwine, *France since 1870: Culture, Politics and Society* (Basingstoke: Palgrave, 2001); Maurice Agulhon, *The French Republic 1879–1992* (Oxford: Basil Blackwell, 1993).

2 Herrick Chapman, 'The Liberation of France as a Moment in State-Making', in Kenneth Mouré and Martin S. Alexander, eds, *Crisis and Renewal in France,*

1918–1962 (New York and Oxford: Berghahn, 2002), p. 174.

3 See Maurice Agulhon, *The French Republic 1879–1992*. Antonia Nevill, trans. (Oxford: Blackwell, 1993), pp. 309–16.
4 Charles de Gaulle, speech, August 1944.
5 Julian Jackson, *France: The Dark Years 1940–1944* (Oxford: OUP, 2001), p. 557.
6 Agulhon, *The French Republic*, pp. 307–9.
7 See Jackson, *France: The Dark Years*, pp. 577–8 for a full breakdown. For a detailed comparative analysis of how the purge unfolded at a local level, see Megan Koreman, *The Expectation of Justice: France 1944–1946* (Durham and London: Duke University Press, 1999).
8 See Vinen, *France 1934–1970*, pp. 83–5.
9 See Vinen, *France 1934–1970*, pp. 111–12, and Sowerwine, *France since 1870*, pp. 274–8 for details of French economic growth through these years.
10 On such proposals, in particular championed by Etienne Clémentel, see Stephen D. Carls, *Louis Loucheur and the Shaping of Modern France 1916–1931* (Baton Rouge: Louisiana State University Press, 1993), p. 128, and John F. Godfrey, *Capitalism at War: Industrial Policy and Bureaucracy in France, 1914–1918* (Leamington Spa: Berg, 1987). Such arguments about Anglo-Saxon liberalism being opposed to a French style of economy were prominent in discussions at the European level, and used as an argument for keeping Britain out of the EEC (see below). See also Vinen, *France 1934–1970*, pp. 115–16 on nationalisation and planning.
11 The Algerian war and decolonisation will not be discussed specifically here, except as a backdrop to other changes. See Chapter 8 for a full discussion.
12 René Rémond, *The Right Wing in France From 1815 to de Gaulle*, 2nd Ed., J. M. Laux trans. (Philadelphia: University of Pennsylvania Press, 1969), pp. 385–91.
13 See also Chapter 8.
14 For a full discussion of May 1968 as a part of the revolutionary tradition, see Chapter 7.
15 See Vinen, *France 1934–1970*, pp. 193–4.
16 Kristin Ross, *May '68 and its Afterlives* (Chicago and London: University of Chicago Press, 2002), pp. 5–6.
17 Michelle Zancarini-Fournel, 'Conclusion', in G. Dreyfus-Armand, R. Frank, M-F. Lévy and M. Zancarini-Fournel, eds, *Les Années 68: Le temps de la contestation* (Paris: Editions Complexe, 2000), p. 497.
18 Andrew Feenberg and Jim Freedman, *When Poetry Ruled The Streets: The French May Events of 1968* (Albany: State University of New York Press, 2001), p. 68, and Zancarini-Fournel, 'Conclusion', p. 502.
19 See Vladimir Claude Fisera, 'Stepping Stone and Shifting Legacy: A few conclusions and reappraisals of May 1968 and its history', in D. L. Hanley and A. P. Kerr, eds, *May '68: Coming of Age* (Basingstoke: Macmillan, 1989), pp. 200–5.
20 See Henry Rousso, *The Vichy Syndrome: History and Memory in France since 1944*. Arthur Goldhammer, trans. (Cambridge, Mass: Harvard University Press, 1991), pp. 98–100.
21 Jean-Louis Violeau, 'Les Architectes et le mythe de Mai 68', in Dreyfus-Armand, et al., eds, *Les Années 68*, p. 258.
22 Michael Seidman, *The Imaginary Revolution: Parisian Students and Workers in 1968* (New York and Oxford: Berghahn, 2004).
23 Ross, *May '68*, p. 6.
24 See, Seidman, *The Imaginary Revolution*, p. 281.
25 Sowerwine, *France since 1870*, p. 351.

26 Even the French right supported the French vision of economic organisation known as dirigisme.
27 Schuman Declaration, 9 May 1950.
28 For a full discussion of anti-Americanism, see Denis Lacorne, Jacques Rupnik and Marie-France Toinet, eds, *The Rise and Fall of Anti-Americanism: A Century of French Perception*. G. Turner, trans. (Basingstoke: Macmillan, 1990); Richard F. Kuisel, *Seducing the French: The Dilemma of Americanisation* (Berkeley: University of California Press, 1993) and Jean-Jacques Servan-Schreiber, *The American Challenge* (New York: Atheneum, 1968).
29 Kuisel, *Seducing the French*, p. xii.
30 Theodore Zeldin, 'Foreword' in Lacorne, et al., eds, *The Rise and Fall of Anti-Americanism*, p. xi.
31 Within Europe, the French have also criticised the British for being too close to the United States, thereby trying to reduce their European influence and leave France as the alternative possible voice for the middle or small sized powers to follow.
32 For a thorough analytical discussion of the concept of French exceptionalism and the notions upon which it is founded, see Emmanuel Godin and Tony Chafer, 'Introduction', in Godin and Chafer, eds, *The French Exception* (New York and Oxford: Berghahn, 2005).
33 Yves Tinard, *L'Exception Française: Pourquoi?* (Paris: Maxima, 2001).
34 See, for example, Christian Saint-Etienne, *L'Exception Française* (Paris: Arman Colin, 1992), pp. 26–9.
35 For more on the way history is used in contemporary political debates, see Claire Andrieu, Marie-Claire Lavabre and Danielle Tartakowsky, eds, *Politiques du Passé: Usages Politiques du Passé dans la France Contemporaine* (Aix-en-Provence: Publications de l'Université de Provence, 2006).

PART II

INVENTING FRENCH EXPERIENCE

The national history covered in Part I is only one element comprising the French nation. This section will examine the invention of French 'experience'. It will include an analysis of the ways in which the French reflect upon their history, the lessons drawn from it about the nature of French society, its composition and evolution, as well as the kinds of lives which have been lived by different identifiable groups which have taken on a national character. It will cover the personally felt links to the historical narrative and the ways personal experience can be understood 'nationally'. Common national experiences which form part of the national memory are often expressed symbolically or through images, and help to bind society together. Yet like history, such national experience is also 'invented' rather than simply 'lived', in the sense that it is selected and interpreted, and can therefore be understood as a part of the national myth. This process may be consciously directed or influenced for similar political reasons as has been described for national history, although it can likewise never be completely manipulated or controlled, preserving some measure of spontaneity and chance.

The experiences which have become part of the national consciousness of modern France can be divided into several types. The first chapter will look at the experience of French society, the kinds of social groups which composed it, and the resulting images of the way in which social interaction and conflict was lived through by the French. The following chapters will examine French experiences of war and expansion, firstly with other nations, and secondly within France, looking at the experience of Revolution as a kind of civil war. The final chapter in this section will examine the French colonies and French experience of colonialism or imperialism, to examine firstly the extent to which the experience of the colonial empire has been considered a national one, and then the ways in which this experience has been marginalised with respect to French national experience.

5

French Society

Societies which comprise nations can be broken up and analysed in a variety of ways, through such prisms as class, race, religion or gender, to name but a few. Rhetoric about the unity of the French people notwithstanding, the identification of a 'typical' French citizen to present as a representative of the nation is impossible. Instead, one needs to examine particular social 'types' which have themselves found a mythical place within the national story as particularly representative of the French nation, or at least of one element of it. Not always corresponding directly to Marxist or other conceptions of class, the social categories which will be employed in this chapter are nevertheless essentially socio-economic.[1] Four specific social types are going to be examined: the peasant, the worker, the bourgeois and the intellectual.[2] While not an exhaustive list, each of these types is a clearly recognisable figure within an idealised French society, acting out roles both in particular circumstances and in the wider evolution of French history. Individual experiences vary, but national memory nevertheless includes participation in social interaction and conflict by defined group, each of which has been invented and re-invented over the past two centuries.[3] Similarly, individual experiences of French society become conceived in terms of positioning within the groups, and encounters with representatives of each of the specific types serve to reinforce the stereotypes.

The Peasant

> I who called myself a magus or an angel, exempted from moral constraints, I have gone back to the land with a duty to find and a rugged reality to embrace.
>
> Peasant — Arthur Rimbaud, *Une saison en enfer*[4]
>
> (justifying his abandonment of his life as an artist and poet)

The associations between the French nation and the peasantry are many. One needs never to look too far, be it in art, literature or film, history or politics, to find images of or allusions to the peasant as representative of France. The popular saying 'ploughing and pasture are the two breasts of France' has been repeated through many generations.[5] One of the first French economists, François Quesnay (1694–1774), expressed the same view in a more scholarly manner: 'the sovereign and the nation must never lose sight of the fact that land is the unique source of wealth.'[6] Even after the French economy and economic theory had dramatically changed as a result of industrialisation, the perception of the French economy and more particularly of French society and national identity remained solidly anchored in images of agriculture.

While such symbolic imagery of the peasant and countryside has indeed attained mythical proportions, it is nevertheless true that the majority of the French population lived in rural areas until after the Second World War, and that agriculture and its derivatives comprise a greater percentage of the French economy than that for other western developed nations. Throughout the nineteenth century and beyond, the number of small, independent landholders was also much greater than that of other European nations. Freed from serfdom during the French Revolution and given the vote in 1848, the peasantry developed a relatively high level of political consciousness earlier than in other European nations, and at the same time aspired to stay on the land as long as possible. France is unusual in that it is one of the few nations where, through to the end of the twentieth century, individuals continued to claim with pride to be 'peasants', where in other nations they would have called themselves farmers, agriculturalists, or some more specific term like dairyman or rancher.

The peasantry and the land they inhabit occupy a huge space at the heart of the French nation. One of the most prominent national images is that of the countryside as providing the familial and material roots of the nation. Poorer families were a few generations at most removed from peasant life, and for the bourgeoisie, the countryside was where the extended families passed their summers, going back again and again to rural family homes. Even after the advent of paid holidays in the 1930s and the desire to pass vacations at the seaside, the rural family home continued to symbolise the links between modern French life and its peasant roots. In his autobiographical novel whose title, *For the Pleasure of God*, is the d'Ormesson family motto, Jean d'Ormesson described the bitterness of his grandfather discovering gradually how much the younger generation preferred holidays in the mountains, at the fashionable seaside resorts or travelling around Europe to the traditional gathering in the family chateau of Plassy les Vaudreuil.[7] The selling of this country house in the 1970s symbolises in the novel the fall of an old traditional French family. As the source of France, the land and its peasantry also represent the concreteness of the nation. In his memoirs, François Mitterrand criticised his rival Charles de Gaulle for thinking of France or the French nation simply as an abstract idea, whereas Mitterrand's France was a material reality, anchored in the land from which the people had sprung, and that he 'loves it like a peasant.'[8]

Although the peasantry was a large group numerically with significant economic and political influence, the experience of 'being' a French peasant, as well as the interpretations of these experiences and their place and significance within the French nation, were diverse if not downright contradictory in some instances. Images of the peasantry were almost exclusively produced by others, most often literate members of the local or indeed national elites, rather than from among the peasants themselves. Such observers portrayed the peasants from a particular angle, depending upon their point of view, but whether romanticising, patronising or downright hostile, their interpretations tended towards the stereotypical. The Frenchness of the peasant emerges through these different images, which need to be examined in turn, beginning with the positive portraits of the virtuous peasant through the simple peasant to the backward peasant. As with much of French history, the positive image of the ideal peasant needs to be subdivided between the ideal republican peasant and the ideal Catholic peasant.

The most positive image of the peasant is as the solid backbone of the French republican nation – hard working, productive, honest, devoted to family and nation, and appropriately in love with the French soil from which he derives his livelihood. Peasant life is seen as wholesome and the countryside idyllic, producing generation after generation of young French men and women whose numbers, energy and virtue constitute the strength of the nation and are the guarantees of French national greatness. The Berry novels of George Sand, written after she had retired to the family home of Nohant, are characteristic of this search and construction by the republican elite of an ideal French peasantry.[9] Thriftiness and innovation occasionally complement this image, which includes the small landholders' adaptation of new agricultural techniques or new types of crops to help develop the rural French economy.[10] The peasant is often associated with other images such as the sheaf of grain, or the bread, be it loaf or baguette, linking every French table with the countryside which produced it. Visual representations of this interpretation of the peasantry will have them dressed simply and cleanly, perhaps in some kind of traditional folk costume. While regional variations exist, a positive image of the French peasant, found throughout the nation, hovers often in the background.

The French villages in which these 'typical' peasants lived are held up as relatively harmonious, picturesque backgrounds for this peasant life, with their typical dwellings, market square, and the ever-present buildings symbolic of national institutions: the parish church and the *mairie* or village hall. Whether presented in conflict or in co-operation, through these symbolic buildings French national life is mirrored in each rural village, and each village participates in national debates. Architecturally, a visible reminder of the nation could also be found in each village after the end of the First World War in the monument to the fallen. The commemoration of the peasants' sacrifice in each locality linked the local with the national in the minds of all of those who saw them. Such a visual pattern of the ideal French village, found throughout the nation with its familiar form and spaces, provides the backdrop in which the ideal French peasants live out their lives.

The very positive image of the ideal peasant, backbone of the nation, also appears in another guise through a close association with the Catholic church, as the loyal defender of traditional Catholic France against the evils of modernity. This image goes back to the Vendée civil wars during the Revolution when French peasants took sides not with the urban, Parisian bourgeoisie, but with their local religious and aristocratic leaders in support of the king. From this standpoint, in addition to the virtues discussed above, the ideal peasant is also credited with faith and loyalty to church and monarch, to 'true France'. Such additional virtue further links the image of the peasant with the long-standing tradition of France as the eldest daughter of the Catholic church.

This presentation of Catholicism as a primary characteristic of the ideal peasant tended to be generated by the French Catholic elites (those who had developed the Catholic vision of French history discussed in Part I) or at least those on the more reactionary, conservative right. This was true during the nineteenth century for such writers as Maurice Barrès, Charles Péguy and even the Comtesse de Ségur, in her portrayal of an ideal rural lifestyle, in which Catholicism was predominant among the peasantry and the elite alike.[11] Another obvious case in point was the championing of rural values which lay at the root of the Vichy government's National Revolution. They portrayed France's defeat in the Second World War as the result of the nation's having strayed too far from the traditional peasant values which had always characterised the best of the French nation. The suggestion was that for a return to greatness, France needed to recapture the work ethic and other values of the ideal French peasant and the land which sustained him, for 'the land doesn't lie'.

While it may be true that the image of the ideal peasant does have its origins predominantly on the right of the political spectrum, it is not the exclusive preserve of the right. As it has been suggested, republicans and those on the left have integrated this positive vision within the republican tradition of France, and although the religious dimension is downplayed, it has also been integrated as something to be overcome. Little attempt was made to mythologise rural origins of the Revolution, even though examples can be found, such as the *Cahiers de doléance*, statements of grievances collected from around France to be presented at the Estates General. At that time, the republican vision saw the peasantry as primarily characterised by its Catholicism. For republicans, it was this

Figure 5 François Mitterrand: presidential election poster 1981 ('silent strength')

Catholicism in the countryside which occasionally stood in the way of the spread of republicanism, from the Vendée wars during the Revolution, through to their regular conservatism, blockage of reforms and unwillingness to support the Republic at such moments as the election of Louis-Napoleon during the Second Republic. But even in their most republican incarnations, such as the heroes of George Sand, most ideal peasants have, among other virtues already discussed, the additional characteristics of faith and regular practice, loyalty to the church, and respect for its priests, rules and traditions.

Thus the two idealised images of the peasantry were not as contradictory as one might think. In both cases, the peasants at the core of the French nation had to be mythified as a strong, stable, loyal, conservative social class. How much it was necessary to insist on Catholicism to get that point through varied, and the religious belief of the peasant could be presented in a positive or negative light, depending upon the Catholicism or anticlericalism of the observer, but the main significance of the image is still the same. In the ideal French society (republican or Catholic), peasants were recognised as socially conservative forces, at the heart of the French nation. Even the socialist François Mitterrand, in his successful presidential bid in 1981, portrayed himself in his main campaign poster with the background of a village with its church spire clearly in evidence (Figure 5). One might have thought that for a socialist a more appropriate backdrop would have been a shining factory, but he and his campaign team obviously thought that it was more important yet to demonstrate that he was in touch with 'authentic' France – the rural world of the peasant from which the majority had their origins. Mitterrand's campaign slogan, 'La Force tranquille' (silent strength), further emphasised his reliability and how deeply rooted he was in the French land and its people.

Linked to the image of the ideal peasant (in both republican and Catholic forms), but not identical to it, is that of the simple peasant. Characterised by a lack of formal education and probably even illiteracy, such simplicity or ignorance can on the one hand be interpreted as another virtue to add to the catalogue, especially by certain members of the reactionary right. Simple peasants were 'unpolluted' by the urban, revolutionary doctrines and called for special treatment. These were peasants who needed to be guided, treated with paternal care, protected from the corrupting influence of the urban areas by the traditional local elites and, for example, instructed in how to vote. Such simplicity excludes part of the positive image – that of the enterprising, progressive peasantry, but does not detract from the Frenchness of the image. Republicans also integrated this image, suggesting that it was simplicity which kept the peasants under the domination of the church, legitimising their policies of mass education as emancipating them from this association. For those in both camps, the perceived simplicity of the peasants could be used as a justification for any attempts to lead, instruct and educate them in one direction or the other.

Shorn of its positive connotations, the simple peasant can also become the backward peasant. Looming as large as the ideal peasant in the imagery of the French nation, the backward peasant comes in for much criticism for the very lack of virtue with which the other image credits him. Ignorant, filthy, greedy, violent, lazy, selfish and untrustworthy, the backward peasant's nature was certainly nothing to be proud of. Sometimes an object of derision, mockery and contempt, sometimes of embarrassment or sometimes simply of mirth and comedy, the backward peasant can be found throughout French literature, examples including Balzac's *Les Paysans* or Zola's *La Terre*.

In many ways the almost savage and uncontrollable being thus presented is the black reverse of the ideal myth discussed earlier. Such an image was already present in the seventeenth and eighteenth centuries, in the writings of La Bruyère or Voltaire.[12] The violence of the Vendée civil war during the Revolution was then held up as further evidence of the backward savages, and used by republicans as a warning in the national memory. As Balzac pointed out in his novel *Les Chouans*, 'the chouans remained as a memorable example of the danger of stirring up the uncivilised masses of any country.'[13] What was new from the nineteenth century onwards was the construction of the positive, idealised counter-myth supposed to annihilate such a danger. Depending upon the attitude of the individual thinking of the backward peasant, what can or might need to be done to help them or prevent their violence or vice from contaminating society also varied. Such peasants may have needed paternalistic care (as with the simple peasant) or indeed a heavy handed legal system to keep them in check. Alternatively, their ignorance and baseness may have represented a challenge to be overcome through education and exposure to republicanism and the values that went with it. By freeing them from the domination of priests and nobles, and providing them with increased opportunities under the republican system, the backward peasant could be transformed, and the nation modernised.

The French peasant of the nineteenth and twentieth centuries, like the 'savage' of the eighteenth century, presented a paradoxical ideal through which French society could examine itself. The fact that these almost opposite visions of the peasant, either virtuous or backward, existed simultaneously also meant that attitudes towards the desirability of the modernisation of the countryside differed. On the one hand it was helping the backward peasant to become enlightened, helping them to overcome all of the hardships which rural life entailed and could only be seen as in their own interest and for their unqualified good. Alternatively, modernisation could be viewed as the shameful destruction of the romantically viewed rural culture, as yet uncorrupted by secular, urban values.

One might have assumed that since attitudes towards modernisation differed, that the exact position of the peasant within the idealised French nation would also differ, yet this has not really been the case. According to the theory of assimilation and integration of the masses into mainstream French society, the implication in many cases is that the backward peasants were in some ways not French, and that a break with the clerical conservative and backwards tradition of provincial society was necessary for the creation of the modern republic. Even the work of historians such as Eugen Weber's *Peasants Into Frenchmen* lends support to this image, and while it is partly true that a certain degree of opposition can be found in the images, in practice, the vast majority nevertheless considered the peasants as at least unquestionably, if not quintessentially French.[14] Even those who lamented the backwards state of the peasantry could as easily claim that they were 'naturally' French and being held back from full participation in the French nation (to which they belonged) by their own ignorance as well as those local leaders who encouraged them to accept their lot and kept them down.

These different images of the peasantry survived through the generations in juxtaposition with real experiences of and interaction with French peasants. In reality of course, French peasants were neither ideal nor completely backward; uneducated does not imply unintelligent, and although as a group they tended towards conservatism, they acted primarily according to self-interest in about the same degree as any other group, which meant progressive at times and reactionary in others. In the images of the modern French nation and the society which makes it up, the peasant in his diverse forms plays a large role as a national symbol of pride and of essential Frenchness, in spite of not having played a great part in the Revolution. Later French people placed the life of the peasant at the roots of the national experience, as the origin of French society and its connection to the land. While links to these peasant roots are lamented in some circles as lost, they can nevertheless be found throughout national imagery right through to the end of the twentieth century.

The Worker

> As for the workers ... He pictured them as the only heroes, the only saints, the only nobility, and the only force which could redeem humanity.
>
> Etienne Lantier, the strike leader in Zola's *Germinal*[15]

Alongside that of the peasant, the image of French society as experienced by the worker is central to any vision of Frenchness. In spite of the relatively greater position of agriculture and the rural world for France compared to Britain or Germany, industrialisation can nevertheless be found at the heart of French identity, with the worker, his activities and experiences unquestionably those of a typical Frenchman.[16] Later than in Great Britain, industrialisation in France began to take off by the mid-nineteenth century, with the construction of a network of railways, the opening up of mines and the development of industrial centres of production. Gradually French cities grew, although the urban population would not surpass that in the countryside until the mid-twentieth century. Several industrial regions developed which would become part of the mythos of the working classes. Perhaps the most famous is the coal-mining basin of the northern Pas-de-Calais, which entered into the collective memory via Zola's novel *Germinal*. Besides the Parisian industrial basin, with its large working-class neighbourhoods and suburbs, workers were also concentrated at the textile factories in and around Lille, the steel producing cities in the east of France and in Lyon, where the workers known as the 'canuts' produced silk and other goods on the legendary hill of the Croix-Rousse. By the Second World War, workers appeared alongside peasants as the symbolic essence of the French nation, jointly called to arms by the resistance anthem 'the Partisan', which can be understood as an attempt to reconcile communist visions of the two groups.[17] In the second half of the twentieth century, when the urban population had at last outstripped the rural one, new mythological workers were added to the canon within the French nation. The 'ouvrier specialisé' of the Parisian suburb Boulogne-Billancourt, where the large Renault factories were located is one such image, who Jean-Paul Sartre famously refused to abandon, preferring to remain within the Communist Party as a sign of solidarity with these workers, and simultaneously hoping to distance the party from the Eastern Bloc. Towards the end of the twentieth century, the extreme left presidential candidate Arlette Laguillier's opening line to each speech 'travailleuses, travailleurs' ('workers' in its female and male forms) may have provoked some humorous commentary from journalists, but it nevertheless demonstrates the importance of the image of the worker in French political culture.

It can thus be said that after the peasant, the worker is the second relevant figure for the national identity of modern France. But unlike the peasants, who through their association with traditional economic activities came to symbolise the historic roots of the French nation, the worker is, throughout the nineteenth and twentieth centuries, associated with a new and modern kind of economic activity: industry. At the same time, through revolution and industrial action, the worker is associated with the struggle for change and improvement. He is the symbol of France as a forward moving, progressive nation, not only one with strong roots; he is a figure of the future rather than of the past. Economically, socially but also politically, the figure of the worker incarnates the ambiguities and complexities of the relationship of post-revolutionary France with modernity and progress.

It should not therefore be surprising that, as with the peasant, images of the French worker are diverse and include both positive and negative versions. Variety originates firstly from the diversity of types of jobs which could be found throughout nineteenth- and twentieth-century France. From the more prestigious coal miner, steel or industrial textile worker to the unskilled labourer, a variety of potential figures and lifestyle experiences could be found. More importantly the variety of images can be attributed to differences of political attitudes towards workers' actions and experiences. The first is the romantic vision of the French worker which originated in the nineteenth century and continued to resonate in various guises throughout the twentieth, an image which itself has two faces: one of suffering and misery, and the other of revolt and progress. Victor Hugo's *Les Misérables* is one of the most famous representations of this vision, where the suffering is transformed into assertive protest.[18] Romantic images of the worker often centred upon the hardship of conditions, either in the workplace or at home. In the factory or mine, they had to work long hours in unsafe and physically demanding environments. At home they were overcrowded, living in accommodation which was often poorly constructed, without proper sanitary facilities or perhaps even easy access to good drinking water.[19] Overall, workers appeared in a variety of different moments in their lives: at work of course, but also on strike or engaged in active protest if not actual revolution, and also at leisure, enjoying a 'well-earned' rest from their labours.

The worker in the factory or down the mine, the worker on the barricades fighting for social justice, romantic images were diverse and plentiful. Even something like the dirt associated with heavy labour, and most particularly of course with coal mining could be viewed in different lights – as a badge of honour and a symbol of hard work and dedication, or as the very filth which characterised the whole of the workers' existence, not only in the workplace but also in their homes, literally and metaphorically.

While the romantically portrayed experience of the worker was one of hardship and perpetual conflict with the French state and the bourgeois industrialists who controlled the workplace, it also included the view that it was the workers' reaction to suffering via revolution and protest which kept France at the forefront of social development and enlightened progress. Workers were not only instrumental in the Revolution itself, but at the core of the French tradition of aggressive and demanding social protest which ensured the advancement of society, and brought prestige to the French nation as self-perceived world leaders in the fight to overcome oppression. Even outside traditional Marxist circles, workers were recognised as a revolutionary force within France.[20] In many ways, looking back at the hardships of earlier workers purveys a sense of accomplishment, of triumph over adversity to those later French citizens who identify themselves with the experience of their worker forebears.

Because of the violence which grew out of this vision of the worker during the second half of the nineteenth century, rival groups within the political elite of France attempted to pick up upon different elements of it, while adapting it to their own particular agenda. Even if they were sympathetic towards and felt guilty with respect to the sufferings of the workers, both the republican and the Catholic bourgeois elites had been severely frightened by the violence of the revolutions, riots and other protests in which the workers had participated. The equation 'Working classes = dangerous classes' was profoundly felt by those who saw in workers degenerate, vagabond, criminal, lazy, uneducated, immoral and violent disrupters of the natural order and whose activities represented a real threat to the stability of French society.[21] The republican vision of the worker remained ambiguous. Accepting that the Revolution and the working classes had contributed to the progress which was manifest in the republic itself, they nevertheless rejected the violence condoned and celebrated by the romantics, suggesting that the era of violent protest was over, and that any remaining suffering or hardship would be overcome in due course through regular reform sanctioned by republican governments. Catholics also rejected the violence of the working classes, hoping to suggest a model similar to that of the peasantry, that paternalism and social Catholicism would be the way to overcome the hardships of the workers, along the pattern illustrated in the novels of the Catholic writer Maxence Van der Meersch.[22] This image was even less successful than the republican one, and, as Bernanos pointed out, the great tragedy of the church during the nineteenth century was its loss of the working class, which was true both in terms of loyalty and participation, as well as in control or manipulation of subsequent imagery. The image which was the most consensual, and the least difficult to maintain in each of these visions was that of the misery and suffering of the workers. This was especially true where emphasis could be placed upon the sufferings of women and children, either in the workplace themselves or as a result of the conditions of their husbands and fathers, for the corollary of violence did not follow them as closely as it did the men.[23]

An alternative portrait was developed by the extreme left and the trade unions, who, backed up by Marxist justifications for violence, built upon the romantic model of worker violence which could lead to progress. Championing the previous revolutions and confrontational strikes and protests, this view credited the workers as the most important positive force within the French nation. This position also suggested that further protest or indeed revolution was the sole way to bring about further change and improvement. Such images were not accepted as readily as the labour leaders hoped, since the negative side of the violence and excesses of past revolutions were difficult to cover up. Looking at the actual historical record, participation in one or another of the official faces of the workers' movement – the trade unions and the socialist parties – was considerably lower in France than it was in Germany or Great Britain.[24] Never as unified, centrally controlled or directed as many of the leaders wished, the French workers nevertheless displayed a great deal of militancy which has contributed to the regular image of the French worker as capable of aggressively rising to a specific occasion in the name of social progress.

In each of the visions of French workers, the diverse experiences of individual workers often became dissolved into the greater experiences of the French working class as a whole; workers were as often perceived as a group rather than as individuals. For the far left, the collective image of the worker is channelled primarily through the vision of the workers' movement, rather than the specific conditions of living and working. Portrayed almost exclusively as a mass movement, individual heroes from the world of the worker were less common than references to the faceless group. Such a vision proliferated images of the development of class consciousness among the workers, with the growth of the trade union movement and the various socialist parities contributing to the co-ordination and channelling of the natural militancy of the worker. The regular return to the barricades to fight for social justice was an important dimension of the workers' experience. For the extreme left, the collective representation has a positive spin – the united working class, expressing its cohesion and solidarity through collective action, co-operation and mutual aid. Alternatively, as in the republican and Catholic visions of the worker, the perceived group can be thought of as an uncontrollable, violent, disruptive mass which lay at the root of social unrest. In each case, specifics give way to collective images. The lack of individuality associated with 'the worker' contributes to the pervasiveness of him as a symbol, with just enough permeability to be evoked in a wide variety of situations, and allowing for identification with a vague generalisation of French workers' experience as one of hardship which provoked coordinated action central and necessary to the advancement of the French nation.

In terms of their actions, their characters and personalities therefore, the typical French workers appearing in histories, art and literature are ambiguous creatures, both positive and negative, but whose experience was clearly central to the French nation, closely associated with each major event, crisis and development. The most obvious, even if not the most significant, is their role in the industrialisation which brought increased wealth to the country and helped to preserve its place as one of the world's leading nations, keeping France at the forefront of modernity. More importantly in terms of their image within the French nation was their central, indeed pivotal contribution to revolutionary progress and the role which workers' activism repeatedly played in social change and advancement throughout the nineteenth and twentieth centuries. From the great Revolution through 1830, 1848 and the Paris Commune down to the protests of May 1968, to mention only the high points, workers were supposedly at the heart of every major crisis. Although the violent social protest was downplayed in the republican and Catholic representations of the worker, who hoped to relegate such protests firmly to the past, it survived in those originating among the extreme left which attributed to it a fundamental political dimension. Identification with these great movements and the progress they brought about, to say nothing of the perceived prestige to the French nation which came with being on the forefront of such social changes has been central to French national identity in all of its guises.

The relationship between the perception of what workers' experience has been and the historical reality of what workers actually lived through is of course imprecise. The sheer diversity of the real professional and personal experiences of workers, especially when taken over such a broad sweep of time, necessarily preclude an accurate generalisation as to what the 'typical' French worker was like or how he or she behaved. That does not stop workers' experiences and actions from constituting an important mythical element in French society and its evolution. The perceived experience of what it was to be a French worker, whether in terms of living or working conditions, can be summarised as the experience of oppression. Fellow feeling with those who have suffered, and an identification with the underdog, became closely associated with belief in social justice and was a significant element of French identity. Also the experience of being a worker was at least in part the experience of participating in protest and revolution. Even the very large protest movements of the late twentieth century can at least in part be understood as carrying on the great tradition of French working-class protest, even if few of the actual participants were themselves workers. They feel an association with the workers of this mythical past and understand their own political actions in light of their belief in 'French' types of behaviour and experience.[25]

By the end of the twentieth century, the traditional working class had in many ways become something of the past. With the fall of the Soviet bloc and the full participation of the whole of the French population in consumer society, Communist rhetoric of the struggle of the workers and the need for a proletarian revolution seems to have lost most of its social as well as emotional relevance. In such a context, the survival of the historic image of the worker becomes something of a paradox. The French Communist party, denounced as recently as the 1980s by the extreme-right leader Jean-Marie Le Pen as a mainstream party – one of the 'band of four' – had become the outsider in French political life. The Socialist party itself had abandoned much of its working-class rhetoric, in its pre-occupation with the fortunes of the middle class, and turned increasingly towards its new Green allies in preference to its historic alliance with the Communist party. The trade unions and the variety of extreme left parties, however marginalised they and their discourse may have become, never abandoned the old images of the worker. Such rhetoric, including the image of the oppressed worker, symbol of revolutionary hope and of social progress, charged with historical meaning, as old fashioned and irrelevant in a white-collared post-modern France as it may appear, still echoes strongly in the French collective memory. A figure of hardship and courage, the worker remains a key image within modern understanding of French society, a powerful symbol not only for the French left, but for French identity in general.

The Bourgeois

> Les bourgeois c'est comme les cochons
> Plus ça devient vieux plus ça devient bête
> Les bourgeois c'est comme les cochons
> Plus ça devient vieux plus ça devient ...'
>
> Jacques Brel, 'Les bourgeois'[26]

The next prominent figure in modern French society with whom every French person had experience is the bourgeois, a pivotal figure from the *ancien régime* through the Revolution to the nineteenth and twentieth centuries. Originally meaning simply town-dweller, the term bourgeois came to describe the members of an economic elite held up as rivals to other groups within French society. During the *ancien régime*, they were portrayed in competition with the aristocracy, in such places as Molière's 'Bourgeois-gentilhomme'. Marx then placed them as the social class which emerged triumphant from out of the Third Estate during the French Revolution, and then went on to dominate French society and firmly establish the capitalist economic system for their own benefit in the decades which followed. The image of the bourgeois best emerges within the context of these conflicts which confer meaning and understanding of successive phases of French society, with the aristocracy up to and during the Revolution, and with the proletariat after that.

Individual representations of the French bourgeois abound, from Monsieur Homais in Flaubert's *Madame Bovary* to Monsieur Bertin as he was painted by Ingres. Most often such portraits are unsympathetic or at least unflattering. Perhaps because of the importance of Marxist mythology in the image of the French bourgeois, and similarly to what we have just seen with the worker, the individual bourgeois is often subsumed within images of the collective bourgeoisie. Julien Sorel, at the end of Stendhal's *Le Rouge et le Noir*, has no doubts that as the educated son of a poor peasant, he will be condemned by his jury to whose 'class he hasn't the honour to belong' and among whom he only sees 'indignant bourgeois'. Such generalisation can be found in the writings of the Catholic Francois Mauriac set in the Bordeaux region, as well as of the Protestant Jacques Chardonne describing the Limousin, whose works describe the overall characteristics of the bourgeoisie as a group. French expressions such as a 'maison bourgeoise', or 'cuisine bourgeoise' further indicate the ways in which the word bourgeois often describes an atmosphere and common values rather than specific individual qualities.

Taken collectively, images of the bourgeois are varied and often ambiguous. Given sole credit in some circles for bringing about the French Revolution and championing freedom, yet much maligned by later socialists as those who exploited the workers, the bourgeoisie, both in characteristics and actions, is extremely difficult to define objectively owing to the tremendous diversity which it includes. Ranging from extremely wealthy industrialists, army officers, civil servants and teachers to petty clerks and small shopkeepers, representing the full spectrum of political and religious beliefs, and possessing diverse social, educational and regional backgrounds, the bourgeoisie cannot but represent different cultural values and behaviour at different times.[27] In his novel *Pot Bouille*, Emile Zola describes the life of a bourgeois building in Haussmann's Paris. He describes in detail the complicated hierarchy that existed within the bourgeoisie, represented in the novel by the different floors of the building, from the wealthy industrial of the second floor to the poor students living in the small garret rooms. He also insisted upon the fact that the bourgeoisie was the class that lives at the front of the building, hiding inside and in the back courts its own misery and that of the poor they ruthlessly exploit. A tacit acknowledgement of purely economic hierarchies and ruthless social conformism appear in the novel as 'typically' bourgeois characteristics. Outside of a value structure which gives a prominent place to wealth and property, coming up with a satisfactory objective definition of the bourgeois is not really the point here. It is to understand the place which images of the bourgeois and the perceived experience of the bourgeois have had within French society, and their part within the invention of the French nation. For that reason we will look at several specific types of bourgeois in turn, and the place of their experience within the French nation.

The first, and arguably most enduring image of the bourgeois is that of the 'grand bourgeois': wealthy, connected, politically active and a member of the regional or national elite. Collectively, it is this grande bourgeoisie whose pressure helped to overthrow the nobility via the French Revolution, and whose access to capital placed them behind French industrial, banking and trade interests. Politically, this is the group which has been identified as dominating the nineteenth or 'bourgeois' century, benefiting from (if not actually precipitating) the transformations of French society following the 1789 Revolution. It is perhaps most closely identified with the July Revolution of 1830 and Orleanism. The bourgeoisie was identified through its support of the restricted franchise in order to keep power in its own hands, and through putting pressure upon successive regimes to defend the interests of individual property ownership, wealth, commerce and industry. Louis-Philippe was called 'the bourgeois king', and even the comfortable, unostentatious style in furniture which bears his name remains popular and symbolic of a certain economic success, as well as of social conformism. Economically, it was the grand bourgeois who modernised the French economy, dominated French trade, manufacturing and finance, and also came increasingly to dominate elite society in France at the expense of the declining nobility. Even the communard Louise Michel concedes some achievement to the grande bourgeoisie, albeit in a manner designed to criticise, when she wrote that 'the bourgeois race was only great for at most a half century after 1789.'[28]

In addition to its wealth, the grande bourgeoisie can also be distinguished by the value structure which it represents. Bourgeois values included respect for private property, individualism, tolerance, the rule of law, caution, prudence, respectability and also a vision of domestic harmony. On the latter point, the bourgeois family, both nuclear and extended, came to be an important part of the image. The bourgeois wife did not work, but respectfully cared for the home and family, appearing decoratively in support of her husband on social occasions, and setting an example of morality and virtue. The extended family was also important, with the establishment of 'grande familles' who passed on business and political traditions through generations. Connections between the great families via marriage further promoted links and solidified the hold of the bourgeois as the dominant class and the setters of values. Family values were reinforced within numerous bourgeois circles by links with the Catholic church. Perhaps even more true for bourgeois women than for men, the bourgeoisie often came down on the side of supporting tradition and the church as symbols of their honesty, trustworthiness and overall respectability.[29]

Although such characteristics and values appear to cover the whole of the bourgeoisie, behind the façade of unity lay a profound social division. Unlike Victorian England with its image of the gentleman, post-Revolutionary French society was never able to reconcile the new bourgeois with the old gentleman to form a representative, coherent social elite. René Rémond identified the political counterpart to this social division of the French elite as that between the legitimist and the Orleanist right. Even well after the return of either monarchy had become impossible, the two conservative socio-political traditions were perpetuated in other forms, right through the twentieth century.[30] This opposition is one of the principle elements of the social commentary in Marcel Proust's *À la Recherche du Temps Perdu*, well over a century after the Revolution, in which the aristocratic world of the Guermantes is opposed to that of the republican grand bourgeois Swann.

Links to Catholicism need also to be viewed in light of these social divisions within the bourgeoisie. The church was associated with conventional morality, the nuclear family and political conservatism which could be found throughout the bourgeoisie, including among republican families. However, it also harboured within it an anti-bourgeois, anti-capitalist tendency which was far removed from the social democracy of the nineteenth and twentieth centuries and was founded upon a pure nostalgia for the *ancien régime*. Inside such Catholic intellectual circles, the bourgeois was despised for his 'greediness' and so called lack of spiritual values, which can explain some paradoxical political shifts from socialism to traditional Catholicism like that of Péguy, or from traditional Catholicism to social democracy or even socialism like that of Mauriac or Mitterrand.[31] Georges Bernanos, in some of his pamphlets like *La Grande Peur des Biens Pensants*, or *Les Grands Cimetières Sous La Lune*, in which he violently attacks Franco's government in Spain, represents this tendency and dares to say very plainly that 'the middle classes have until now been the only ones to produce genuine imbeciles.'[32]

In opposition to this very traditionalist anti-bourgeois Catholic feeling was the republican bourgeoisie. It of course included anticlericals and atheists, even though in many respects, particularly when it came to family and morality, mainstream Catholicism was still a widespread value. The republican bourgeoisie, while harbouring a passive Catholicism, also contained a more freethinking trend, one which was also tolerant of, and capable of integrating Protestants, Jews and freemasons. While some interaction took place between these two sub-groups of the grande bourgeoisie, in practice they remained socially closed to one another, existing in parallel. Each had its own elite schools in which they would form their own members: Louis le Grand and Henri IV for the republican bourgeoisie, St Genevieve or Stanislas for the Catholics. Each had its own press, its own clubs and, as was suggested by the example of Proust already referred to, married and socialised among themselves. As it became less and less a compliment to be called a bourgeois, each of these two groups had a tendency to accuse the other of being the real one.

Criticised and mocked therefore from the right, from the left and from within, by the nobility for being overly vulgar in their tastes, by the radical left for standing for oppression under the veneer of the discourse of freedom of the individual, by alternative groups for being too much under the influence of the church, or not enough, and by intellectuals of every stripe for being too conservative, the image of the grande bourgeoisie nevertheless became a key symbol within the French nation. Described as 'an ocean of nothingness', 'all that thinks basely' or simply as an obstacle to the spread of genius, the bourgeois was prominently represented in all accounts of French society, primarily as that to which the peasants and workers were opposed.[33] The image of the grand bourgeois was at least sometimes accorded a kind of begrudging respect for economic and political achievement, and in helping to ensure that France remained great internationally, but not very often, and usually by those who wanted to present themselves as heirs. Occasionally a positive, central figure within the French nation, but most often that which blocked the progress and self-fulfilment of the nation, the grand bourgeois represents in every case a central figure. Interaction with, if not opposition to such individuals was a key experience for the collective perception of French society.

The grand bourgeois is not the only example to have attained mythic status within the French nation. The 'petit bourgeois', be it shopkeeper or perhaps more commonly a member of the growing state administrative structure, known as a 'fonctionnaire' or civil servant, also figures large within the experience of French society. Partly a symbol of opposition for the lower classes, as with the grand bourgeois, or occasionally on the side of the people, images of these middling characters fill accounts of French society. The civil servant appears as the symbol of upward mobility or of thwarted ambition, or indeed as the personification of the state bureaucracy, in all of its negative, regulation-following, form-filling inflexibility with which every French person came face to face at some time or another.

Within the regional context, in the myriad of restricted societies of provincial France, the bourgeois often came under the category of 'local notable'. Among the very restricted local elites in villages and provincial towns, such an individual may in fact be a genuine grand bourgeois, or simply a petit bourgeois, one generation removed from the peasantry, but who has gained significantly in status within the small local community to which he belongs. This may be the local schoolteacher, the priest, or indeed the most recent heir to an old, land-owning family. The rivalry between such individuals for status and influence within local communities is a widespread image, with positive and negative stereotypes abounding. Possibly associated with regionalist movements, or made fun of as hick provincials within the national context, they are an interface between different elements of French society.

During the twentieth century, critiques of the bourgeois and of traditional bourgeois values were renewed and increased. Marxists repeatedly attacked the ideology of private property and the capitalist system which guaranteed the domination of the bourgeoisie. Feminists and youth movements (often linked to the left), via the resistance and later in the protests surrounding May 1968, also criticised bourgeois society as inappropriately hierarchical and without spiritual life. That being said, as the century progressed, an ever increasing percentage of the population entered the middle classes, and even the socialist party could be accused of having become a bourgeois party, supported by what became known as the 'gauche caviar' (the 'caviar left', similar to the 'champagne socialism' jibe against supporters of Tony Blair after 1997). Particularly after the fall of communism, values such as freedom on issues of race and gender, political correctness or environmental awareness can be seen to have crept into mainstream bourgeois acceptability. While some degree of social democracy also became acceptable, the fundamental bourgeois values of private property, individualism and a largely capitalist economic structure were no longer seriously questioned outside increasingly marginal extremist circles. Late twentieth century images or symbols of the bourgeois within French society include not only the 'BCBG' (Bon Chic Bon Genre) which refers to well-dressed, conservative, traditional thinking young bourgeois (read also 'boring' by those who were critical), but also the 'bo-bo' which stands for 'bourgeois-bohème' (bohemian-bourgeois), and suggests a juxtaposition of the unconventional, unpredictable or even artistic with the conventional and conservative. Such images suggest the extent to which bourgeois respectability and conservatism have become commonplace in French society, at the same time as the desire to continue to think of themselves as daring or at least unconventional thinkers.

Late twentieth-century French society, although composed mostly of individuals who would have to be called bourgeois, in one way or another, certainly did not often identify itself primarily with the historic image of the bourgeois in French society. French society has been understood since the Revolution as characterised by a mistrust of its new elites, most often personified in the figure of the bourgeois. Opposition to and criticism of the bourgeoisie and bourgeois values came from all sides of the social and political spectrum. The place of the bourgeois in French society is certainly central, but as a figure standing in opposition to the progress championed by the Revolution and enlightened sections of French society, keeping workers and peasants down, and rendering vulgar the positive achievements of French cultural elites and French high culture. While the French nation had extensive experience of the respectable bourgeois, it was as the figure within society against whom all progressive or positive and valuable forces were ranged. Even those clearly within the bourgeoisie routinely sought to create alternative images which labelled their opponents as bourgeois and themselves as having a more positive role within French society.[34] As Roland Barthes put it, the bourgeoisie can be defined as 'the social class which does not want to be named', and which presents its values and norms as universal.[35] This is particularly true of the final segment of French society to be examined in this chapter, the intellectual.

The Intellectual

'Je suis tombé par terre
C'est la faute à Voltaire
Le nez dans le ruisseau
C'est la faute à Rousseau'

Gavroche's song in Victor Hugo's *Les Misérables*

Although not a 'class' in any traditional sense, intellectuals occupy a prominent place within French society, and their influence at the cusp of cultural and political life has earned them the status of 'national icons'.[36] While the term has several connotations, intellectual in France has come to mean those writers, scholars, poets, artists or scientists who put their work or their name to the direct service of a particular political position or cause, and hope that by so doing they will confer extra prestige or success upon it. It is a distinguishing feature of French society to have intricate connections between the artists and men and women of letters on the one hand and the political and economic elite of the French nation on the other. From Voltaire to Bourdieu, via Chateaubriand, Hugo, Péguy, Aragon, Sartre and Camus, countless members of the French cultural elite have even considered that it was their duty to have their say in French political life rather than to restrict themselves to their academic or cultural work. The relationship between intellectuals and the course of French political history have been the object of numerous studies, and their position within modern French society has always been a highly visible one.[37]

Far from resenting the interference in politics of writers and thinkers, the participation of intellectuals in politics and political debate has long been recognised as an essential and indeed necessary part of national life by the French public, and interaction with their ideas a common experience of French society. In France's crucial historical moments – the fight for or against the republic, the years leading up to the First World War, the period of collaboration with Germany during the occupation, the Cold

War, the wars of decolonisation, and perhaps more so around specific issues like the Dreyfus Affair, the question of torture by the French military in Algeria, the Papon trial or the 'foulard affair', members of the French intelligentsia have been expected to voice their opinion and to lead their fellow citizens towards what they think is right and true.[38] The French intellectual symbolises the intersection and inseparability of the political and cultural life of the nation. As Balzac expressed it: 'what Napoleon started with the sword, I will finish with the pen.'[39] Such high expectations led, for example, to the well-publicised criticism of Camus' silence during the Algerian crisis, once he realised there could be no peaceful compromise, and acknowledged that he did 'believe in justice but would defend his mother before Justice'.[40] His inability to choose his camp was held against him from all sides, for as a French intellectual he had a duty to speak out. Political leaders themselves acknowledge the specific duty of the intellectuals. Charles de Gaulle's refusal to pardon Robert Brasillach from his death sentence after the liberation, in spite of the lengthy petition signed by many of France's leading citizens, is such an instance. De Gaulle stated that Brasillach's status as an intellectual made his opinion far different from that of an average citizen, and that as an intellectual he had leadership duties and responsibilities: 'the sin of the intellectual' – leading his fellow Frenchmen into disaster – was unpardonable.[41]

The popular use of the term intellectual in French political life began at the time of the Dreyfus Affair. The most visible Dreyfusard was novelist Emile Zola, whose article 'J'Accuse' precipitated the escalation of the crisis. It was Clemenceau who introduced the word intellectual to describe those who had first signed the petition circulating in favour of Dreyfus, essentially academics and students, as well as a small number of artists, who gravitated around the Sorbonne and the *grandes écoles*. The word became well-known after Barrès, one of the most admired writers of his generation, also used it pejoratively to describe the same group in the widely-circulated paper *Le Journal*.[42] The Affair saw the eventual success of this minority, the voice of the intellectuals, and the term entered mainstream usage, symbolic of the network of thinkers ever-present in French political life.

Highly developed ties between elite circles of writers or artists and French politics pre-dates the term intellectual, however. The eighteenth-century philosophers had certainly hoped to influence political life by their work, and were recognised by revolutionary France as their spiritual leaders. The romantic writers and poets of the nineteenth century also believed in their political mission as members of the literary and scientific elite. French political leaders liked to have fully worked out theoretical justifications for their actions, and sought to enhance and justify their movements through association with prominent writers. These writers themselves came to expect the people to follow their lead, as for instance in the young Victor Hugo's appeal: 'Peoples! Listen to the poet! Listen to the blessed dreamer! In your darkness, his forehead alone brings light.'[43] In a later poem, Hugo compares the poet (himself) with the Old Testament political and spiritual leader Joshua, who by the sheer power of 'the horns of thought' would one day bring down the walls of oppression and injustice.[44] The close ties between intellectuals and political parties in France contrast strikingly with the anti-intellectual pragmatism which characterises British and North American politics.

Many intellectuals went beyond the influencing of French political life through the medium of their art, and sought an active political career, often including high elected office, although this occasionally meant the end of their purely artistic career. Examples include Lamartine's leadership during the 1848 Revolution and the early Second Republic, Victor Hugo's years in the French Senate or André Malraux's position as Minister of Culture under de Gaulle. Many others pledged loyalty to a party or a cause, like Hugo through his defence of republicanism, or Aragon and many others who became members of the French Communist Party. Some, like Jean-Paul Sartre, described themselves as mere 'Fellow Travellers', keeping themselves at a critical distance from an official party structure, but nevertheless acknowledging solidarity with the cause. But whatever the specific form of their commitment, being an intellectual in the French nation meant more than simply being a writer or artist, it also implied having, or at least seeking political responsibility and leadership.

In the romantic tradition as expressed by Hugo, the artist and specifically the poet are described as new spiritual leaders, and deserve the share of the credit they received for their contribution to the Revolution, political change and social progress. For this role, they have often been represented by themselves and by others as a new kind of secular clergy.[45] In a country with a strong Catholic tradition like France, the need for priests and spiritual leadership, taken with the conflicts between the republican regimes and the traditional Catholic clergy, can partly explain the nature of the intellectual's place within myths of French society. The reverence with which their writings are quoted by politicians and the people, the vocational devotion and sense of duty they apply to their work, as well as the prestigious niche they occupy among the elite in French society can all be compared to that of a priest in a traditional village. Even after direct parallels with the clergy had faded, priest-like behaviour could still be observed, such as the almost blind loyalty to the Communist Party which characterised many twentieth-century intellectuals, and could be compared to a vow of obedience, or in the celebrity status accorded to intellectuals which makes them akin to movie stars or sports heroes.[46]

Part of their celebrity status derives from the strong connection between the intellectual and the avant-garde, between politics and not only theory, but also innovation in art. Being an expert in the classics is not enough, an intellectual should also be a creative force, and the term could apply to writers, actors or musicians as much as to academics operating within the sphere of universities. Those with academic training such as Sartre or Simone de Beauvoir became genuine French intellectuals when they also became creators of a new philosophical school, or avant-garde literary works. Even among fully-fledged artists, however, the image of avant-garde was difficult to sustain. In the 1950s, Jean Vilar, the founder of the Avignon festival and the National Popular Theatres (TNP), designed to bring theatre to the lower classes, and his principal actor Gérard Philippe symbolised the intellectual avant-garde. Refusing to be an entertainer only producing 'boulevard' plays, Vilar developed an ambitious programme of popular high-quality theatre very much linked to his political engagement with the Communist Party. It did not take long, however, for such work to become a respected French institution, seen as a part of the establishment. As the new cultural avant-garde of the 1960s was moving off in different directions, both Vilar's theatre and his politics began to appear old-fashioned. To be a true French intellectual, with an influence in politics, meant keeping to the progressive edge of the avant-garde.

The generally positive image did not preclude criticism of the French intellectuals and their symbolic place in French society. Of course political (and intellectual) opponents often criticised the positions taken by individuals, who could be vilified as misleading France through the misuse of their position, but that would not be a criticism of intellectualism per se. In spite of the general acknowledgment of their right (even their duty) to play a political role, intellectuals were also more generally criticised and mocked for their inability to be realistic political leaders or even advisers, lost in their utopias and lacking common sense. The positivist rationalism or more precisely the Kantian spiritualism that dominated the Sorbonne in the late nineteenth century came to symbolise their philosophical stance, but was condemned by Péguy, very much in the Barrès spirit, who affirmed 'the Kantians have pure hands because they have no hands'. Such criticism led intellectuals not only to defend themselves, but to go out of their way to prove the contrary. The fascination of many right-wing intellectuals of the 1930s with fascism or later left-wing intellectuals with the Stalinist version of communism has a lot to do with a refusal to be seen as mere abstract thinkers, out of touch with reality. Such feelings also led to intellectual defences by the ultra-collaborators of Nazi violence, or by communist intellectuals of the 1950s, 1960s and 1970s of Soviet, Maoist and also Vietminh actions. Over thirty years after Péguy's death during the first days of the First World War, Sartre was still taking issue with him when he wrote a play about the necessity of pragmatism in the emerging communist bloc entitled 'Dirty Hands'.[47] Responding to Péguy's earlier attack, Sartre argued that communist intellectuals were precisely the ones that did understand social and political realities.

While most political positions within France had their intellectual supporters, their reputation is primarily as the defenders of progressive, universal and humanist ethical values such as truth, freedom or justice, most often associated with the left of the political spectrum. Michel Winock significantly entitled his book on nineteenth-century intellectuals *Voices of Freedom*.[48] Such a conception does not preclude the presence of intellectuals of the right, from the already-mentioned Barrès, through Catholic traditionalists like Bernanos or Maritain to the ultra-collaborationists like Brasillach or Drieu la Rochelle. As Venita Datta shows, these two groups may have differed in their specific political aims, but grew out of the same closely-knit social and cultural milieu, communicating regularly with one another and sharing the desire to act as the moral and spiritual leaders of the nation.[49] The youthful friendship of Aragon with Drieu la Rochelle shows clearly just how the borders between right and left-wing intellectuals were porous and helps to explain the ease with which more than one was able to shift from one extreme to the other. Even after the shock of the occupation and collaboration led the highly visible tradition of right-wing intellectuals quickly to evaporate, their longer-term influence and ability to have their ideas carried forward should not be underestimated, especially given the proximity of the two groups in the first place. The impact of Barrès on Mitterrand has long been recognised, and many of the specific values of right-wing intellectuals were reintegrated by the left after 1945. As John Hellman shows in *The Knight-Monks of Vichy France*, even individuals who had been trained in the special Vichy leadership school at Uriage, with its anti-communist and anti-liberal traditions, were able to reintegrate left-dominated French intellectual and administrative circles after the war.[50]

Intellectuals are a highly visible, distinguishing feature of modern French society. Although they are forever arguing with one another as an extension of political conflicts, intellectuals come from a self-conscious, closely-knit group which shares roots and numerous personal affiliations. Their very presence, taken alongside their avant-garde, progressive positions is a source of pride and prestige for France, and central to the self-image of the French nation as permeated with progressive thinking. Intellectual contributions to French nationalism come from all sides of the political spectrum, and they share ideas such as anti-Americanism or indeed a tendency to be anti-bourgeois. As with the peasant, worker and bourgeois, all of the French have experience of interaction with intellectuals, or at least their ideas, and they figure prominently amongst the list of the 'greats' of the French nation.

Conclusion

Most phases of the national history covered in Part I have at some time been analysed in terms of class conflict, with different social groups seeking to either preserve their power or to upset the existing system by increasing class awareness and challenging the existing order. Even if rejecting the notion of class conflict, the French nation has been regularly conceived, envisaged and represented as a composite of numerous social and highly mythologised types, four of which have been discussed in detail here, into which the French can project themselves. Experience of French society leads individuals to identify with or against each of these types at different times. They carry on the traditional experience of the peasant when they eat French food or go on a rural holiday, and of the worker when they participate in a strike or a protest march. They feel opposition to the bourgeois with each unsatisfying experience with the State bureaucracy, yet identify with them at every tax increase. Similarly, they may feel personal connections with intellectuals whenever discussing politics, whilst despising those intellectuals who defend their political opponents. Individual experience, be it through film, literature or with real people, includes a significant component of interaction with these and other social stereotypes, reinforcing mythical conceptions of French society as a whole. Conceiving the French nation in terms of its composite groups, reproducing images of each type and the way they interact with others throughout French history is an important part of the process of inventing the nation, of attributing mythical national qualities to commonplace social types.

Notes

1 The other ways of dividing French society alluded to, race, religion or gender, will be discussed in other chapters.
2 Others, such as the soldier, the civil servant or the 'cadre', have not been given full sections for reasons of space, but as sub-categories of bourgeois have similarly symbolic roles within the experience of French society.
3 For a history of French nationalism from a class-based perspective, see Brian Jenkins, *Nationalism in France: Class and Nation since 1789* (London and New York: Routledge, 1990).
4 'Moi qui me suis dit mage ou ange, dispense de toute morale, je suis rendu à la terre avec un devoir à chercher et la réalité rugueuse à étreindre. Paysan.'
5 'Labourage et paturages sont les deux mamelles de la France.'
6 'Le souverain et la nation ne doivent jamais perdrent de vue que la terre est l'unique sources des richesses.'
7 Jean d'Ormesson, *Au plaisir de Dieu* (Paris: Gallimard, 1974).
8 Quoted in Régis Debray, *A demain de Gaulle* (Paris: Gallimard, 1990), p. 106.
9 See George Sand, *La Petite fadette* (1848) and *Les maitres sonneurs* (1853). While her main characters are always the traditional republican idealised peasants, her presentation of the countryside is complex and includes diversity and opposition. See also Michelet, *La sorcière* (1862) for a similar description.
10 For a historical example of peasant development of the rural economy, see Peter McPhee, *Revolution and Environment in Southern France: Peasants, Lords and Murder in the Corbières 1780–1830* (Oxford and New York: OUP, 1999).
11 See, for example, Comtesse de Ségur, *Les vacances* (1859), *Les deux nigauds*

(1862) and *Jean qui grogne et Jean qui rit* (1865), Charles Péguy, *Dialogue de l'histoire et de l'âme charnelle* (1912), or Maurice Barrès, *Un Homme Libre.* (1889).

12 See La Bruyère, *Les caractères* 128 (1688), and Voltaire, *Essais sur les moeurs et l'esprit des nations* (1737).

13 Balzac, *Les chouans* (Paris: Livre de Poche, 1983).

14 Eugen Weber, *Peasants into Frenchmen: The Modernisation of Rural France 1870–1914* (Stanford: Stanford University Press, 1976). See also James R. Lehning, *Peasant and French: Cultural Contact in Rural France During the Nineteenth Century* (Cambridge: CUP, 1995).

15 Zola, *Germinal.* P. Collier, trans. (Oxford: OUP, 1993), p. 521.

16 For a general history of workers and their place in French society, see Gérard Noiriel, *Les ouvriers dans la société Française XIXe–Xxe siècle* (Paris: Seuil, 1986).

17 'The Partisan' was written by the Gaullists Maurice Druon and Joseph Kessel.

18 Victor Hugo, *Les Misérables* (1862). The factory is a place of humiliation and degradation, the last step before prostitution, yet the presence of workers in revolutionary Paris is a sign of hope.

19 See Victor Hugo's poem 'Joyeuse vie' (1853), *Les châtiments* (Paris: Livre de poche, 1985) describing the working class slums in Lille. 'Caves de Lille on meurt sous vos plafonds de pierre'.

20 See, for example, Arthur Rimbaud's poem 'Le forgeron', *Oeuvres completes* (Paris: Garnier Flammarion, 1987), p. 6.

21 See Louis Chevalier, *Classes laborieuses et classes dangereuses à Paris dans la première moitié du dix-neuvième siècle* (1958).

22 See Maxence Van der Meersh, *Quand les sirènes se taisent* (1933) reprinted in *Gens du Nord* (Paris: Presses de la cité, 1993), pp. 111–278, describing a strike in the textile factories of greater Lille.

23 See Victor Hugo, 'Melancholia', *Les contemplations* (Paris: Garnier Flammarion, 1986), p. 129.

24 Roger Magraw, *France 1800–1914: A Social History* (Harlow: Longman, 2002), pp. 65–6.

25 See Danielle Tartakowsky, *Le Pouvoir est dans la rue: Crises politiques et manifestations en France* (Paris: Aubier-Montaigne, 1998).

26 Jacques Brel, 'Les bourgeois' (1962), *Tout Brel* (Paris: Robert Laffont, 1982), p. 250.

27 For a good discussion of the diversity of the bourgeoisie and how to define it, see Magraw, *France 1800–1914*, pp. 13–15.

28 Louise Michel, *La Commune, histoire et souvenirs*, IV, 1 (1898).

29 See Carol E. Harrison, *The Bourgeois Citizen in Nineteenth-Century France: Gender, Sociability and the Uses of Emulation* (Oxford: OUP, 1999) for a good description of the way in which bourgeois society and its value structure evolved and developed.

30 René Rémond, *The Right Wing in France from 1815 to De Gaulle.* James M. Laux, trans. (Philadelphia: University of Pennsylvania Press, 1969).

31 For more on the relationship between different strands of Catholicism and French politics, see Chapter 10.

32 Georges Bernanos, *Les grands cimetières sous la lune* (Paris: Plon, 1938), p. 13.

33 Les Goncourt, *Journal* (5 September 1867), Gustave Flaubert quoted in Robert Tombs, *France 1814–1914* (London and New York: Longman, 1996), p. 280, and Baudelaire 'Le musée classique du bazar bonne nouvelle', *Curiosités esthétiques II* (Paris: Garnier-Flammarion, 1986), pp. 87–96.

34 For a critical analysis of this position, see Tzvetan Todorov, *On Human*

Diversity: Nationalism, Racism and Exoticism in French Thought (Cambridge, Mass.: Harvard University Press, 1993), pp. viii–ix, 3–4.

35 Roland Barthes, *Mythologies*. Annette Lavers, trans. (London: Vintage, 2000), pp. 138–42 (first published 1957).

36 Venita Datta, *Birth of a National Icon: The Literary Avant-Garde and the Origins of the Intellectual in France* (Albany: State Univeristy of New York Press, 1999).

37 See, for example, Pascal Ory and Jean-François Sirinelli, *Les Intellectuels en France, de l'Affaire Dreyfus à nos jours* (Paris: Armand Colin, 1986), Michel Winock: *Les Siècle des Intellectuels* (Paris: Seuil, 1999), Christopher Flood and Nick Hewlett, eds, *Currents in Contemporary French Intellectual Life* (Basingstoke: Macmillan, 2000) and David Drake, *Intellectuals and Politics in Post-War France* (Palgrave, 2002).

38 For a specific comparison of the role of intellectuals in two of these, see: David Drake, 'Intellectuals, demonisation and exclusion in the Dreyfus Affair and *l'affair du foulard*', in Kay Chadwick and Timothy Unwin, eds, *New Perspectives on the Fin de Siècle in Nineteenth- and Twentieth-Century France*, Studies in French Civilisation, Volume 15 (Lewiston: The Edwin Mellen Press, 2000), pp. 43–60.

39 Balzac, quoted in Julie Pellegrin and Christiane Grosbois, *L'épée et la plume, catalogue de l'exposition au chateau de Saché* (Service des monuments et musées départementaux d'Indre et Loire, 2004), pp. 4, 17.

40 Acceptance speech for the Nobel prize for Literature, (December 1957).

41 Tzvetan Todorov, *Devoirs et délices: une vie de passeur: entretien avec Catherine Portevin* (Paris: Seuil, 2002), pp. 258–9.

42 Maurice Barrès, 'La protestation des intellectuels!' *Le Journal* (1 February, 1898).

43 Victor Hugo, 'fonction du poète', *Les rayons et les ombres,* 1840. 'Peuples! Ecoutez le poète! Ecoutez le rèveur sacré! Dans votre nuit sans lui complète, Lui seul a le front éclairé'.

44 Victor Hugo, *Les châtiments* VII, 1 (1853), pp. 271–2. 'Les clarions de la pensée'.

45 On intellectuals as modern 'clerics', see Julien Benda, *La trahison des clercs* (1927), and Régis Debray, *Le Pouvoir intellectuel en France* (1979).

46 See the distinction established by Tzvetan Todorov between committed intellectuals and responsible intellectuals, fully analysed in Richard J. Golson, 'Tzvetan Todorov, the "Responsible Intellectual", and the New World Disorder,' *Modern & Contemporary France* 12, 3 (2004), pp. 299–311.

47 Jean-Paul Sartre, *Les Mains Sales* (Paris: Gallimard, 1948).

48 Michel Winock, *Les voix de la liberté. Les écrivains engages aux XIXème Siècle* (Paris: Seuil, 2001).

49 Venita Datta, *Birth of a National Icon: The Literacy Avant-Garde and the Origins of the Intellectual in France* (New York: State University of the York Press, 1999).

50 John Hellman, *The Knight-Monks of Vichy France: Uriage, 1940–45*, 2nd Ed. (Liverpool: Liverpool University Press, 1997).

6

Militarism and War

The experience of war in the formation of the French nation has been drawn from both the experience of actually fighting the wars, as officers, soldiers and the families of those same officers and soldiers, and the experience of the army as an institution within French society. It includes the perception of France as a military nation, forged through war and conflict, covered with glory and honour, with its heroes, traditions and status as a 'great power' within Europe and the wider world. Military conflict, as well as the surrounding negotiations with future or former enemies and allies, repeatedly conferred a sense of the national self through this experience of other rival nations or peoples. The very fact of having enemies has often served to sustain and enhance perceptions of the greatness of the French nation, to galvanise and temporarily unify conflicting elements within French society faced with an external threat, and to confirm that the values of the French nation, because they are threatened, must be worth defending. The different wars across the centuries have had different roles in the creation of the French nation, including the particular experience of the other which each conflict conferred, the lessons learned at the time of the war, as well as the place they were accorded later in the national history. This chapter will begin with an examination of several of the wars in which the French nation has engaged, from the Revolutionary and Napoleonic wars, through the limited wars of the nineteenth century, the First and Second World Wars, to a section on the wars of colonisation and decolonisation, ending with the Cold War. It will then turn to examine French society and war to reveal the place of military conflict and the external enemies with respect to the invention of the experience of the French nation. The discussion will include an examination of military imagery, from specific heroes to the unknown soldier, the place of military leaders, veterans and the army as an institution within French society, as well as a discussion of conscription, the idea of the 'citizen-army', and the experience of the civilian in war. What becomes evident with war and the enemies of the nation is that the actual experience which individuals may have had is of secondary importance compared with the perceived experience and the way in which such experience has been remembered and entered into the national story.

The Revolutionary and Napoleonic Wars

Although overshadowed by the Revolution itself, and the domestic conflicts which surrounded it, throughout many of the years which followed 1789 France was at war with one or more of its European neighbours. Beginning as a fight against foreign allies of the monarch who were perceived to be plotting to restore the absolute powers of the Bourbon king and reverse the 'gains' of the Revolution through military intervention in France, these wars grew into a massive conflict of European conquest and domination on the part of the French armies. In the space of a few short years, France fought wars with Austria, Prussia, Great Britain, the Dutch Republic, Spain and Russia. Ironically, given that the war was begun in the hopes that it would resolve the uncertainty of the power struggles within France, the pressure of these external wars contributed significantly to the radicalisation of the Revolution after 1792, to the establishment of the reign of Terror, and helped to prevent any definitive stabilisation in the domestic regime throughout the first decade following the Revolution.[1] It also made possible the rise to prominence of military men, in particular the seizure of power by Napoleon Bonaparte in 1799 and the creation of the French Empire five years later.

The French army of the Revolutionary years was an army of citizens, created both through conscription and through a response to the cries of the country (*la patrie*) in danger. The mass mobilisation of the French population, the *levée en masse*, saw as many as three-quarters of a million men integrated into the French army and take to the field in 1793, whilst also encompassing the overt mobilisation of the civilian population for war. In the words of the revolutionary Barrère: 'all the French, both sexes, all ages are called by the nation to defend liberty.'[2] Victories of this mass or citizen-army were subsequently interpreted as the triumph not only of the French nation, but also of the principles of the Revolution and republicanism. The French could also therefore continually reconstruct their enemies as hostile to their nation and to everything that they stood for. In part, the rhetoric supporting the wars played up the idea that the mass army was aiming to liberate other nations from their tyrannical rulers, just as the French had already liberated themselves, but by and large the wars were promoted and the war effort of the mass army sustained through the image of the external enemy hostile to the nation and revolutionary principles.

The French did not need to exaggerate when depicting the number of their enemies, or the extent of the glory of their own military achievements. Over the years of war, four European anti-French coalitions were formed and most of the territory of continental Europe was conquered by the French at one time or another, leading to the annexation of territory to France, as well as the setting up of French satellites ruled by Napoleon's brothers across Europe. Eventual defeat and the loss of not only all of the territorial gains they had made on the continent, but the colonial empire of the *ancien régime* as well, could not completely overcome the pride in the military achievements of the French nation and its mass army. Napoleon as the leader received much of the retrospective credit, but the links between French military greatness and the citizen-soldier of the mass army were also firmly embedded in national imagery. Physical reminders of the experience of these wars and victories were embedded in the French landscape, from the Arc de Triomphe to the streets all over France bearing the names of battlefields where the mass army was victorious.

The experience of the Revolutionary and Napoleonic wars coloured future attitudes towards war within the French nation. Memories of French greatness were important, but so were memories of the anti-French European threats which were perceived (accurately in part) to have been set up because they were opposed to French republicanism and the principles of the French nation. External threats and enemies could be held up to the population as a reminder of what unified them, ever hearkening back to the experience of the nation in battle.

Nineteenth-Century Wars

The wars which were fought by France throughout the remainder of the nineteenth century were much more limited in scope than those of the Revolutionary and Napoleonic period. They were also much less significant in the consciousness of the French population, which was much more preoccupied with domestic concerns and the changing of regime at almost every generation. Throughout the century the perception of France as a glorious military nation was sustained in spite of the lack of any notable victories (except, perhaps, in the colonies), and indeed of a significant, humiliating defeat for France by Prussia in 1870–71. Focussing upon an external enemy could be used as a tactic by political leadership as a means to break out of domestic conflict, to de-legitimise potential opposition, to bring about some temporary unity, or occasionally to help prevent revolution. Napoleon III in particular hoped to use external conflict as a means to bring his Empire out of trouble and divert domestic frustration outwards. Potentially a good strategy, it backfired when his armies were defeated and he himself was captured at the battle of Sedan in September 1870.

The imagery of the French nation in arms continued to be used as a recruitment tool, as can be seen most clearly in the Franco-Prussian War literature. Calls to join the fighting explicitly used rhetoric from the

Revolutionary years, referring explicitly to the popular response to invasion in 1792, comparing the nation's enemies to criminals and calling Frenchmen to arms in defence of freedom.[3] While it is far from obvious that the population was warmly receptive of such thinking, over 600,000 men were nevertheless forthcoming. Military technology had advanced to the state, however, that the citizen-army was no longer as effective as it had been during the revolutionary years, and one of the chief lessons learned from the defeat was that the nation in arms needed to give way to properly trained troops (even if they were chiefly conscripts trained through military service).[4] The blame for the defeat, however, was not with the army of the nation, but with the leadership of Napoleon III, who was neither to return to power himself, nor to see his descendants on the throne. The French nation went on to store up the defeat in the national memory, repeatedly reminding itself who the enemy was, while setting up full-scale republican military service in the hopes of an eventual opening to gain revenge and to recapture the lost provinces of Alsace and Lorraine.

At a secondary level, the defeat of 1870–71 was also interpreted in several quarters as a sign that the values of the French nation were failing, and that the nation needed to recover its fundamental values in order to recover from the loss. If victory showed the triumph of French values, then defeat must also show that the French nation had in some way taken the wrong turning. For Catholics, this meant returning to God, and the building of Sacré Coeur in Paris and Notre Dame de Fourvières in Lyon – great monuments on the top of visible hills – was designed to atone for the nation's sins in the eyes of God by showing their extreme devotion. For republicans, this merely showed that republicanism had not penetrated deeply enough into French consciousness, and that further efforts were needed to solidify the links between the nation and its republican values.

Overall, the wars of the nineteenth century did not really diminish either the perception of France as a great military nation, or the belief in the nation-in-arms to defend its principles against the perceived foreign invader, hostile to the nation and to its freedoms. Taking the century as a whole, the actual experience of war with foreign armies was restricted to a small number of individuals, and largely preserved through the continued discourse of the foreign threat to the nation and periodic requirements of the people to be called to arms to defend the nation.

The First World War

The experience of the First World War differed from all previous wars by the extent to which the entire nation really was influenced, directly or indirectly, by the fighting. Almost an entire generation of men went to the front and met the enemy in combat. The home front watched their men leave, in many cases never to return, and every village had to adapt, experience rationing and become a part of the national war economy. The real lived experience of the soldiers in the trenches was not widely communicated during the war itself, nor was much of the population aware of the full extent of the death toll or the true nature of the fighting until after the war was over, the survivors returned from the front, and the mourning and commemoration began. The scale of the war was such that it was not called the Great War for no reason: all sections of society – men and women, young and old, rural and urban, rich and poor – felt themselves to have been involved personally.

The war was not what had been anticipated beforehand, that is to say a short, glorious victory, although the rhetoric used to support the war and the calls for volunteers still used the language of the *patrie en danger*. The war cry was thus once again to defend the nation from the invading foreigner, to save the French from foreign tyranny, rather than to get revenge for the previous defeat and to recapture the lost provinces. The first phase of the war is the one moment of genuine political unity in French history since the Revolution, during which the 'Sacred Union' drew together representatives of all parties, including even the socialists who had previously threatened to attempt to prevent any workers from going to fight in the name of international solidarity with other workers. The popular response to the declaration of war was far less enthusiastic than has often been portrayed, however, and more characterised by resignation and determination than by genuine enthusiasm or joy at the prospect of revenge. Even the more enthusiastic outpourings tended to be reassuring forms of traditional public rituals, rather than spontaneous acts of excitement.[5]

In spite of the perceived closeness of the population to the combat during the First World War, actual experience of the enemy was limited to those doing the fighting, as well as those in the occupied north and east. For the remainder of the population, the only real experience of the enemy came through stories and reports in the press. During the early years of the war, propaganda was devoted to the vilification of the German barbarian, justifying the reality of the threat presented to the nation, and seeking to increase support for the war effort and unity of the population. Tales of atrocities committed towards civilians, women and children were widespread, and even if not wholly believed, nevertheless contributed to feelings of hostility toward the foreign enemy, increasing solidarity with the other members of the French nation which was under threat.

The lived experience of the enemy by civilians in the occupied sections of France behind the Western Front was quite different from that of the rest of France. In addition to the humiliation of being occupied, and in many cases cut off from other family members, the population suffered from numerous general hardships, the most significant of which was the shortage of food and the resulting hunger and malnutrition, the effects of which would be felt long after the war had ceased. There were also requisitions, reduced medical and other benefit services, administrative frustration, and the necessity to billet Germans. The occupying rule was also strict, hostages were taken from among the civilians to ensure good behaviour, and civilian workers were conscripted and often deported to work, including adolescents, which was against the Hague convention.[6] Although hardship was great and the Germans did breach international agreements with respect to treatment of the civilian population, they were far from committing the kind of atrocities which were being reported in the French press (no bayoneting of French babies...). The difference between the war experience of those in the occupied zone and that of the rest of the population tended to be lost in the memory after the war, with the main experience of war being defined as that in the main part of France or those in the army fighting at the front.[7]

The memory of the war as a national experience, as a national sacrifice in which the entire population played a part began to grow and develop from the time that the last shot was fired. The former war zone was filled with cemeteries, a visible reminder of the cost in terms of lives. Memorials to those who had died for the nation were also put up in communes all over the country, creating what would become a familiar feature in the physical landscape of France, a common reminder of what every village or town had sacrificed. Similarly, the anniversary of the armistice, 11 November, was instigated as a public holiday to commemorate all those who had sacrificed their lives for the nation, and in particular the common soldiers. Veterans' organisations became widespread, and while they in part served to allow those who had really experienced the fighting to meet with those who had shared the experience, they also kept the memory of the war alive, and were an active social force throughout French society. The result of the war was to glorify the entire nation, since all sections of the population had contributed to the war effort, and to reinforce national solidarity after having been faced with an outside enemy.

The Second World War

The Second World War was a different experience for the French nation, and although the fighting did not last anywhere near as long as the First World War had done, nor were the casualties as extensive, the entire population did have face to face experience of the enemy. Militarily, the actual fighting during the German invasion went so quickly, and everyone was taken so completely by surprise, that there was little time for the population to experience any feelings other than panic before France was defeated. The defeat was humiliating, of course, but the Armistice was nevertheless greeted by widespread relief throughout the nation. It was soon followed by occupation, at first of a large section of the north and west, and then the whole of metropolitan France from November 1942 until the liberation. Thus contact with the enemy during this war was much less as a fighting, but rather as an occupying force, and real face-to-face experience of the enemy extended through most of the population.

The initial reaction to meeting with German soldiers and officers was much surprise at how 'correct', polite and well-behaved they were. Early resistance propaganda had repeatedly to stress to the population that it did not matter how nice or cultivated they seemed, the French had continually to be on their guard and to remember that they were the enemy, that they were 'not tourists'.[8] The short story *The Silence of the Sea* portrayed exactly such a situation, with a wonderfully cultured, polite and handsome German officer billeted in a French household, the members of which must continue to resist because as long as the officer wears the German uniform (and even when out of it), he represents Hitler's overt aims to destroy the French nation and its culture, even if he is unaware of them or does not agree with them himself.[9] Such reminders were necessary because the actual lived experience in occupied France, at least at first, encouraged complacency, if not friendliness towards the 'former' enemies. After several years of occupation, however, as reprisals against civilians for resistance attacks became more numerous, deprivations and frustrations at the continuation of the war greater, and hopes for an allied victory over Germany rekindled, then the focus of resistance propaganda shifted towards the genuine necessity to resist more actively (even if maintaining polite relations with the enemy on the surface was necessary to cover for secret resistance).

After the war, the memory of French attitudes towards their German enemies needed to be re-cast, in order to find a way to ignore the period of cooperation and relative harmony. They tended to concentrate therefore on what relations were like at the end of the occupation, rather than what they had been during the first couple of years. Furthermore, once the full horror of the Holocaust became known, the remembered enemy became the ideology of Nazism, hostile not only to the French nation, but to civilisation in general. It was the ideology itself, and those in leadership positions who had created it or encouraged it to flourish who were the true enemies. The individual Germans who had behaved so well when posted to occupied France and who had become allies by the post-war period were primarily guilty of having not resisted Nazism. Perceptions of France as a nation of resisters during the Occupation also meant that not only had the entire population made a contribution to the victory, as with the First World War, but that it was also a military one. Secret operations, tricking the enemy, or even helping to demoralise them through proud silence or non-cooperation could all be held as contributing directly to the war effort. The construction of this version of memory began with de Gaulle making great speeches about the resistance of the entire nation, and with local resistance movements throughout the country erecting monuments to local martyrs and resistance activity, further consolidated through film and writing.[10] Although alternative and critical interpretations to the myth of national resistance existed, the remembered experience of the Second World War was one of hardships and an ever-present enemy, being fought by the entire nation from its weak, vulnerable position, in the defence of the land, the people and the values of the French nation.

Wars of Colonisation and Decolonisation

Throughout the nineteenth and twentieth centuries, France, like other European powers, fought numerous large and small-scale wars across the globe, which can be brought together under the heading of 'colonial'. Slightly offstage with respect to what have been considered as the 'main' wars which took place in Europe with immediate neighbours, these were nevertheless wars, and meant that the army at least was engaged in conflict much more regularly throughout the modern period than might be thought if concentrating simply upon the European wars. Through the course of these wars, the French conquered and colonised a vast territory, bringing vast numbers and varieties of peoples under French rule. Many of these colonies went on to fight wars of independence, or decolonisation, in the mid-twentieth century, in which the French armies also participated extensively.[11]

Although the soldiers in the colonial section of the French army themselves had some experience of colonial wars, the general populous of the nation experienced them in a much more secondary way, and certainly not as 'the nation in arms'. This is even more true in terms of experience of the 'enemy', who in perception was as often as not a rival colonial power, rather than the actual native population whose army was being fought. By the twentieth century, awareness in France of the wars of decolonisation was higher than it had been for the wars of colonisation, but only slightly, with the one exception of the Algerian War. Unlike the wars in the other colonies, Algeria was (fictively and legally) not considered a colony but a part of France, and in 1956 conscripts were used outside of Europe for the first time. This direct involvement, coupled with keener interest and emotional attachment, the presence in France of post-war migrants and the fact that it had provoked a full-scale constitutional crisis in 1958 contributed to raise the profile of the conflict among the mainstream population. Although it inspired a wide range of writing and film, much of the Algerian war remained a 'taboo' subject, being labelled the 'war with no name'.[12] In terms of the experience related, the limitation can be seen in the fact that in the range of French films with the Algerian War as either the background or the main subject, in almost none does 'the Algerian', much less 'the enemy' appear at all.[13] The Algerian War notwithstanding, however, widespread consideration of the colonial wars as 'national experiences' was nevertheless far less than for the European wars. Although defeat (or even simply lack of victory) in the colonies could bring down governments or even constitutional regimes, emotional involvement with a perceived enemy was never high among the press, the public or indeed most of the leadership of the nation.

A lack of feeling of common experience and personal involvement did not mean that there was no interest in France in the outcomes of the colonial wars, since the greatness of the French nation and its prestige within the world of European colonial powers were at stake. Victory in the colonies was a good thing, and it was perhaps even more important in the wars of decolonisation, when ironically colonies were no longer the sign of national greatness that they had once been. In the climate of the 1950s and 1960s, France needed to compensate for the defeat of 1940 and therefore tried harder to hold onto its colonies than other colonial powers such as Britain were doing, to preserve as best it could the stature which had been lost in defeat. As with some of the limited wars of the nineteenth century, however, none of the wars in the colonies besides Algeria was so significant in French consciousness as to be felt to be the 'nation' in arms, but only evidence of the nation's power, prestige and merit.

The Cold War

Although not exactly a war by some measures, the Cold War did present an external 'enemy' to the nation through several decades of the twentieth century. The image of the Soviet Communist menace was not as strong in France as it was in the United States, due to the presence of a strong Communist Party in France, but the external enemy was still an opponent to the French values of republicanism and individual freedom, and was perceived to be undermining France from within as well as threatening from without. The presence of native French communism, although diminishing the purely external dimension of the communist threat, did not mean that internal anti-communist propaganda did not play upon the external threat posed by the Soviet enemy. On the contrary, fears of external enemies became a weapon to discredit the French Communist Party, portraying them as beholden to a hostile foreign power. This was not the first time that internal opponents could be labelled as traitors because of perceived links to external enemies. During the 1789 revolution, the European coalition against France had as one of its objectives to restore the French monarch to his throne. Thus an external enemy had a preoccupation with the internal organisation of France, with internal and external enemies to the nation overlapping. In the case of the cold war the opposition came from the left, rather than the reactionary monarchist right, but the fundamental pattern of an external enemy hostile to the nation and its values remained consistent with earlier wars.[14]

The Cold War also presented a context within which France was able to assert its military influence on the international scene, and recapture the prestige and importance tarnished by the loss of its former colonies (at least in the eyes of the French). This was particularly true during the period of de Gaulle's presidency of the Fifth Republic. He insisted on developing an independent French nuclear deterrent, with the first test carried out in Algeria in 1960. Alongside the development of an atomic bomb, he developed a fleet of Mirage aircraft and nuclear submarines, and began work on nuclear missiles. Refusing to simply gravitate within the American sphere of influence and accept American decisions as less than a full partner, he formally pulled France out of the command structure of NATO in 1966, although keeping France within the alliance. These are the military facets of what was a wider programme of competition to keep France in the forefront of global affairs, not just military and diplomatic, but scientific and industrial as well. France put its first satellite into space in 1965, and developed nuclear electric generating plants as well as bombs.[15] Peaceful rivalry notwithstanding, the desire for France to remain powerful alongside the superpowers of the Cold War had significant military undertones, and was the context within which the French experienced the globalisation of the second half of the twentieth century.

French Society and War

Independent of the experience of individual wars, there is a wider experience of France as a military nation, both through the army as a national institution and through the militaristic policies and discourses developed in the two centuries which followed the Revolution. France has often been described as a 'peace-loving' nation both by its members and by observers, with periods of war as supposedly unusual and certainly undesired. Given the regular alternation between peace and war which characterised the post-Revolutionary period, it is difficult to conclude that war was simply an anomaly, and peace the 'natural' state of things for France, or indeed for Europe.[16] Desire for peace was certainly widespread, and nowhere more so than among war veterans, but this did not alter the fact that war was an inescapable dimension of the political realities of modern Europe, a regular experience for much of the French population and an integral element in their conception of the nation. The military cannot be conceived as separate from the remainder of French society, since it has never operated in a vacuum, or had a parallel existence to the rest of the nation. After occasional wartime conscription, compulsory military service for men went through a variety of phases (from lottery to compulsory) and lengths, and spending time in the army became a right of passage to manhood not abandoned until the end of the twentieth century. Stories of military campaigns brought back by veterans or related through the press, nationalist propaganda calling the people to arms when France was 'threatened', images of the soldier found throughout popular culture from literature and song to posters and illustrations, as well as the presence of military figures in most areas of social life, from the veterans in the local communities to the senior officers in the government, are all examples of the interconnectedness between the military and the people.[17] Since the creation of the national holiday, military parades have been a key feature of 14 July celebrations, and after the end of the First World War the commemorations of 11 November meant that these twice yearly holidays kept the army and military images as a part of the background for French public life. Thus even in a 'peace-loving' society, war and the army were nevertheless central elements in the experience of the entire population.[18]

The French nation has a strong cult of the hero, and among the national canon can be found a large number of military figures. The most widely represented is certainly Napoleon, who led the people's army to victory across Europe, and who has been represented in books, films, statues, paintings, posters, and commemorated on buildings and streets more than any other figure in French history. A major part of the Napoleonic legend was his status as a strategic genius and hero whose very presence on the battlefield was an advantage to French troops. The Arc de Triomphe and his tomb, in what became the military museum in Les Invalides, are merely the two most prominent physical reminders erected to the memory of the military glory he brought to France.[19] Other victorious military leaders have also been given the status of national hero, the most notable being Charles de Gaulle following the liberation and defeat of Germany in 1945, and Marshals Foch and Pétain following the French victory in 1918. Even Pétain's disgrace following the Second World War was not enough to end his celebration as a French military hero, with the Presidents of the Republic commemorating his achievements on 11 November throughout the twentieth century.

Slightly different, but as large an image as the individual military heroes already referred to was the '*poilu*', or simple French soldier. This 'hero' was depicted in numerous ways and times, with increasing frequency particularly after the First World War, and praised for his anonymous heroism. Commemorated at the local level around France in memorials dedicated to the fallen from each village, and at the national level through the tomb of the unknown soldier, the fallen *poilu* was celebrated for his virtues of courage and self-sacrifice for the good, indeed the very life, of the French nation. By his death, he sanctified and rendered holy the cause for which he fought, drawing religious feelings together with military nationalism.[20] He represented France's strength, appearing not only in images of the active fighter or the fallen soldier, but also in the person of the war veteran (especially if he was wounded during the war) who was accorded a special status within French society for his service to the nation-in-arms. As late as the 1990s, Parisian metro carriages had signs indicating that the seats were first of all reserved for war wounded, secondly for pregnant women and thirdly for children, and had a full cabinet-rank Ministry for War Veterans (*Ministère des Anciens Combattants*). For all veterans, war decorations could be worn proudly, and membership in the prestigious Legion of Honour was a further way of publicly recognising the outstanding contributions made by individual heroes to the military glory of the nation.

Similar to the hero, the victorious battles also became symbols in their own right. Perhaps the two most well known are the battle of Valmy on 20 September 1792, when the revolutionary mass army – the people in arms – halted the advance of foreign troops (Figure 6), and Verdun, where the French army held onto the fortress throughout the First World War, in spite of incredible German pressure.[21] Memory of the victorious experience of these and other victories has been kept alive through commemoration as the names of streets, metro stations and other public places, as well as through education and the general national discourse.

Figure 6 The battle of Valmy

France also experienced itself as military nation through the important social and political role of military figures, be it as individual leaders or more generally through active veterans' organisations. Military leaders were often significant political actors throughout modern French history. The most significant and obvious examples have already been discussed – Napoleon, his nephew Napoleon III, Marshal Pétain and General de Gaulle, each of whom took power amid a wave of popularity and then had the previous constitution thrown out in favour of a new regime.[22] These more spectacular examples were not the only ones, however, and military figures could be found among the political elite through the various regimes. Many of the Revolutionary leaders had participated in the wars, and General Lafayette had been an important figure in the early phases of the Revolution. Marshal MacMahon, in spite of the recent defeat of his armies by Prussia, became President of the Third Republic in 1873. In the late 1880s, amid a wave of popular enthusiasm which was so significant as to acquire the label 'Boulangism', General Georges Boulanger became Minister of War, with many of his supporters hoping that he would lead a Bonapartist-style 'coup d'état'. The fact that it came to nothing does not belie the significance of the military presence and high visibility among the elite of the nation.

The opposite kind of situation occurred as well: civilian leaders hoping to increase their reputation through their bellicosity, resolve and ultimate success. Léon Gambetta's dramatic escape by balloon from Paris in 1870 to try and rally troops to liberate encircled Paris from the Prussians, Georges Clemenceau's political will to continue the First World War until the victory, and Napoleon III's efforts to lead the armies personally during the Franco-Prussian war are all examples of attempts to seek an increase in political capital through military success. At a more modest level the organisation of war veterans into social organisations gave them not only a visible presence in French society, but also a voice which could be heard and potentially mobilised. The most notable examples are the veterans of the Napoleonic campaigns in Restoration France, and those from the First World War, whose active political role during the inter-war period was significant in shaping the growth of pacifism and had an influence upon the course of French foreign policy.[23] It is also true that following the Second World War, former 'resisters' also had a special social status conferred upon them. In addition to the Resistance Medal, Companionship in the newly-instituted Order of the Liberation became the most prestigious distinction available.

Not only was French society shaped and influenced by the presence of military figures, its status as an international power and the prestige accorded the French nation within the realm of international relations was directly influenced by its military qualities and fortunes. Although suffering from periodic setbacks, it was the alternating phases of success that kept France a place among the 'great powers' or the 'concert of Europe' or the 'permanent members' of the UN Security Council, depending upon the period. It was the belief that the French nation was great, and needed to be great to remain France which motivated leaders such as Clemenceau or de Gaulle to keep on fighting.[24] It was this belief which led to France's independent stand within NATO and to the perceived necessity of possessing an independent nuclear deterrent. Throughout the modern period, France's military greatness, real and perceived, was a significant symbol within the French nation of its rights to international importance, and thus the deeply-held conviction of France being 'great' can never be completely dissociated from its experience as a military nation.

The key link between French society and the experience of war is the army as an institution. From the *levée en masse* onwards, in each generation there was a degree of mass participation in the army, either through volunteering or conscription during wartime, or via military service at other times. While never achieving the kinds of success and popular enthusiasm portrayed in the propaganda, passing through periods of reluctance on the part of large segments of the population and in some cases provoking genuinely hostile reactions to the State's claims on individuals for military service, all levels of society were exposed to the discourse and reality of the mass army.[25] Likewise, notwithstanding significant regional variations in volunteering or resistance to conscription, all French regions were touched by local participation in the army.[26] For republican nation-builders, the 'citizen-army' was one of the primary links between the people and the State, and although not by any means always positive, a vast segment of the population had real direct and indirect experience of, if not exposure to the French army.[27]

In many ways, democratic principles prevented the acceptance of a genuinely 'professional' army, because of the importance accorded to the citizen-in-arms as an essential pillar of the French nation, but also for fear of the political power such an army could potentially have, and which might be used against the Republic. Voices calling for the professionalisation of the army, such as Charles de Gaulle in the early 1930s, were in a distinct minority even among military and civilian leaders from the French right.[28] On the other side of the political spectrum, left-wing republicans, socialists and anarchists were very much against any extension of the powers of the army, and many hoped that the reduction of armies would go hand-in-hand with international working-class cooperation which would in turn prevent large-scale war.[29] Between the fear of royalist links among the aristocratic senior officers in the army which might lead them to support a restoration or oppose a popular uprising, and the fear of another Napoleon Bonaparte who would use his military prestige to suppress the Republic, the necessity both to limit the power of the army and to keep its composition as close as possible to the republican citizenry was evident to the republican nation-builders.

Fears of the power or role of the army can perhaps best be illustrated with the Dreyfus Affair of the late 1890s. Not long after the height of General Boulanger's populist movement had fizzled out, the army discovered that military secrets were being leaked to the Germans. After an investigation, they tried and convicted a Jewish staff officer named Alfred Dreyfus in 1894, sentencing him to deportation and imprisonment for life. Over the next few years it slowly leaked out that the trial had not been conducted properly, that evidence had been forged, that military secrets were still being leaked and that, in fact, Dreyfus was not the guilty party. At the time, the army felt that its honour and prestige would be compromised too greatly if it were to admit that it had caught the wrong man, could still not identify the guilty party, and therefore preferred to continue to assert Dreyfus' guilt and to deny the possibility of re-opening his trial. Public pressure mounted until it finally exploded in January 1898 when the novelist Emile Zola published an open letter to the President of the Republic entitled 'J'Accuse' in which he directly accused a long list of military leaders by name of consciously committing a criminal act of injustice with regard to Alfred Dreyfus. The army stuck to its original verdict, and although forced to re-open the trial, repeated the guilty sentence after a few short days. The issue was surrounded by a great deal of furore and newspaper coverage from all points of view, involved resignations, suicides, and contributed to the defeat of the Opportunist Party and the victory of the Radicals in the 1898 elections. After a Presidential pardon, Dreyfus' case was eventually revisited and in 1906 he was cleared, reinstated in the army, promoted and given the Legion of Honour.[30]

Beyond the surface question of Dreyfus' guilt or innocence, the underlying tension of the Dreyfus Affair stemmed from the rivalry between the French army and the civilian authorities. The army resented interference by politicians and many of the republican (especially the Radical) politicians mistrusted the army and sought to restrict its independence. From this point of view, the principal result of the Dreyfus Affair was the passing of a law which explicitly recognised the civil authority as superior to the military one, which is to say that the army had to take orders from the government and parliament. It is also interesting to note that while ultimately 'victorious', the Dreyfusards (those in favour of re-opening the trial and believing in Dreyfus' innocence) were nevertheless in a minority among the wider French population. The majority of the public, never completely informed or assured of the accuracy of the propaganda from both sides, tended to display moderate anti-Drefusard sympathies. This position can primarily be attributed to the belief that when unsure and without considerably stronger evidence of his innocence made public, it was most reasonable to have confidence in the army, and certainly not to adopt opinions which would embarrass or humiliate it in the eyes of the nation and of other nations watching with interest. Antisemitism of course played a part in many circles, presuming Dreyfus' guilt because he was a Jew, but it was also true that many segments of the population felt that it was important not to weaken the army, and that the strength of the French army and its ability to preserve prestige and maintain 'order' was more important even than justice for one individual. His sacrifice was worth it for the greater good of the nation, measured in terms of the importance of the prestige of the army among the public.

Conclusion

Throughout the two centuries which followed the Revolution, the French nation had a wide diversity of experiences of war – at home and abroad, in Europe and in the colonies, victory and also defeat. Under a variety of leaders at different times, the French nation-in-arms had shown what a glorious and powerful force it was, fighting for the principles upon which the nation was founded, as well as defending itself from outside attack. Citizens from all over France participated and could claim pride in the victories of the French armies over the years, with the soldier an important national hero. Every memory was not completely positive, for the nation did have experiences of military defeat, which included disorientation, dislocation, soldiers' separation from family, shock and surprise. The overall perception of the nation's military fortunes over the long term, however, was of a nation historically victorious and militarily powerful, characterised from time to time by a 'setback' (a recurrent theme in French history), but always rising from the ashes to show her true greatness.[31]

A key dimension of the experience of war was the experience of the enemy, the external 'other' who was being fought, and who helps to define the nation. This experience derived in part from the genuine personal encounter on the part of French soldiers with the enemy soldiers across the line, but also from the more general perception in the wider population that the nation as a whole had enemies, and that it correspondingly represented something worth defending. The presence of external enemies also helped to diminish any internal differences which could be made to seem less important in comparison with external threats. Such perceptions help to create and to reinforce support and positive feelings for the nation and its army on the home front, solidifying and galvanising it in the minds of individuals, while at the same time glorifying the nation whenever its armies should be successful. Whether or not particular French men or women ever actually came into contact with these enemies personally is in many ways beside the point. The perceived national experience of war, as related and constructed through state propaganda and regular commemorations, the tales of veterans, letters, the press or other means, is what counted in the long term. France was a glorious nation, regularly, if not perpetually, under threat by foreign enemies.

Military conflict and international negotiations with others represent a significant means in which the French have conceived themselves as a nation in opposition to other nations, in a world filled with perceived enemies or possibly allies. The fact of having fought so many wars, and of thinking of the nation so often in terms of potential attacks by other nations contributed not only to the presence of national feeling, but also to the nature of the French experience as one of conflict. Keeping alive the memory of wars and military conflict caricatured the development of the nation and was often a priority of nation-builders, who sought not only to extend national feelings, but also to keep the national population in readiness to participate in future conflicts. The refrain of the national anthem, the Marseillaise, is led by the cry 'Aux armes citoyens' (To arms, citizens), and the experience, real and perceived, of past wars kept alive the sense of hostile national enemies. The citizen-soldiers had ever to be ready to defend their nation, as it was always liable to attacks from without, for numerous 'others' were always on the lookout for any sign of French weakness or a way to bring down the French nation.[32] The military tradition (lived and imagined as past military success) also provided a tradition of national greatness which then needed to be lived up to. As with many of the social types seen in the last chapter, it was not necessary to have actually experienced a battle with an enemy oneself, hearing about it in terms of the national 'we' was enough to ensure that it was collectively remembered as a kind of lived national experience.

A lengthy tradition of military success is one of the key elements in the national mythology of France, with victories conferring credit not only on the army, but the French nation as a whole. These national myths also defined the enemies of the nation, perpetually poised to bring down the French nation and all that it stood for. The enhancement of perceptions of a continual external threat helped not only to solidify national unity, but could also be used by particular political groups seeking internal support as a weapon against their internal rivals. War, or even the discussion of potential war, could be used as a means of de-legitimising political opposition.[33] External conflict could also be used as a means to forestall, or to prevent if possible, internal conflict, civil war or revolution, which is the subject of the next chapter.

Notes

1 On the origins of the revolutionary wars in 1792, see J. M. Roberts, *The French Revolution*, 2nd Ed. (Oxford: OUP, 1997), pp. 46–7, and Colin Jones, *The Great Nation; France from Louis XIV to Napoleon* (London: Penguin, 2002), pp. 454–7. See also T. C. W. Blanning, *The Origins of the French Revolutionary Wars* (London: Longman, 1986).

2 Quoted in D. M. G. Sutherland, *France 1789–1815: Revolution and Counterrevolution* (London: Fontana, 1985), p. 201.

3 For one such example, see B. Taithe, 'Reliving the Revolution: War and Political Identity during the Franco-Prussian War', in Bertrand Taithe and Tim

Thornton eds, *War: Identities in Conflict 1300–2000* (Phoenix Mill: Sutton Publishing, 1998), pp. 142–3.

4 Brian Bond, *War and Society in Europe 1870–1970* (Phoenix Mill: Sutton Publishing, 1998), p. 17.

5 For more on the early attitudes to the call to war, see Regina M. Sweeney, *Singing Our Way to Victory: French Cultural Politics and Music during the Great War* (Middletown, Conn.: Wesleyan University Press, 2001).

6 For more detail on the occupation zone, see Helen McPhail, *The Long Silence: Civilian Life under the German Occupation of Northern France, 1914–1918* (London: I. B. Taurus, 1999).

7 See Annette Becker, *Oubliés de la Grande Guerre: humanitaire et culture de guerre 1914–1918, populations occupées, déportés civils, prisonniers de guerre* (Paris: Editions Noêsis, 1998), and Timothy Baycroft, 'The Versailles Settlement and Identity in French Flanders', *Diplomacy and Statecraft 16, 3* (2005), pp. 589–602.

8 Jean Texcier, 'Advice to the Occupied,' tract, 1940.

9 Vercors, *The Silence of the Sea/Le Silence de la Mer* (Oxford: Berg, 1991).

10 See Jackson, *The Fall of France*, pp. 601–5, and also Chapter 3.

11 For more on the experience of the colonies in general, not just in war, see Chapter 8.

12 See Martin S. Alexander, Martin Evans and J. F. V. Keiger, 'The "War without a Name", the French Army and the Algerians: Recovering Experiences, Images and Testimonies,' in Alexander, Evans and Keiger, eds, *The Algerian War and the French Army, 1954–1962: Experiences, Images, Testimonies* (Basingstoke: Palgrave, 2002). This work shows the extent of representations of the Algerian War, which is somewhat greater than often supposed, but still nothing in comparison with the two World Wars.

13 Guy Austin, 'Representing the Algerian War in Algerian Cinema: Hamina's *Le Vent des Aures*', *French Studies* LXI, 2 (April, 2007), pp. 182–95.

14 For more on internal enemies, revolution and the Communist Party, see Chapter 7.

15 On nuclear mystique in France, see Gabrielle Hecht, *The Radiance of France: Nuclear Power and National Identity after World War II* (Cambridge, Mass.: MIT Press, 1998).

16 For more on the relationship between war and peace, see B. Taithe and T. Thornton, 'Identifying War: Conflict and Self-definition in Western Europe', in Taithe and Thornton, *War*, pp. 1–18.

17 For examples of images see David M. Hopkin, 'Sons and lovers: popular images of the conscript, 1798–1870', *Modern & Contemporary France* 9, 1 (2001), pp. 19–36.

18 See Julian Jackson, *The Fall of France: The Nazi Invasion of 1940* (Oxford: OUP, 2003), pp. 224–7.

19 See Chapter 1 for a more complete development of the Napoleonic historical myth, as well as Sudhir Hazareesingh, *The Legend of Napoleon* (Granta, 2004), idem, *The Saint-Napoleon: Celebrations of Sovereignty in 19th-Century France* (Cambridge, Mass.: Harvard University Press, 2004) and idem, 'Napoléon et son mythe,' *Notre Histoire* 218 (February, 2004), pp. 16–41.

20 For more on the links between religion and the experience of war, see Annette Becker, *War and Faith: the Religious Imagination in France 1914–1930*. Helen McPhail, trans. (Oxford: Berg, 1998).

21 On Verdun, see Antoine Prost, 'Verdun' in Pierre Nora, ed., *Les Lieux de Mémoire* 2 (Paris: Quarto-Gallimard, 1997), pp. 1755–80.

22 Napoleon III was less a genuine military leader, although he actively sought to have himself portrayed as such and built upon the military reputation of his

name, and is thus included here.

23 For a full discussion, see Antoine Prost, *In the Wake of War: 'Les Anciens Combattants' and French Society 1914–1939*. Helen McPhail, trans. (Oxford: Berg, 1992).

24 Jackson, *The Fall of France*, p. 239.

25 For more on the theory and implications of mass mobilisation, see Daniel Moran and Arthur Waldron, eds, *The People in Arms: Military Myth and National Mobilisation since the French Revolution* (Cambridge: CUP, 2003); see also Alan Forrest, *Conscripts and Deserters: The Army and French Society During the Revolution and Empire* (Oxford: OUP, 1989).

26 For a comparison of regional attitudes towards conscription, see David M. Hopkin, *Soldier and Peasant in French Popular Culture, 1766–1870* (Woodbridge: The Royal Historical Society – The Boydell Press, 2003) on Lorraine, a heavily participating region, and Louis Bergès, *Résister à la conscription, 1798–1814: Le cas des départments aquitains* (Paris: Editions du Comité des travaux historiques et scientifiques, 2002), where reluctance was high.

27 See also Chapter 11.

28 Jackson, *The Fall of France*, p. 225.

29 See Paul B. Miller, *From Revolutionaries to Citizens: Antimilitarism in France 1870–1914* (Durham and London: Duke University Press, 2002) for more on left-wing desires to reduce the civil power of the military.

30 For a full account of the Dreyfus Affair, see Martin P. Johnson, *The Dreyfus Affair: Honour and Politics in the* Belle Epoque (Basingstoke: Macmillan, 1999), or Eric Cahm, *The Dreyfus Affair in French Society and Politics* (London: Longman, 1996).

31 For the Gaullist articulation of this vision of the French military, see Jackson, *The Fall of France*, p. 239.

32 The blurring of the distinction between citizens and soldiers can be interpreted also as a part of a wider trend in the modern era of total war; see Jean-Yves Guiomar, *L'Invention de la guerre totale: XVIIIe–XXe siècle* (Pais: Le Félin Kiron, 2004).

33 On the use of war during the revolutionary years, see Jones, *The Great Nation*, p. 457. On more general links between republicanism and the military tradition, see Antoine Prost, *Republican Identities in War and Peace: Representations of France in the 19th and 20th Centuries*, Jay Winter with Helen McPhail, trans. (Oxford: Berg, 2002).

7

Revolution or Civil War

France is the 'revolutionary nation' *par excellence*. Not only was the French nation 'born' out of the 1789 Revolution, but during the two centuries which followed it, France underwent numerous other revolutions (successful and unsuccessful), as well as protests, strikes and a wealth of internal conflicts which were understood and interpreted primarily in terms of the Revolution and what became sanctified as the national revolutionary tradition. As a parliamentary enquiry concluded in 1871: 'Other people have had revolutions more or less frequently; but we have revolution permanently,'[1] and even the most reactionary regime of the period – the Vichy government – actively sought to associate itself with the revolutionary tradition when it labelled its domestic programme the 'National Revolution'.

One can distinguish between the Revolution as an historical event with a central place in the history of the nation and the subsequent attitude of revolution which characterised and permeated all areas of French politics for the next two centuries. The revolutionary tradition became the lens through which the whole of French History, every subsequent dispute or new political movement were viewed and interpreted. Even the participants themselves in all subsequent political conflicts with a popular dimension, from armed revolts to peaceful marches, thought of themselves and interpreted their own actions and objectives in terms of their relationship to the revolutionary tradition.

Because so many subsequent events and political discourses have been understood in terms of the Revolution, each and every individual French person can thus be said to have personal experience of revolution (even if only as a spectator), further encouraging them to understand and interpret their own and others' actions as a part of the continuing tradition. Even a purely literary event, such as the birth of the romantic movement, was reinterpreted in terms of revolutionary politics, as Victor Hugo asserted when he wrote: 'Je fis souffler un vent révolutionnaire./Je mis un bonnet rouge au vieux dictionnaire.'[2] Through identification with and praise of the revolutionary tradition, the French nation gained its identity and individual French men and women confirmed their personal links with their nation's history. This attitude manifests itself within French politics in violent bipolarisation, accompanied by overtly confrontational discourses and vocabulary, the extremity of which is often surprising and inexplicable to outside observers of French politics, as well as in a kind of messianism on the part of every political faction.

As we saw in the previous chapter for external conflict, internal conflict is also linked to 'moral' self-righteousness which manifests itself in this messianism which characterises French political movements. The principles behind the revolution, and by association any further internal conflict which could claim the revolutionary tradition as its inspiration, stemmed from moral virtues such as justice, liberty, equality, fraternity and so on. To be an enemy of the revolution, therefore, implies opposition to these positive virtues and also pushes those resisting the revolution to seek moral justifications for their position. In this way, each crisis (revolution or civil war) can, and has regularly been interpreted as a kind of moral crisis of the nation, rather than simply as a conflict about different political positions. Charles Péguy, whose political conscience grew out of ethical concerns during the Dreyfus Affair, ended up breaking from the political left in what he viewed as a moral crisis of his natural political family. Over the years, he felt bitterly disappointed when he saw political pettiness take precedence over the ethical issues he thought he had been fighting for.[3] Almost a century later, in 1974, during their first televised debate, Valéry Giscard d'Estaing chose to attack François Mitterrand on what he knew was the left's biggest strength: their perceived moral high ground on the political scene. Rather than question the validity or practicality of the socialist's programme, he proclaimed: 'vous n'avez pas le monopole du coeur'.[4] The effects work both ways, and those in the counter-revolutionary camp, through force of circumstance, also developed moral justifications for their positions, needing to vilify republicanism and the revolutionary values at times in the process, as a way of fighting fire with fire. The messianism of the revolutionary tradition, seeking converts to the political cause while at the same time hoping to bring about complete moral conviction in the principles behind it, parallels Catholic practices in many ways. The church had regularly maintained ambiguous links to politics, both in discourse and in the quest for converts. The Catholic tradition, like the revolutionary one, retained its messianic characteristics (religious and political) throughout the nineteenth century, when the vast majority of the world's missionaries were French in origin.[5] The existence of the other group routinely encouraged them in their domestic campaign for support and conversion, adding to the urgency of their respective rhetoric.

Describing the revolutions, revolutionary movements and traditions as the central experience of the French nation is only part of the story, however. The language of revolution has become filled with pride and positive connotations, yet the violence and extreme bipolarisation of such revolutionary movements have also be interpreted as signs simply of perpetual conflict, division or indeed of civil war. Robert Tombs holds that a conservative estimate of those killed or seriously wounded by political violence in France during the nineteenth century is over 60,000.[6] Historians have become increasingly interested in the question of national trauma resulting from such regular and intense internal conflicts, especially in light of the experience of the Second World War.[7] Whether the history of the nation is one of regular, glorious revolutions, each bringing greater levels of freedom or progress to France, or alternatively a seemingly endless series of internal battles, each one more extreme than the next, constituting what has been known as the 'Franco-French war', is a matter of interpretation. An entire section of the *Lieux de Mémoire* collection is devoted to internal political conflicts – from Catholic and Republican through to Gaullist and communist.[8]

Where the difference between revolution and civil war is important is of course from the perspective of unity as a national characteristic. The dominant republican vision of the French nation has always placed unity at the very centre, regularly defining the French Republic as 'one and indivisible'. Such a vision can be compatible with revolution and a revolutionary tradition, since enemies of the revolution can be few in number and 'outside' of the nation, independent of their actual origins. In this way the French aristocracy was not considered part of the French nation at all at the time of the Revolution, but as traitors.[9] Such thinking inspired an entire host of further conspiracy theories and paranoia about the nation's enemies plotting to overthrow the national order, from royalists and Jesuits to freemasons, Jews or Protestants.[10] Since these perceived 'conspirators' were considered outside the nation, revolution and unity thus remain potentially compatible. Without this mechanism, one is left simply with 'civil war', with which it is much more difficult to reconcile a history of unity. For republican nation builders, therefore, negative experiences on the part of the masses stemming from internal conflict need to be downplayed; suffering must not be thought of as a futile consequence of civil war, but part of the necessary sacrifice for the progress of revolution.

Although the interpretation of French history as containing episodes of civil war intrudes from time to time, the pressure for moral justification and the need to preserve an enduring image of national unity has meant that it is Revolution which forms the background for understanding and interpreting political conflict since 1789. Whether relatively peaceful political rivalry, or explosively violent confrontation, most of the later episodes have in one way or another been traced back to the original revolutionary and counter-revolutionary movements and their heirs. The remainder of this chapter will examine specific revolutions and outbreaks of political violence which can be interpreted in light of the revolutionary tradition or the Franco-French war: the successful revolutions of 1789,

1830, 1848 and arguably 1968, failed revolts such as the Paris Commune of 1871 and the 'National Revolution' of the Vichy government, and general movements dedicated to renewing revolutionary activity, including republicanism in opposition and communism. Each case will be examined to discover the ways in which the particular event or set of events were experienced and contextualised within the revolutionary tradition, and their contribution to the subsequent continuation of the tradition. Other kinds of political protest and social unrest which have been understood at least in part in their relationship to the revolutionary tradition, such as strikes or rallies will also be examined, as well as the ways the domestic revolutionary tradition coloured and modified the ways external European influences, such as Marxism or fascism, were assimilated in the French context.

Major Revolutions

The most important revolutionary experience for the French nation was that of the great Revolution of 1789. It was described by each successive generation of French men and women as 'our' revolution, the one in which 'we' fought to defend the universal rights proclaimed in the revolutionary slogan 'liberty, equality and fraternity' against the tyrannical defenders of absolutism and the enemies of the people, as well as to promote all enlightened and progressive thinking. Throughout the nineteenth and well into the twentieth centuries, French politicians were bitterly divided by those who felt themselves heirs to the revolution, although the memories of the experience of revolution differed depending upon the political position of the individual or group in question. Following the Second World War, the details of the enormous differences which had divided the country for decades faded slowly in favour of a unified general national experience. From the early Revolutionaries of the Third Estate through the Girondins, the Jacobins and the Sans-Culottes, from those who were in favour of a limited or constitutional monarchy to the 'regicides' who voted in favour of the execution of the king, the memory of the experience of the French people as a whole slowly receded to become simply that of those fighting for liberty and against the foreign invaders seeking to re-establish the monarchy from without. The 'rights of man' and the enlightenment writings of Voltaire and Rousseau, presented as a unified evident truth, became central to French history teaching, replacing even the 'grand siècle' of Racine and Corneille as the most significant in French cultural history.[11] It was clear in 1989 at the celebration of the bicentenary that the official commemorations promoted this consensual rather than divisive vision of the Revolution.[12] In spite of the efforts of minority groups and political parties to commemorate the more divisive aspects of the Revolution, what captured the public imagination was indeed this unified vision of the revolutionary experience of the nation, for 'the Revolution no longer drove a wedge into the heart of French politics.'[13] By the late twentieth century, most French people would even have agreed that the Terror was excessive and unnecessary, primarily the fault of a handful of individual tyrants at whose hands the nation also suffered for the good cause of general liberty, a view which would have been completely unacceptable for a republican of the late nineteenth century.

Implicit in the general consensus around the meaning and interpretation of the 1789 Revolution is a diminution of the place of marginal experiences as well as external views of the Revolution, at least insofar as they touch the historical imagination of the French public. Groups such as the Chouans or the pre-revolutionary right may be represented in films or studied historically, yet their experiences are not a source of personal identification for later generations. For many of those living in the Vendée, the home of the counter-revolutionary uprising put down during the Revolution, the 'experience' of the Revolution was even more so one of oppression by the tyrants who had carried the Revolution too far. It was an experience of violent civil war, political positions intensified by religious fervour, and one for which the memory was long-lived.[14] For each of the revolutionary and counter-revolutionary movements, the fact that the vast majority of the population at the time in fact did not actively participate at all was neither here nor there, it was remembered as a formative national experience with which each member of the nation can continue to identify. External perspectives have a correspondingly marginal place in the way in which the revolutionary experience is remembered. Whether historical fiction, popular or academic work, writings on the Revolution by nineteenth or twentieth-century foreigners such as Mary Wollstonecraft's *History and Moral View of the Origin and Progress of the French Revolution*, Charles Dickens' *Tale of Two Cities* or Hannah Arendt's *On Revolution* have been quietly ignored, in spite of the fact that their works on the whole are well known in France and recognised as those of progressive authors.

The July Revolution of 1830 can in some ways be compared to the early stages of the 1789 Revolution. It included a popular dimension and had its usual share of barricades and street unrest, but was led essentially by the liberal opposition among the elite who feared outright republicanism which might simply de-stabilise the country, but who sought greater parliamentary control and changes to the constitution. Frustrated with Charles X and his reinstatement of an *ancien régime*-style monarchy and its absolutist rhetoric, they found in Louis-Philippe a reasonable leader who would bring about the liberalisation they sought, combining moderate reforms with claims to popular legitimacy without over-extending the democratic franchise or relying too much on the unruly masses. The outcome of the 1830 Revolution can therefore be viewed precisely as an explicitly conceived 'bourgeois monarchy', such as that of the early 1789 Revolution that collapsed in the 'regrettable' violence of the 1791–1792 years.[15] As with the entire July Monarchy, the 1830 Revolution inspired mostly indifference in its legacy (as opposed to hatred or active identification), coupled with a more general anti-bourgeois sentiment within society. It can be held as a part of the great revolutionary tradition only insofar as it was successful in changing the regime, rather than because subsequent generations held this particular revolution to be a defining national experience.

For different reasons, the 1848 Revolution has also had a limited place in the national experience, beyond simply providing further evidence of the continuing successful revolutionary tradition. Drawing much more upon the popular masses, rhetorically representing values central to the republican revolutionary tradition and putting a programme in place in practice more radical than the July Monarchy, the subsequent failure of the regime it inspired (and worst of all, because that failure was due to its very democracy) meant that the 1848 Revolution was more of an embarrassment, becoming under-represented in the symbolism of later French Republics. Many of the images, events and heroes more specifically related to the events of 1848, such as the first introduction of universal male suffrage in Europe, the abolition of slavery, Liberty Trees, the *Fête de la Fraternité,* Alphonse de Lamartine, Louis Blanc, the insurgents of the June days, the successful reconciliation of the Catholic church and the revolutionary heritage within a Republican constitution; each could have become an integral part of the dominant republican historical myth, but did not. They were later passed over in favour of symbols from the early phases of the 1789 Revolution, leaving 1848 very much in the background of French national consciousness.[16]

Thus on their own, the 1830 and 1848 Revolutions did not inspire anywhere near as much attention, discussion or emulation as the 1789 Revolution had done, but they did serve very much as evidence of the revolutionary tradition: that the people of the French nation could regularly be called on to revolt if previously won freedoms had been suppressed, or if greater ones were demanded. Each included a popular dimension, with which 'ordinary' French people could identify, and as often as not even positively recruited defenders of order such as the National Guard to join the revolutionaries when the incumbent powers had 'betrayed' the people. These revolutions also served as references for the general national experience of revolution, with its powerful image of the people in arms, manning the barricades, defying and then triumphing over authority in the name of liberty and the nation.

Failed Revolutions

In the meantime, other unsuccessful revolutions had also taken place which can be counted among the experiences leading to the revolutionary tradition. Following the successful revolution in 1830, small revolts took place by republican agitators unhappy with the regime of Louis-Philippe, hoping not only for the demise of absolutism but for the downfall of all monarchy and the re-establishment of the Republic. These revolts were measured in strength by the number of barricades that the insurgents managed to construct in the many narrow streets of Paris, using the cobblestones of the streets or any other materials which came to hand to block off one street at a time and force the authorities to fight through for every short section of road. Inspired by a romantic consciousness of emulating their forebears of 1789 (and 1793), the would-be revolutionaries believed themselves capable of transforming the world by reliving the revolution and using similar violent urban social protest to bring about change.[17] The most famous of these failed revolts occurred on 5 and 6 June 1832 following the death of General Lamarque, later recounted in Victor Hugo's *Les Misérables*. It was, however, but one example of several such protests during the first half of the July Monarchy, erupting again later even more powerfully to bring about its fall in the successful revolution of 1848. The power of the revolutionary images upon French imaginations helped engender a prominent political culture characterised by belief in recourse to street violence and long-term institutional instability.

Given the tradition of regular revolts, sometimes localised in one particular neighbourhood and occasionally sweeping the entire capital city, and their impact upon the political life of the whole country (more than once had revolutions caused the national government to collapse), measures were taken that shaped not only France's political structure, but also its landscape and urban structure in Paris. Napoleon III felt that, in addition to the regular plebiscites that he used to confirm his legitimacy, the best way to prevent future revolutions was through the reorganisation of the entire layout of Paris. Once he had secured his hold on power, wide, straight avenues were pushed through the city under the direction of Baron Haussmann, razing the previous street plan and thereby making it much more difficult for insurrections to take place. Wider avenues were of course more difficult to barricade, requiring many more paving stones and other rubble, and the long, straight avenues also permitted the use of cannons by the army. Previously ineffectual in narrow, winding streets with multiple corner barricades, the authorities' ability to use cannons meant that insurgents were theoretically at an extreme disadvantage from that time onwards. The before and after of this tremendous transformation have their representation in two of the great literary collections of the nineteenth century – the old Paris of Balzac's *Comédie Humaine,* the historical city whose streets and neighbourhoods has slowly emerged over many centuries and which can be neatly contrasted with Emile Zola's *Rougeon Macquard* series, depicting the new city artificially created by a political power in order to control the masses. Thus the specificity of the city of Paris and the impact of the Parisian-led revolutions on the French national psyche is deeply imbedded in the literary tradition and even in the very map of the city.

Not long after the fall of Napoleon III and the Second Empire, the new urban landscape was to be tested as an obstacle to leading a successful revolution when the newly born Third Republic almost immediately faced a significant revolt in the form of the Paris Commune of 1871. Although drawing part of their inspiration from International Socialist doctrines surrounding a working-class revolution, the Communards understood themselves to be participating in the great French revolutionary tradition, of which they were simply the most forward thinking and progressive to date. They were building upon the experience of previous generations of French revolutionary leaders to take the revolution further than it had been taken before. While working-class imagery was also used, links to the history of the French people-in-arms, to the revolutionary French nation were prevalent and strong. Bertrand Taithe goes even further and suggests that after two decades of dictatorship with few channels for moderate or constructive opposition, armed demonstration including the use of barricades was 'the only technique of dissidence with which the revolutionary forces were familiar.'[18] Men and women from across the Parisian working classes joined forces in the creation of an armed revolt which replicated all of the familiar forms of the revolutionary tradition.[19] During the Bloody Week of May 1871, the French army fought its way through the newly opened up Paris, violently crushing the Commune and condemning its final partisans to execution or exile. In this context, the experience of martyrdom for so many revolutionaries was understood in terms of the longer national tradition of popular sacrifice for the revolution.

After the fall of the Commune, the new Paris of Haussmann lost a great deal of its political power within the French nation, while the legacy of revolution continued to have an influence upon the urban landscape. For fear of further challenge to the national government by municipal authorities setting themselves up as rivals, the city was denied a mayor until 1977, when Jacques Chirac was elected as the first mayor of Paris in over a century. The legacy of suspicion of the popular working classes who might at any time provoke another revolutionary bloodbath also led to the creation, not of urban ghettos in 'downtowns' such as those found in many other countries, but working class suburbs or 'banlieues' which would remain bastions of popular agitation into the early twenty-first century, but at a much safer distance from the centres of power than if they had been allowed to grow up in the city centres.

Protests

Although agitation was not to produce another full-scale revolution in France after 1871, the revolutionary tradition was understood to be continued through industrial action, strikes and mass protests, heavily coloured by its commingling with Marxist ideology. Although some French socialists were reluctant to participate in the internationalist movement since they had 'their own' revolutionary tradition, Marxist thinking was important for the French left. Marxism itself, as a philosophy of history, was of course significantly influenced by the French revolutionary tradition, Marx having written important books on both the Revolution and the Paris Commune. From French history Marx concluded that the capitalist system carried within it the seeds of its own destruction, and would eventually be brought down by revolution if the cause were never abandoned. The Commune had simply come too soon, capitalism was not yet ripe, and the workers in the French army had not been convinced to join with the Communards, rather than the bourgeois government.[20] The influence of Marxist thinking on the French socialist (and later communist) political parties as well as the trade union movement, when combined with the national revolutionary tradition, was such that the whole of the French left, although working within a republican democratic system, remained fully devoted to revolutionary ideology and imagery well into the twentieth century. Long after the principal objectives of the early revolutionaries had been achieved (such as the abolition of privileges, and manhood suffrage), the revolutionary tradition was kept alive by altering the aims in accordance with Marxist doctrines.

Regular strikes punctuated the peacetime decades between the various major wars with Germany, from smaller scale industrial action to general strikes and national protests. Throughout the Third Republic and beyond, those French men and women who experienced such strikes or protest marches believed they were continuing the revolution, and thought of their personal experiences as direct links between themselves and the longer tradition. Evidence for this link can be found in the repeated use of revolutionary songs and slogans by the protagonists, whether their opponents were the State itself or simply a particular employer or set of employers. Examples of individual moments of protest abound, from calls for wider revolution in response to Clemenceau's violent actions against strikers in 1907 through to the mass protests and strikes in response to the Matignon agreement in 1936. From the beginning of the Third Republic onward, the revolutionary tradition became a regular feature of social and political culture in France, a kind of rite of passage whereby any individual or political group had to go through a phase of protest understood in rhetorical terms as revolutionary.

The turmoil of the 1930s and its relationship to the revolutionary tradition merits some special discussion. The marches by the Leagues were certainly mass movements of violence aimed at overthrowing the parliament-dominated Third Republic which was perceived as too weak. Coming as they were from the right, they were inspired partly by the success of European fascism and can be understood more in the Bonapartist than the revolutionary tradition within French history. The popular reaction to the rise of the Leagues, however, brought about renewed cooperation (if not unity) on the left and led to even greater mass demonstrations culminating in the victory of the Popular Front in 1936. This coalition between socialists, radicals and communists certainly drew upon revolutionary rhetoric, and its success could be interpreted as a kind of revolution before the fact: preventing an authoritarian takeover from happening rather than waiting and having to stage a revolution afterwards. Political battles were fought on the street throughout the decade, if not in bloody armed combat, then in demonstration of the capacity of rival political groups to gain mass support, manifested through popular descents into the streets. Thus as much as the impact of the economic depression and the rise of fascism in neighbouring countries were significant, the national revolutionary tradition of acute political crises and civil war gave the broad continental rise of an authoritarian right during the 1930s its specific political flavour in France. It is furthermore through the ideological prism of the struggle between the forces of progress and the forces of regression that the events have since been principally understood, inscribing them within the revolutionary tradition rather than within the European fascist and Popular Front movements. For most of the French public (and even to a certain extent for French intellectuals and academics) there was no French fascism, but simply the same counter-revolutionary far right that had been plaguing France since the aftermath of 1789. This image is a further example of what has already been discussed in earlier chapters, that for the period up until 1940 French history is still almost exclusively seen and understood in light of the Revolution.

Wartime did not spare the French nation from internal protests inspired in part by the revolutionary tradition. The Paris Commune had arisen in the context of the Franco-Prussian War, severely handicapping the government's ability to prosecute the war and then to negotiate the peace, while having to deal with revolution in the capital. A generation later, various representatives of the workers' movement had threatened non-obedience before the outbreak of war as a way to help prevent it. The socialist leader Jean Jaurès had tried to mobilise the International against war, and rallied hard in France up to his assassination on 31 July 1914 on the very eve of the First World War. Such efforts did not stop the people answering the call in 1914, with the support of the socialist leadership. By 1917, however, frustrated by the conditions in the trenches and the lack of leave time, many soldiers engaged in a mutiny, the results of which actually led to the improvement of conditions for the soldiers (once a handful of individuals had been punished as the leaders and deserters). Just over twenty years later, following the rapid French defeat during the spring of 1940, the signing of the Armistice and the establishment of a collaborationist government in Vichy, mass protests would again be a feature of wartime, not just peacetime. Reacting to the difficult conditions imposed by the occupation and in spite of the presence of the occupying army, even in the occupied zone traditional labour strikes and protests continued to colour French experience.[21] Furthermore, the resistance made use of revolutionary imagery and song as a means of interpreting their own actions as a part of French nationalist tradition.

Perhaps the most obvious example of wartime use of revolutionary imagery and vocabulary can be found in the name given to the overarching domestic policy of Marshal Pétain's government during the years of the occupation, the 'National Revolution'. Attempting to latch on to positive connotations of the republican revolutionary tradition, this programme preached national renewal through such policies as back-to-the-land, the promotion of traditional family values, maternity, service, respect for order, hierarchy and tradition, added to strong militaristic nationalism and general xenophobia. Absent was much of the familiar rhetoric of the classic 'revolutionary' values and objectives such as individual freedom or equality. By calling itself a revolution however, those who favoured it, however passively, could feel themselves a part of the longstanding national tradition, and seek to woo those traditionally on the left over to their vision for a renewed French society. It goes to show how very central revolution is to the French nation when even the most reactionary government of the century felt the need to present itself and its policies as 'revolutionary'.

Following the liberation of the nation and for some time after the end of the war, French society went through 'the purge' in which those perceived as collaborating were brought to trial and convicted of treason against the nation. While a special system of courts was set up to deal with the number of cases, many were dealt with unofficially by local groups of resistors: scenes of mob violence and summary executions occurred in many parts of France, carried out by those in the resistance (and others) who could not, or would not, wait for the courts. The nation appeared on the brink of falling apart. Many feared that de Gaulle's provisional government would not be able to stem the flood of violence, and that civil war would break out. For some time before the Liberation, de Gaulle had been preparing to create a national political structure able to overcome the 'civil war' and potentially unstable if not revolutionary situation that would undoubtedly emerge after the collapse of the Vichy government. His choice of Jean Moulin, whose far-left credentials were indisputable, to federate the various internal resistance movements was a far-sighted attempt to bridge the smouldering future crisis, and contributed, along with Stalin's choice not to push for a communist-led change of regime in France, to the reduction in the scale of the 'civil war' and the absence of a full-scale communist-led revolution in the aftermath of the Liberation. De Gaulle went on successfully to create a government of national unity which included communist ministers, and pushed for a new constitution which would facilitate the task of the government.[22] At the same time he did not push for a full-scale administrative purge which would further reduce stability, but simply maintained most of the administrative structure of the Vichy government. These various measures allowed de Gaulle temporarily, at that crucial point in France's history, to overcome the French nation's historical nemesis: yet another violent revolution. By 1946 however, with the Fourth Republic in place and de Gaulle in self-imposed political purgatory, it was clear that neither the threat of revolution nor the presence of revolutionary language and imagery in political discourse had gone away entirely. The revolutionary tradition remained an important interpretive framework for understanding French politics and national experience, but from that time forward it was no longer the only one.

One further event in the second half of the twentieth century requires discussion in terms of the revolutionary tradition, and that is the student (and also worker) protests of May 1968. Combining public marches and even a few barricades with the trade union action of strikes, the protagonists of May 1968 saw themselves very much as continuing the revolutionary tradition. The protest began with students in the Parisian suburb of Nanterre, before spreading to the heart of the Latin Quarter. Unhappy with overcrowded conditions and the general unresponsiveness of universities to expanding student numbers and changing economic conditions, discontent also spread to include diatribes against capitalism, materialism, American participation in the Vietnam War, and the authoritarian, conservative ideology which the government of Charles de Gaulle symbolised in their eyes. While the articulated aims were not always coherent (and in some cases downright contradictory), the French protests were unusual among the student demonstrations of that era because of the subsequent participation of workers. Although they were not very comfortable with the students' lyricism and Maoist or Trotskyite rhetoric, the national trade unions were quite rapid in trying to capture and turn the spirit of protest to their interest and advantage. They joined the students marching in Paris, and initiated a wave of strikes, seeking to use the momentum generated by the students to further their claims for higher wages and concessions from employers, the most significant of which was the French State itself. The union leadership did manage to gain enough control of an apparently unstoppable movement, identified a few concrete, pragmatic aims or political goals, and convinced workers and students of the words of communist leader Maurice Thorez, that 'il faut savoir terminer une grève'.[23] The medium-term results were a general wage-rise for workers of seven per cent, with an even greater increase in the minimum wage, and the passing of an education reform bill which increased the capacity of universities. Although, following his defeat in a referendum in April 1969 on the unrelated subject of regional and Senate reform by 53.2 to 46.7, President de Gaulle himself resigned, the right ironically solidified their hold on power for more than a decade following the events.

Whether the events of May 1968 constituted a 'revolution' is a matter of debate among analysts and participants. Some cite the sheer scale – over 10 million workers – of those who participated in the strikes as evidence that it was a bona fide revolution. On the other hand, the limited impact of the protests upon the political elite, either in composition or policies, lead others to conclude that this was merely one more, if very large and well-publicised, example of protest among a host of political and trade union activity throughout the twentieth century. It was principally those who looked back on it in retrospect who defined the May 1968 events as revolutionary, and who sought to present the protests as the latest resurgence of the French revolutionary tradition, through which their own experience could be equated to the 'greatness' achieved by earlier national revolutionaries.[24] The mock-revolutionary events of 1968 came to symbolise something which was new in France: the individualist, liberal, permissive, consumerist society. That this transformation needed to be seen to be born out of a self-proclaimed revolution demonstrates the extent to which the myth of the 'revolutionary nation' was still powerful in a society that had not actually known a revolution for almost a century.

Thus although no single event since the Paris Commune has come to be called a Revolution by absolutely everyone looking back on it, scenes of extreme violence continued to occur between groups of French people, including those perceiving themselves to be outside the main power circles and acting in the name of justice, progress or enlightenment in the good revolutionary tradition. Some were general strikes, as indicated above, but other examples can be found. Richard Vinen has described the France of the entire middle decades of the twentieth century as perpetually on the brink of civil war,[25] and many historians' work has been aimed at analysing and understanding France in terms of crisis and civil strife.[26] Even if it did not erupt into open war or revolution, tension was a part of the lived atmosphere of modern France. The threat of revolutionary conflict was real, coming from several points on the political compass and aimed at producing at least significant change or reform, if not overthrowing a particular political faction holding power or indeed the entire constitutional structure. Thus throughout the twentieth century, the vocabulary of revolution and protest was alive and strong, as was the legacy of political extremism and instability which had grown out of the revolutionary tradition.

Although not 'revolutions' as such, both political protest marches and the strikes, especially by the French public service employees or 'fonctionnaires', which continued at regular intervals well into the twenty-first century, were still very much considered as links to the revolutionary tradition. The French nation has continually seen itself very much as the nation which will 'descend into the streets' at the slightest provocation or whiff of injustice. Examples may be economic, such as wages which are considered too low, job conditions less than satisfactory, insufficient job security or holiday time, or indeed because of unequal treatment of different social groups or employment categories. Alternatively, such protests may have been motivated rather by desire for political change in the form of the repeal of a particular bit of legislation, the resignation of an individual politician or a change in government policy in a controversial area of domestic or foreign affairs in which the perceived injustice can be found. In the words of Phil Cerny, the revolutionary tradition became 'absorbed into the dominant political culture' of the French nation.[27] Jack Hayward adds that modernisation in France occurred through the medium of protests, which were not 'anachronistic and retrograde, disruptive and dysfunctional parts of the French problem', but simply the vehicle for change and progress, based upon an alternative vision of society to that of other countries.[28] While the nature of protests may have altered throughout the twentieth century in terms of the motivations and types of organisations leading the movements, what remained constant was the use of mass protest for political ends and the involvement of large segments of the French population.[29]

By participating in any strike or protest march, individual French men and women were linking their own experience to the national experience of Revolution. Up to the end of the twentieth century and beyond, the politics of protest retained 'a vitality and a sense of historical purpose' unlike that which can be found elsewhere.[30] A striking feature of the French tendency to protest is the degree of solidarity between groups, different job categories and unions. The number of unions who have gone on strike out of pure solidarity with others is surprising, as is the way in which large-scale strikes which halt public services can on occasion receive significant public support and sympathy even among those not only unconcerned but also inconvenienced by the strikers.

Regular opportunities to associate experiences of serious domestic conflict with the revolutionary tradition were prominent due to their frequency throughout the period, yet ironically they did not fundamentally undermine a simultaneous sense of national unity. Part of the reconciliation between the images of unity on the one hand and civil war on the other comes from the perception that the regular protests or strikes were really aimed at a restricted group of industrial or political leaders who had led the nation down the wrong path or used their position inappropriately or irresponsibly to abuse the trust of the masses, and who in the minds of the activists were associated with the tyrants of the *ancien régime* during the Revolution. Such associations can be made of despised political leaders of the moment, of companies, business leaders, or simply the faceless state itself, and reinforce the feelings of participation in the revolutionary tradition. It is also not unheard of for the protests to be aimed against leaders from their own 'revolutionary' constituency, who are felt not to be serious enough in their challenges to authority, from trade unions unwilling to push negotiations far enough to political parties not behaving radically enough for their members. The Matignon agreements between trade unions and the Popular Front government which brought about the most significant gains for workers at that time in Europe, were nevertheless greeted by further strikes hostile to the working-class leaders who had not achieved more. During the protests in May 1968, there was much dissatisfaction with the Communist Party, encouraging radical students to turn to Maoist or Trotskyite groups, or at the very least to take matters out of the hands of the official 'revolutionary' leadership and into the hands of the people, further reinforcing the experience of the participants as authentically revolutionary.

Conclusion

Revolution has been a central experience for the French nation since 1789. French men and women of every generation experienced insurrection and protest, and often lived their own individual and collective experiences as a part of the great national tradition of revolution spanning the two centuries. The power of revolutionary images upon French imaginations helped engender a distinctive national political culture characterised by moral self-righteousness, street violence, extremism and political instability often akin to civil war, and even had a significant impact upon the urban structure of Paris and other regional cities. Through its centrality, the mainstream experience of revolution has meant downplaying the experiences of marginal groups (such as opponents to or victims of revolution), and the perception of France as having unique features in its political culture, including the way it responds to, absorbs and modifies Europe-wide ideological changes.

In spite of the power of the revolutionary imagery in France since 1789 and its importance in the character of French political tension and instability right into the twenty-first century, it has to be said that another trauma has also come to the fore of the national political psyche: the experience of the collaboration of a French government with the Nazi occupiers. By 1968, the young French 'revolutionaries' were no longer comparing the CRS (French riot police) to the *ancien régime* mercenary armies, but to the German SS. In twentieth-century communist influenced jargon, the right wing capitalist enemy of the proletariat was usually called 'fascist'. Gradually, even in French minds, the emotional content of the experience of Nazi-occupied Europe has reduced (but by no means eliminated) the place of the mythology and images of the French Revolution within French social and political discourse. Thus the complex soul-searching process that led to the trials of Paul Touvier, Klaus Barbie and Maurice Papon has gradually gained pre-eminence over the 1789 Revolution in terms of contemporary relevance. It may be that a similar process will take place because of the next ghost in the nation's history – its former colonial expansion and the myriad of consequences which came from it – and that is the subject of the next chapter.

Notes

1 Parliamentary enquiry, 1871, quoted in J. M. Roberts, 'The Paris Commune from the Right', *EHR* supplement 6 (1973), p. 7.
2 'I caused a revolutionary wind to blow. /I put a red hat on the old dictionary.' Victor Hugo, 'Réponse à un acte d'accusation', *Les Contemplations*. Autrefois, I, 7 (Paris: Gallimard, 1943), p. 43. Written in 1834.
3 Péguy asserted, in *Notre Jeunesse* (1910) that 'Tout parti vit de sa mystique et meurt de sa politique.' 'All political parties live on their mystique, and die from their politics.'
4 'You do not have the monopoly of the heart.'
5 Of the European missionaries in the nineteenth century, 80% were Catholic, of whom 70% were French.
6 Robert Tombs, *France 1814–1914* (London and New York: Longman, 1996), p. 8.
7 See, for example, Jean-Noël Jeanneney, 'The Legacy of Traumatic Experiences in French Politics Today', in Gregory Flynn, ed., *Remaking the Hexagon: The New France in the New Europe* (Boulder, CA: Westview Press, 1995), pp. 17–29.
8 Pierre Nora, *Les Lieux de Mémoire 2* (Paris: Gallimard, 1997). The section on political divisions contains nine chapters, pp. 2246–601.
9 See Abbé Gregoire, *What is the Nation?*
10 For a full discussion of the paranoia resulting from conspiracy theories in nineteenth-century France, see Tombs, *France 1814–1914*, pp. 88–94.
11 It is extremely ironic that Voltaire and Rousseau, who were bitter enemies, have their ideas presented as if they were simply two ways to present what was fundamentally the same truth, as if their vision, and that of the many on the side of the revolution fit together unproblematically.
12 See Robert Gildea, *The Past in French History* (New Haven and London: Yale University Press, 1994), p. 14.
13 Ibid, p. 15.
14 For more on the Vendée, see Arno J. Mayer, *The Furies: Violence and Terror in the French and Russian Revolutions* (Princeton: Princeton University Press, 2000), pp. 323–70.
15 See Sarah Maza, *The Myth of the French Bourgeoisie: An essay on the social imaginary 1750–1850* (Cambridge, MA: Harvard University Press, 2003), pp. 161–92 and Chapter 5.
16 See Timothy Baycroft, 'Commemorations of the Revolution of 1848 and the Second Republic', *Modern & Contemporary France* 6, 2 (1998), pp. 155–68.
17 See Jill Harsin, *Barricades: The War of the Street in Revolutionary Paris, 1830–1848* (New York: Palgrave Macmillan, 2002), pp. 15–16.
18 Bertrand Taithe, *Citizenship and Wars: France in Turmoil 1870–1871* (London and New York: Routledge, 2001), p. 33.
19 For women's participation, see Gay L. Gullickson, *Unruly Women of Paris: Images of the Commune* (Ithaca: Cornell University Press, 1996).
20 Karl Marx, *The Civil War in France* (London, 1871).
21 Lynne Taylor, *Between Resistance and Collaboration: Popular Protest in*

Northern France, 1940–45 (Basingstoke: Macmillan, 2000).

22 In the latter task he did not succeed at the time, but resigned, only to come back and achieve his constitutional aims in 1958.

23 'You have to know when to stop a strike.'

24 See Chapter 4 for a more complete discussion of May 1968 in the context of the national historical narrative, as well as Kristin Ross, *May '68 and its Afterlives* (Chicago and London: University of Chicago Press, 2002) and Michael Seidman, *The Imaginary Revolution: Parisian Students and Workers in 1968* (New York and Oxford: Berghahn, 2004).

25 See Richard Vinen, *France 1934–70* (Basingstoke: Macmillan, 1996).

26 See, for example, the essays in Kenneth Mouré and Martin S. Alexander, eds, *Crisis and Renewal in France, 1918–1962* (Oxford: Berghahn, 2002), Michel Winock, *La fièvre hexagonale: Les grandes crises politiques 1871–1968* (Paris, 1986) or Philip G. Cerny, ed., *Social Movements and Protest in France* (London: Frances Pinter, 1982).

27 Phil Cerny, 'Introduction: The Politics of Protest in Contemporary French Society', in Cerny, ed., *Social Movements*, p. vii.

28 Jack Hayward, 'Dissident France: The Counter Political Culture,' in Cerny, ed., *Social Movements*, p. 7.

29 For changes towards the end of the twentieth century, see Sarah Waters, *Social Movements in France: Towards a New Citizenship* (Basingstoke: Palgrave, 2003).

30 Cerny, 'Introduction', in Cerny, ed., *Social Movements*, p. viii.

8

Colonies and Imperialism

Source of national prestige and evidence of French global significance, the French colonial Empire was second only to that of Great Britain at the end of the nineteenth century.[1] Most of the colonial Empire that France had acquired during the *ancien régime* had been lost by the end of the revolutionary years,[2] but during the next century, in spite of all of the distractions of revolutions, domestic upheaval and changes of regime, France was nevertheless able to muster the resources to conquer a vast amount of territory spread throughout the world. By 1945, the French colonial Empire covered 12 million km^2 spread over four continents and comprised 65 million inhabitants. The original motivations for that conquest were largely political and ideological, as, unlike in Britain, no serious economic or social motivations for colonial expansion existed in France.

The extent to which colonial expansion and the subsequent management of empire constituted a defining or all-pervasive national experience is a subject of debate. On the one hand, the French colonial Empire was large, quite a few of the French had personal experience of the colonies, and the presence of colonial immigrants and representations in metropolitan France was widespread throughout the period. On the other hand, the acquisition of a colonial Empire was ideologically defended only by a small but determined and articulate minority within the elite who were perfectly convinced of France's mission to enlighten the world and of its need to procure colonies to demonstrate and enhance national greatness. Their vision was that the peoples and territory of the Empire would be assimilated directly into the nation, thereby transmitting the enlightened French republican values throughout what would be termed 'Greater France'. On the other hand, notwithstanding the size and presence of the colonies, and the discourse defending them as an integral part of France, in the long run they did not really penetrate deeply into the French psyche as central to the essence of the French nation, occupying only a small place in the national mythology.[3] To national history, national debates, national principles, national culture or in definitions of what constitutes

Figure 7 Recruitment poster for the colonial army

the French nation, the colonial Empire is most striking by its absence, occupying a far less important place in the national imagination than one would expect given the extent of the colonial Empire and the material and ideological resources devoted to it throughout the modern period. Such an attitude was perhaps most obvious when, following the defeat in 1940, Marshal Pétain and his followers chose not to pursue the war from the colonies because they did not want 'to leave France', General Weygand summing up the position when he stated: 'L'empire, c'est de l'enfantillage'.[4] In this instance, Pétain merely symbolised the hexagonal vision of the French nation, for after the military defeat, no more than 20 deputies and senators boarded the *Massilia* to sail for Casablanca to carry on the war, all of whom were eventually arrested and charged with desertion.

This chapter will examine the national experience of the colonial Empire, such as it was captured in the dominant republican vision of the nation. It will aim to analyse and appreciate its place within the other experiences of society, war and revolution already covered, and will also try to understand why the colonial experience was so very much on the periphery of the mainstream national one, given the place that it once had within republican discourse on the nation. The chapter will begin with a basic chronology of the French colonial Empire, dividing the period into three phases – the acquisition of Empire, decolonisation and the years following the end of the colonial Empire. Following a more detailed look at Algeria, the most significant of the French colonies, it will then turn to examine the various representations of the colonial Empire within French national imagery, including the presentations of Empire at the international exhibitions, colonial images in advertising, literature and elsewhere.

The Chronology of Empire

In terms of the national experience of the colonial Empire, the two centuries since the French Revolution can be divided into three periods: the acquisition and consolidation of the colonial Empire, the period of decolonisation, and the decades which followed the end of most of the formal colonial Empire, in which France attempted to come to terms (both practically and ideologically) with its colonial past. In the first phase, France slowly conquered territories at various 'strategic' locations around the globe. Some regimes were more preoccupied than others by the issue of outright overseas expansion, but all devoted enough resources to the colonial Empire at least to hold onto it and to keep it running, even if they were not interested at that particular moment in further extending the conquered territory. The Restoration and July Monarchies, Second Empire and Third Republic all had their moments of interest, each contributing to the expansion of the colonial Empire.[5] Interestingly, concern for the colonial expansion of France is perhaps the only significant political question where the national political divisions throughout the nineteenth century did not coincide with the main 'revolutionary-republican' and 'counter-revolutionary' (left-right) cleavage. What became known as 'the colonial party' was a collection of individual politicians drawn from across the political spectrum from left to right who favoured further colonial endeavours for France. At the same time, opposition to any policies of colonial expansion could also be found within the main political parties of both the left and the right. Such opposition tended to be because of a feeling of higher priorities (such as the re-conquest of Alsace and Lorraine or the restoration of the monarchy), or that colonies were a waste of time and money, rather than significant principled objections.[6] Those who refused to forget the blue line of the Vosges (towards Alsace and Lorraine), primarily from the nationalistic right but found throughout the political spectrum, had their position summarised by the nationalistic poet Deroulède who felt offended at having 'lost two sisters and being offered 20 servants' in exchange. Thus, although never really commanding a solid majority of support within the French political elite until at least the late 1890s, a handful of colonial enthusiasts were able to encourage successive French governments to continue to expand the

French colonial Empire. Through this gradual expansion pushed forward by the colonial party, by the end of the century France had major colonial possessions in North Africa around Algeria, East Africa, Indochina and New Caledonia, with further colonies in the islands of the Pacific and Indian Oceans, the Caribbean, the Middle East, India and South America.[7]

Throughout the phase of colonial expansion and consolidation, the belief in a specifically French style of imperialism pervaded French thinking about their colonies. French colonialism was predominantly a business of the State rather than of private French individuals, entrepreneurs or companies. France's attitude was also characterised by its desire to assimilate the colonies as a part of the centralised State, undifferentiated from any other regions. The colonies were described as extensions of France, eventually to be treated as any other parts of the French nation, as opposed (for example) to the British colonies which were always recognised as distinct and separate from the mother country.[8] For this reason, the French colonial Empire came to be understood as 'greater France' (*la plus grande France*). The belief that colonies could become French in the same way that various regions of France were French could be found, for example, in some of the great republican champions of the colonial Empire, such as Jules Ferry, who was also the architect of the republican schools to spread national ideas throughout the hexagon.[9] Looked at another way, the colonial French subjects were to be thought of like those peasants and workers in France before the franchise had been extended to include all men over 18 – in training for full citizenship, which would come later when they were 'ready' and fully assimilated. In practice, however, indigenous peoples for the most part remained outside of citizenship throughout the colonial period, and the plans for their assimilation into the nation were overtaken by decolonisation. While the French assimilationist discourse led to significant incoherencies and contradictions in the long run, it cannot be dismissed as a purely rhetorical device, since it was sincerely believed by those who were advocating it from within the colonial party.

Like other European colonial powers, French colonialism had a great deal of messianism or at least messianistic rhetoric lurking behind its expansionist policies, although it differed in substance from the 'white man's burden' as articulated by Rudyard Kipling with respect to the British Empire. In the case of the republicans, this messianism was significantly influenced by the belief in the French mission to spread the enlightenment and the values of the French Revolution – liberty, equality and fraternity – throughout the world. Colonies were of course an excellent means to this end. By showing them the true nature and benefits of liberty first hand, they too could profit from the lessons the French nation had learned, and become as free and enlightened as they were. In this way, French colonialism also had a slightly different timbre than other European countries, in that it was not just about spreading religion and civilisation, but also about the specificity of the French enlightened republicanism, through the particular republican model of integration of the territory and assimilation of the population into the French nation.[10]

In spite of the rhetoric, French values were rarely spread through the colonies by representatives of a pure or even diluted republicanism. Those promoting French colonialism on the ground included a significant number of Catholic missionaries whose priorities were indeed religious rather than republican, and whose messianism was thus more on a par with the representatives of other colonial powers than one might infer from the discourse of the French colonial party, in spite of the differences between Protestant and Catholic missionaries. During the nineteenth century, Catholicism, and French Catholicism in particular, was a particularly missionary religion. Even the anticlerical republicans themselves were happy to send religious missionaries to the colonies, feeling that their contribution to French colonialism was positive, in that at least they were spreading the French language and education, and that Catholicism was one step in the right direction towards their objectives. Furthermore, given the regular tension and instability within France, republicans did not have the men to spare themselves, and by sending the fervent Catholics to the colonies, they removed them from the schools within the hexagon (one of their objectives anyway).[11]

As an experience, individual participation in the colonies during the phase of expansion and consolidation was primarily restricted to some relatively specific categories of individuals, such that in many ways it was and remained a marginal experience. As already mentioned, a large number of the missionaries were drawn from Catholic circles. Military personnel would often do a spell of duty in the colonies as a part of their career trajectory, as did some categories of administrative civil servants. As in many other countries, French colonial personnel also had their share of adventurers looking for something more exciting, or those who for some reason or another felt ostracised within metropolitan society, and therefore sought the colonies as a more practical alternative. Bernardin de Saint Pierre's novel *Paul et Virginie*, published in 1788 and regularly re-edited since, presents an idyllic Rousseauist and pre-romantic vision of the simple and natural life, in which all of the white heroes of the novel are in one way or another social outcasts unable to find their place in French society, seeking the colonies as a refuge.[12]

The ability of France to support not only its own population, but an immigrant one as well, combined with the lowest birth rate in Europe, meant that there was no push factor for ordinary French people who did not feel ill at ease within France to seek the colonies. As a general rule they could remain in France if they chose, and have full and satisfying careers in the junior civil service, in industry or on the land without the need to do a spell in the colonies. For the very ambitious, a tour in the colonies could be a valuable experience, and a means to gain more rapid promotion back in the hexagon, but not always talked about in detail when they had returned. In both phases of colonial expansion, France did not really have settlement colonies (as Britain had in North America or Australia), and a significant long-term feature of French colonialism was the lack of French emigrants in large numbers. Politically, colonialism was presented as a 'mission' and sometimes as a 'duty', but it was never a necessity or a means to deal with a problem of surplus population in the mother country. Thus the individuals who had actual first-hand experience of the colonies were mostly for one reason or another marginal within French society, either because they were from the Catholic right (in the Church or the army), a social circle which was gradually losing its influence throughout the period, or because as individuals they were not comfortable in French society, and thus chose the colonies as a way to get out of France. The fate of the poet Arthur Rimbaud who left Parisian artistic circles by the time he was 20 for a life of adventure in Abyssinia is a well-known example. Even more typical, though, is the sheer incomprehension that still surrounds his decision to emigrate back to metropolitan France. His destiny is usually understood as the tragedy of the 'artiste maudit', rather than as the natural fate of 'l'homme aux semelles de vent', as his friend Verlaine nicknamed him.[13] Many of those who left because of their marginality, of course, did not return to France, further limiting the communication of their experiences to the rest of the nation.

To suggest that the experience of French colonies was limited during what we have called the first phase is not to suggest that the French were not aware that they had colonies, or indeed that the French were not interested in the colonies. As we will see in more detail below, representations of the colonies were abundant, often presented in such a way as expressly to promote the vision of the colonies as an integral part of 'greater France'.[14] The question of the nature of the fascination with the colonies, of the conclusions which the population drew regarding whether the colonies were an integral part of France, a part of their own personal national experience or rather as something which was separate and outside of themselves – parallel to the national story as opposed to central to it, leads to much debate, and has certainly been coloured by hindsight after decolonisation. Much of the interest, even in the earlier phase, stemmed simply from curiosity about that which was exotic or different, and reinforced, if anything, the view that the colonies were still 'other'. Nevertheless, the population was quick to recognise the prestige which came with possessing colonies, proud of its successful civilising mission and the rank in world affairs which having colonies conferred upon it. To some extent they were even prepared on the surface to believe the official line that they were a part of France and that this was a great benefit for the nation. Those in the colonies however, whether 'natives' or those who had come from metropolitan France, notwithstanding the rhetoric of inclusion which permeated official French colonialist thinking, were never quite considered as 'us', and the preoccupation with domestic political tension over the nature of the regime often prevented the colonies from integration into the French mental space which was the nation.

The middle decades of the twentieth century constitute a second phase in the national experience of colonies, one of conflict over their relationship to the mother country that included both peaceful negotiations and lengthy, violent conflicts. The Brazzaville conference can be considered the turning point between the two phases. Held in January 1944, it drew together representatives from France's African colonies in order to discuss the future of the French colonial Empire once the war was over. During the Second World War, the colonies had for the first time temporarily acquired a centrality in French affairs due to the fact that they were the first to follow de Gaulle and the Free French, and served as a base for the raising of French armies to help the allies in the liberation of France and the final victory over the axis powers. While one might point out that the military contribution of these armies within the overall allied war effort was small, their very existence allowed France a place at the table of the victors and helped to salvage French pride which had suffered greatly after the defeat in 1940. When combined with the administrative autonomy which the colonies gained in practice (since they were cut off from Paris), the central role of the colonies during the war years and the contribution made by colonial troops towards the war effort created an expectation of greater recognition for the colonies within the French colonial Empire following the war through increased representation in Paris and a greater degree of autonomy in their own affairs. These expectations had not arisen out of nowhere, for already during the First World War France had called upon colonials to help in the war effort. In 1917, when faced with a disappointingly limited response to the call to arms, the government had more or less promised French citizenship to anyone who would volunteer to fight. The refusal to grant citizenship to veterans after the war led to disappointment, meaning that by the Second World War, frustration at unfulfilled expectations of France on the part of the inhabitants of the colonies had already been growing for some time. With this background as its context, de Gaulle had called the Brazzaville conference to discuss the future for France and her colonial Empire.

Increased expectations on the part of the colonial peoples in this context proved difficult to reconcile with the traditional French principles of individual assimilation and administrative and political centralisation across 'greater France'. The resolutions of the Brazzaville conference tried to cover up this contradiction (hypocrisy) through ambiguity, which only served to heighten tensions in the long run. Although flirting with models of association and hinting that colonies would have greater freedom in managing their own affairs, the idea of future self-government was categorically rejected and the political authority of France confirmed as applicable throughout the territory. The ambiguities were thus never resolved, and while the French authorities felt that they had clearly asserted that the future French Empire, re-baptised the French Union as a way of indicating the progress in policy, would remain a single block, many of those in the colonies felt they had been promised greater autonomy, which led to a sense of betrayal when that autonomy was not forthcoming. At the same time as raising expectations for the colonial peoples, the Brazzaville conference angered many of the French residents in the colonies and those with commercial interests in the colonies by suggesting that, in future, local life and liberties should be respected, education increased and forced labour brought to an end.

The next few decades saw the gradual disintegration of the French Empire, with individual colonies obtaining their independence one after another, sometimes following relatively peaceful referenda, while at other times following several years of intense fighting in wars of independence. In the immediate aftermath of the Second World War, France became involved in the War of Indochina, fighting a losing battle against communist nationalist insurgents over several years, largely with the aid of American funds, which led to French defeat and final withdrawl in 1955.[15] Faced with further independence movements, the government of Pierre Mendes-France was willing to let Tunisia and Morocco go, but drew the line at Algeria, where another war of liberation broke out, which would continue to escalate until Algerian independence in 1962. By the late 1950s, it had become clear that the French model of centralisation and unity across the colonial Empire was not working as well as its architects had hoped, and other colonies were offered a choice by referendum on 28 September 1958 – either to become assimilated into France as fully-fledged departments, to remain in what was to become the French Community with democratic self-government, or to have complete independence, but without any future French aid.[16] Only Guinea opted for complete independence in the first instance, with the greatest number of the colonies opting for the second choice. Most had achieved a significant degree of independence by 1961, and by the early 1980s, only ten territories remained a part of France, comprising the DOM-TOM (Départements d'Outre-Mer – Territoires d'Outre-Mer).[17] These departments and territories became, from a legal point of view, fully integrated parts of the French State with complete citizenship rights for all of the inhabitants.

If not at the conclusion of the Algerian War in 1962, then at least by the end of the 1960s the phase of decolonisation was essentially at an end, France having grudgingly accepted the reality of colonial independence. In terms of a national experience of the colonies, decolonisation could be considered more significant than the process of acquisition of colonies for a number of reasons. Firstly, because decolonisation brought direct experience of the colonies much more closely to the heart of metropolitan French society than had previously been the case. Conscripts were used to fight in the Algerian war, meaning a significant number of young Frenchmen had a direct and very often negative experience of the colonies, over which they had been given no choice and which they then brought back. Terrorist tactics and the threat that violence would become widespread inside the hexagon also made the conflict more real and personal for the average French citizen. Furthermore, as a result of decolonisation, many of those settlers and colonial administrators had returned to the hexagon after colonial independence. In some cases, such as the *pieds noir* from Algeria, they arrived in large numbers, keen to have their colonial experiences widely known. Secondly, decolonisation had a significant impact upon the political situation in France, not only bringing about the fall of numerous ministries, but of the Fourth Republic itself, directly resulting in de Gaulle's return to power, a new constitution and the creation of the Fifth Republic. Decolonisation also took place in a period when interest in and awareness of events beyond the metropole was steadily increasing, even when the events did not have a direct bearing upon France itself, both because preoccupation with the revolutionary legacy and the inherent primacy of domestic affairs were already diminishing, and because mass communication was becoming more widespread. Finally, in some ways decolonisation was a rejection of the French, of French ideas, morality and republicanism, which by being rejected could have forced some elements of the nation to question the original objectives more closely than in earlier periods when French superiority was far more taken for granted. The fact of several French military defeats as well as the failure of the French colonial project touched a few national nerves which its earlier successes had not been able to do. As is partly clear from this discussion so far, it was decolonisation in Algeria which was the most significant experience for the French nation, and a full discussion of both colonisation and decolonisation of Algeria follows below.

The final phase in this rough chronological division comprises the years following decolonisation, from the late 1960s to the present. Notwithstanding the loss of its colonies, France sought to maintain its former global sphere of influence through economic and linguistic means, as well as through a francophone bloc within international forums such as the UN. Most of the former colonies continued to use the French language and to preserve economic ties to France. The western African currency was shared across several former colonies and pegged to the French Franc.[18] At a time of increasing globalisation, an association of francophone states called 'la francophonie' was set up that includes primarily, but not exclusively, former French colonies, and which has its own institutional structure designed to promote cooperation, provide benefits and increase the influence of its members.[19] For France itself, the francophonie was conceived in part as a way of perpetuating French influence in world affairs in a similar way to Great Britain via the Commonwealth, while at the same time encouraging the development of francophone culture, such that the French language and sphere of economic and cultural activity would remain significant at the global level.[20]

The years which followed decolonisation also saw the earlier history of French colonialism rewritten. What had earlier been conceived as part and parcel to nation-building was reinterpreted as 'simply' colonisation, to which de-colonisation was then presented as an almost inevitable conclusion. This rewriting of the nation's past is what Todd Shepard described as 'the invention of decolonisation', reinterpreting the history of French colonialism as something which would lead to decolonisation, rather than to full integration in the French republican nation, thereby pushing the colonial past to the periphery of the national experience.[21] In this way French colonialism could be viewed as something which in any case was bound to be temporary, as opposed to a genuine desire to find a permanent arrangement which then went wrong. Kristin Ross writes of the 'instant archaism' of France's colonial policy – one day colonial history was central to France, and the next it was something outside national history, 'nothing more than an "exterior" experience that somehow came to an abrupt end, cleanly, in 1962.'[22] The fact that the colonial project of national integration had had many opponents all along made this reinterpretation that much easier to swallow during the decades which followed 'decolonisation'.

Ironically, it is not in the years immediately after the end of the colonial Empire that the French nation began most seriously to question and reflect critically upon its own colonial past. At the time of the wars of decolonisation and following the return to France of settlers from the former colonies, the self-examination of the French conscience was primarily preoccupied with the occupation, collaboration and France's role in the deportation of the Jews and the Holocaust, leaving little room for a serious examination of France's colonial past. It was not until the final decade of the twentieth century that the history of French colonialism began to be seriously questioned by the wider public. This self-reflection was sparked partly by the wave of immigration from the former colonies and the rise of Jean-Marie Le Pen's National Front with its anti-immigration discourse and corresponding public debates within France, and partly by the rise of Islamic fundamentalist terrorism across the globe. Contemporary problems encouraged French intellectuals, artists and the general public to take an interest in the colonial past as a way of achieving greater understanding of their present crisis. By this time, debates about the Holocaust had also led to questions about crimes against humanity in other contexts, one of which was former colonial empires across the world. Thus such problems as the use of torture by the French army during the Algerian war received wider publicity and encouraged further national reflection about the French colonial past. Given the centrality of events in Algeria for all three of the periods of French colonialism, and in particular the last two, we will now examine Algeria as a case study of the experience of colonies, before turning to the wider impact of the mass of colonial images in modern France as a whole.

Algeria

Given the diversity of the colonial Empire, no individual colony can be considered 'typical' in every respect, but it will be useful to examine this single colony and the way it contributed to the overall experience of colonialism for the French nation. While never acquiring a label such as the 'jewel of the Empire' as India was for Great Britain, Algeria can be considered the most important of the French colonies, not only because of its size and proximity to the hexagon, but also because of the fact that it was the closest France had to a settlement colony, and that the process of decolonisation was the most acute, painful and had the most far-reaching consequences for the French nation. Algiers and much of the coastline was taken in 1830 by Charles X in an (unsuccessful) attempt to save the Restoration Monarchy, with the remainder gradually brought under French domination over the next 40 years. By the start of the Third Republic, there were almost 300,000 European settlers living in Algeria, and its 2.4 million km^2 made it the largest single French colony (even if most of this was desert).

As the only real settlement colony in the French colonial Empire with a high population of European immigrants (although many were not French), Algeria benefited from a special administrative regime, much more closely integrated into France, with the territory divided into three departments. The laws of citizenship were complex, and designed to distinguish legally between the French citizen, the 'indigenous person' and the 'foreigner'. The idea was the separation of nationality from citizenship, such that the indigenous population became French subjects, without the rights of citizens.[23] When scrutinised closely, such a policy is completely incompatible with republican discourses about rights and citizenship, but was a way of creating a legal loophole to permit the official, juridical and administrative treatment of the colony as if it were French, by simply according the majority indigenous population a separate status to guarantee that they remained inferior. Under this regime, the capacity to grant citizenship in individual cases, where cultural assimilation had taken place and loyalty tested first, permitted the French government to hold up naturalisation as a reward, meanwhile preserving a democratic majority.[24] In spite of the slowness of the process, much of the French republican leadership in Paris held a vague but sincere belief that the republican system would work and that assimilation, naturalisation and citizenship would be the genuine result of the colonial policy, in the long term. In the shorter term, however, frustration on the part of the indigenous population at what they perceived as repeatedly withheld promises of citizenship, combined with unreasonable requirements of religious conversion before naturalisation were significant contributing factors in the rise of the nationalist movement which would eventually lead to the Algerian War.

In addition to their belief in the republican colonial system, French pride in the 1950s, already suffering from the defeat in 1940, was also unwilling to suffer another blow. This was the time of the early Cold War and the emergence of a world dominated by superpowers, a context in which France was even less inclined to suffer change in its colonial Empire which might remove it from the forefront of the international scene or suffer it to lose prestige. Of all of its colonies, Algeria was the least likely for France to want to relinquish, given not only its size but also the powerful lobby in Paris representing the wealthy settlers from the costal region, numbering 1,250,000 by this time. Nationalist demands from indigenous leaders were ignored and promised reforms not forthcoming, hence the outbreak of armed revolt in 1954. The fighting went in waves, and overall can be characterised as a war in which guerrilla tactics, extreme violence, terrorism and the use of torture all played their part. One dimension of the subsequent national self-examination regarding this war was due to the intensity of the violence and the justifications given for the tactics used.

Within the French camp, objectives differed significantly over what would be an acceptable outcome of the Algerian War, and a great deal of distrust built up between the settler population (known as the *pieds noirs*), the army and the French government, each of whom feared that the others might act in a way that would betray their interests. The *pieds noirs* feared a negotiated settlement, the army feared withdrawal of government support, and the government feared that the war would escalate out of control, or that the army leadership would act on its own initiative or even stage a coup. Meanwhile the pressure from anti-colonial intellectuals and the public was increasing upon the government to negotiate peace and to end the war, giving up 'French Algeria' if necessary.[25] Following the seizure of power in Algiers and the setting up of a Committee of Public Safety on 13 May 1958 under the leadership of General Massu, de Gaulle was able to use the ensuing confusion to return to power supported by all sides, each of whom felt that he would be able to bring about a solution to the war to their satisfaction. In spite of having given the opposite impression at first, once in power, de Gaulle stalled for some time, eventually pursuing a policy of negotiated peace followed by gradual withdrawal leading to the end of the war and the recognition of Algerian independence in 1962.

The aftermath of Algerian independence was to leave a feeling of betrayal among the *pieds noirs* population as well as segments within the army, both of whom had sacrificed a lot for their vision of a 'greater France' which included Algeria, only to be let down at the last moment. Many returned to France, bringing their frustration and disillusionment with them, as well as a lingering longing for that which had been lost, now referred to in this context as 'Nostalgérie' (Nostalgeria). In spite of the inconsistencies, ambiguities and downright contradictions between theory and practice, over the years large amounts of energy and resources had gone into making Algeria 'French', and seeking a way to ensure that it was considered an integral part of the French nation itself.[26] For many among the republican elite, this key colony could become a normal French region, thereby demonstrating the efficiency of the republican nation-building project and the French model of integration and citizenship, visibly proclaiming its success to the world.

Algerian independence epitomised the failures already described for colonialism generally – not only that of the colonial project, but also that of French nation-building in general. It is furthermore symbolic of the altered vision of France; no longer 'greater France', even in the rhetoric, but simply the French nation reduced to the metropole. The fact that one could claim that the failure of what can be called the national project in Algeria could be simply downgraded to the failure of the colonial project was thus a face-saver for French republicanism.[27] In this sense it was not the republican model of nation-building itself, based on gradual individual assimilation through education that failed (which might force a questioning of key republican values!), it was only that these values were incompatible with a project of colonialism. Faced with failure in Algeria, French leadership conveniently 'forgot' that for well over 100 years Algeria had been seriously considered as more than a mere colony, but as a part of the nation itself.

The national experience of French colonialism in Algeria, given the centrality it had once had for nation-building in 'greater France', has meant that feelings run deeper with regard to Algeria than any other former French colony. While many among the French political elite would love to see the subject drop, underlying unease repeatedly manifested itself in both cinema and the interest of intellectuals, artists and scholars in questions of torture, collaboration, and the French experience of colonialism in Algeria. Memoirs and other writings emanating from those who experienced it, including those in former leadership positions seeking to justify their position, encouraged greater public reflection, especially upon the war years.[28] The contemporary issues of immigration from the Mahgreb and the tensions surrounding Islamic fundamentalism, both within France and across the globe, also served to increase interest in these questions of past French behaviour as a colonial power. While the general interest in the history of the French colonial past has been heightened because of Algeria, changing attitudes toward former French colonies in light of decolonisation meant that by the end of the twentieth century the colonial experience in general has come to be thought of as 'how France behaved' (externally and towards 'others'), as opposed to a part of the internal experience of the French nation.

Colonial Representations in France

The fact that the dominant discourse in France, particularly after 1962, presented the French colonial Empire as marginal to the French national experience in the modern period, does not imply that images and representations of the colonies were not widespread. On the contrary, colonial imagery can be found in all areas of French cultural life throughout the three periods described above. From literature and music, cinema and theatre through to cuisine, architecture, museum displays, advertising and public commemorations, evidence of French colonial heritage can be found. Sites of adventure, excitement and mystery, the colonies serve as the setting for countless works of fiction (textual and visual), drawing upon the fascination of the public with the exotic. In addition to writers and filmmakers, other artists and composers also found inspiration in the colonies, combining colonial images or traditions with their own work in search of greater inspiration and as a way of pushing outwards the boundaries of their own work.[29] All sorts of commercial goods, exotic and otherwise, were advertised using images from the colonies,[30] food from around the colonial Empire was slowly introduced into metropolitan France,[31] and colonial places, events and heroes were commemorated in the French landscape through such means as street names.[32] Found in so many areas of national cultural life, the sheer volume of references to the French colonies meant that a significant proportion of the French population had at least experienced the images of the colonial Empire and had an awareness of it through the prism of representation.[33]

While many of the representations of the colonies appeared spontaneously through literature, art or business, the state also produced propaganda for the promotion of the colonies and the colonial agenda within France, both to encourage simple support for their colonial policy of national expansion, as well as to help recruit Frenchmen to do the work on the ground in the colonial Empire.[34] The colonial pavilions at the Great Exhibitions were among the most popular, encouraging the authorities to host an entire 'International Colonial Exhibition' in the Bois de Vincennes in Paris in 1931, in order to showcase the achievements of France in its colonies, and to enhance the knowledge and involvement of the French population in the project of 'greater France'. Perhaps the best confirmation of the quest to conceive of the colonies as an integral part of the nation can be found in the inaugural speech for the exhibition given by Marshal Lyautey, in which he stressed the idea of union: 'union among the European powers, union among the French in support of the colonial enterprise and union between France and the colonial races.'[35] Between the Exhibitions, displays in permanent museums were available for public consumption. Following the heightened interest in the colonial past, a new museum was inaugurated in early 2006 which brought together the collections from several other museums, presented in a way which corresponds to new attitudes towards the French colonial past.

The material which was presented in the more serious representations of the colonies was informed by the work of explorers and scientists, for whom the colonies were subjects of extensive research, made available to the educated elites as well as in a more diluted form to the general public. Courses on anthropology included studies of the colonies and colonial peoples, and some of the most famous French scientists had work published which included work on 'colonial peoples'.[36] Scientific enquiry and to some extent artistic endeavours to represent the colonies were fuelled by a desire to capture 'authenticity' from the colonial experience.[37] Conclusions were used to support the racial theories of the day, and there was much debate about the implications of racial difference in terms of the ability to genuinely assimilate and adopt 'French' values.[38]

Representations of the colonies could be found throughout French artistic, scientific, literary, visual, private and public culture during the period, often supporting the desire by authorities to use such imagery to promote the idea of 'greater France' as a unified whole. By the middle of the twentieth century, the sheer pervasiveness of images certainly increased familiarity with the colonies. After decolonisation, as discussed for the specific case of Algeria, it is easy to look back and see the representations as increasing familiarity while at the same time reinforcing the sense of difference, otherness or at least marginality of those in the colonies, rather than their 'Frenchness'. It is always difficult, given the alterations resulting from hindsight, to distinguish between representations of 'other' and representations of diversity within the category of 'self', both of which could certainly apply to the representations of the French colonies during the years before decolonisation. It is certainly not true though, that the French colonies were considered as marginal simply because of ignorance or lack of interest, as the quantity and variety of interest in the colonies throughout the period was manifestly great, but it was a fascination with 'other' rather than self.

Conclusion

In spite of the rhetoric of 'greater France', the word which perhaps best sums up the colonial experience for the French nation is marginality: colonialism was marginal politically and marginal in the sense of those within French society who participated in it. Representations often portrayed it as marginal (if not downright 'other'), and the great historical reinterpretation which followed decolonisation has been oriented towards stressing the marginality of the colonial experience for the French nation. In this sense, it parallels the Revolution, where marginal experiences have been repeatedly downplayed in the construction of national experiences. French colonialism, in official discourse at least, was not marginal for the longest time, but has been reinterpreted as such given its subsequent failure, presenting the colonial story as having always been outside the main nation's experience, rather than admitting to an inherent flaw in earlier concepts of the nation.[39] Following decolonisation, colonialism became dissociated from mainstream republicanism, and the colonial Empire replaced 'greater France' both as label and concept. In many ways it is the legacy of the colonial Empire which has been problematic for France, more than the reality had ever been, as the nation increasingly questioned its colonial past and its implications.

However much attempts to deny it have become accepted, the colonial experience is nevertheless important for modern France, be it 'unconsciously' as asserted by Elizabeth Ezra,[40] or as a result of the increasing interest in the colonial past as the years went by.[41] One of the principal complications in the relationship is that colonial attitudes were founded upon the French sense that the underlying objective was to take French liberty to the rest of the world, freeing their peoples through education and assimilation into French republican culture. The process was motivated by the belief 'in the existence and value of a unique French identity which could be transferred to other countries and other peoples, and the consequential belief in the universality of the French scale of values.'[42] There was never any sense that the French might learn something themselves, so their experience of the other was always as a kind of parent or tutor. When the messages were not received, or not received well, there may have been puzzlement, but it took a long time to arrive at the next step of wondering why. Even then, many of the questions are simply vaguely curious, not motivated by the suspicion that perhaps something was wrong with the republican message in the first place. The moral self-righteousness that underpinned French colonial messianism was partly abandoned as if it had not happened, as much of the debate shifted to immigration and regionalism and the partial internal breakdown of the republican assimilationist model. The next section of the book will examine French identity, and some of the diverse images which have been captured within it.

Notes

1 Note that throughout this chapter, the terms used will be 'colonial Empire' and 'colonial imperialism' as distinguished from 'Empire' and 'imperialism' which are often used to describe the internal organisation of France into an Empire under the Bonapartes.

2 By 1815, only Martinique, Guadeloupe, French Guyana, Réunion, Saint-Pierre and Miquelon, as well as fishing rights in Newfoundland and a few trading posts in Senegal and India remained from France's first colonial empire.

3 The general disdain for colonial issues was described by Flaubert in his *Dictionnaire des idées recues:* 'colonies s'affliger quand on en parle'.

4 'The Empire is only a childish fantasy.' Weygand felt that the colonies were nowhere near advanced or equipped enough to support the kind of military campaign which would be necessary to turn the tables on Germany.
5 The exile of the revolutionaries of 1848 as well as that of many Communards to the Empire contributed also partly to its incoherent image in France well into the twentieth century.
6 Clemenceau for instance used to loudly denounce the cost of the imperialistic project: 'cette charge formidable dont notre malheureux budget est écrasé' and to claim 'une politique du pot au feu'. But Jacques Marseille has shown how much that argument was flawed (until at least the 1930s) in *Empire colonial et capitalisme francais, histoire d'un divorce.*
7 For a general history of French colonialism, see Robert Aldrich, *Greater France: A History of French Overseas Expansion* (Basingstoke: Macmillan, 1996), and for a less conventional approach to French colonial history through biographies, see Barnett Singer and John Langdon, *Cultural Force: Makers and Defenders of the French Colonial Empire* (London: University of Wisconsin Press, 2004).
8 See Jean Bouvier, René Girault and Jacques Thobie, *L'impérialisme à la française 1914–1960* (Paris: Editions de la Découverte, 1986) for a thorough comparison of British, German and French styles of colonialism.
9 For a more complete comparison, see Timothy Baycroft, 'The Empire and the Nation: The Place of Colonial Images in the Republican Visions of the French Nation', in Marin Evans, ed., *Empire and Culture: The French Experience, 1830–1940* (Basingstoke: Palgrave, 2004), pp. 148–60.
10 For more on the republican attitudes, see Alice L. Conklin, *A Misison to Civilise: The Republican Idea of Empire in France and West Africa 1895–1930* (Stanford: Stanford University Press, 1997), and Nicolas Bancel and Pascal Blanchard, 'Les origins républicaines de la fracture coloniale', in Blanchard, Bancel and Sandrine Lemaire, eds, *La fracture coloniale: La société Française au prisme de l'héritage colonial* (Paris: La Découverte, 2005), pp. 33–43.
11 For more on the debate surrounding schools, see Chapter 2.
12 See also Chateaubriand, *Atala* and even more so *René* (1802) for further examples.
13 'The condemned artist', 'The man with soles of wind'.
14 For two excellent studies of the changes over time of the place of the colonies within visions of the French nation, see Herman Lebovics, *Bringing the Empire Back Home: France in the Global Age* (Durham and London: Duke University Press, 2004) and Elizabeth Ezra, *The Colonial Unconscious: Race and Culture in Interwar France* (Ithaca and London: Cornell University Press, 2000).
15 For more on decolonisation, see Anthony Clayton, *The Wars of French Decolonisation* (London: Longman, 1994), Raymond F. Betts, *France and Decolonisation 1900–1960* (Basingstoke: Macmillan, 1991), Rod Kedward, *La Vie en Bleu: France and the French since 1900* (London: Allen Lane, 2005), and also below on Algeria.
16 Algeria also had a referendum, but was not given the third option.
17 'Overseas Departments and Overseas Territories'. For more on the DOM-TOM, see Robert Aldrich and John Connell, *France's Overseas Frontier: Départements et Territoires d'Outre-mer* (Cambridge: CUP, 1992).
18 See J. F. V. Keiger, *France and the World since 1870* (London: Arnold, 2001), pp. 211–13.
19 On the institutional structure of the francophonie, see William W. Bostock, *Francophonie: organisation, co-ordination, evaluation* (Melbourne: River Seine Publications, 1986).
20 On politics, linguistics and culture, see B. Jones, A. Miguet and P. Corcoran,

Francophonie: Mythes masques et réalités. Enjeux politiques et culturels (Paris: Publisud, 1996); on francophone literature and culture by world region, see Kamel Salhi, *Francophone Post-Colonial Cultures: critical essays* (Lanham: Lexington Books, 2003). For evidence of the longevity of French thinking on the matter, see Auguste Viatte, *La francophonie* (Paris: Larousse, 1969).

21 Todd Shepard, *The Invention of Decolonisation: The Algerian War and the remaking of France* (Ithaca and London: Cornell University Press, 2006).

22 Kristen Ross, *Fast Cars, Clean Bodies: Decolonisation and the Reordering of French Culture* (Cambridge, Mass.: The MIT Press, 1995), pp. 9, 196.

23 See Laure Blévis, 'Droit colonial algérien de la citoyenneté: conciliation illusoire entre des principes républicains et une logique d'occupation coloniale (1865–1947)', in *La guerre d'Algérie au miroir des décolonisations françaises* (Paris: SFHOM, 2000), pp. 87–103; and Emmanuelle Saada, 'Citoyens et Sujets de l'Empire Français: Les usages du droit en situation coloniale', *Genèses: Sciences socials et histoire* 53 (Dec 2003), pp. 4–24.

24 See Laure Blévis, 'La Citoyenneté Française au miroir de la colonisation: Etude des demandes de naturalisation des "sujets Français" en Algérie coloniale', *Genèses: Sciences socials et histoire* 53 (Dec 2003), pp. 25–47.

25 For more on this debate see James D. Le Sueur, *Uncivil War: Intellectuals and Identity Politics During the Decolonisation of Algeria* (Philadelphia: University of Pennsylvania Press, 2001).

26 See Jonathan K. Gosnell, *The Politics of Frenchness in Colonial Algeria 1930–1954* (Rochester: University of Rochester Press, 2002), and Nabila Oulebsir, *Les Usages du patrimoine: Monuments, musées et politique coloniale en Algérie (1830–1930)* (Paris: Editions de la Maison des sciences de l'homme, 2004).

27 See Shepard, *The Invention of Decolonisation.*

28 See, for example, Sylvie Thénault, *Histoire de la guerre d'indépendance algérienne* (Paris, 2005), Martin S. Alexander, Martin Evans and J. F. V. Keiger, eds, *The Algerian War and the French Army, 1954–62: Experiences, Images, Testimony* (Basingstoke: Palgrave, 2002); Philip Dine, *Images of the Algerian War: French Fiction and Film 1954–1992* (Oxford: Clarendon Press, 1994); and Jean-Pierre Rioux, ed., *La Guerre d'Algérie et les Français* (Paris: Fayard, 1990).

29 See, for example, Annegret Fauser, *Musical Encounters at the 1889 Paris World's Fair* (Rochester: University of Rochester Press, 2005).

30 See Dana S. Hale, 'French images of Race on Product Trademarks during the Third Republic', in Sue Peabody and Tyler Stovall, eds, *The Colour of Liberty: Histories of Race in France* (Durham and London: Duke University Press, 2003), pp. 131–46.

31 This was not always successful, but nevertheless happened. See Erica Peters, 'Indigestible Indo-China: Attempts to Introduce Vietnamese Food into France in the Interwar Period', in Evans, ed., *Empire and Culture*, pp. 91–102.

32 Robert Aldrich, 'Putting the Colonies on the Map: Colonial Names in Paris Streets', in Tony Chafer and Amanda Sackur, eds, *Promoting the Colonial Idea: Propaganda and Visions of Empire in France* (Basingstoke: Palgrave, 2002), pp. 211–23.

33 For further examples of colonial images, see the numerous excellent chapters in Evans, ed., *Empire and Culture*, covering film, photography, food, music, dance and propaganda.

34 For several perspectives, see the many good chapters in Chafer and Sackur, eds, *Promoting the Colonial Idea.*

35 Dana Hale, 'The "Ballet blanc et noir": A Study of Racial and Cultural Identity during the 1931 International Colonial Exhibition', in Ibid., p. 103.

36 See Daniel J. Sherman, '"Peoples Ethnographic": Objects, Museums, and the Colonial Inheritance of French Ethnology', *French Historical Studies* 27, 3 (Summer 2004), pp. 669–703, and Emmanuelle Sibeud, '"Negrophilia", "Negrology" or "Africanism"? Colonial Ethnography and Racism in France around 1900', in Chafer and Sackur, eds, *Promoting the Colonial Idea*, pp. 156–67.

37 On authenticity in music and opera, see Fauser, *Musical Encounters*, pp. 143, 217–20, and for links between the racial theories of the day and music, see p. 73.

38 For more on race, see Chapter 10 on immigration.

39 Shepard, *The Invention of Decolonisation.*

40 Ezra, *The Colonial Unconscious.*

41 See Lebovics, *Bringing the Empire Back Home* for a full analysis of the place of the colonial experience in modern France.

42 Denis Ager, *'Francophonie' in the 1990s: Problems and Opportunities* (Clevedon: Multilingual Matters Ltd, 1996), p. 87.

PART III

INVENTING FRENCH IDENTITY

The common national historical narrative as well as the meaning of the experiences described in the first two sections were perpetually invented and reinvented, in part by the republican nation-builders in order to create a coherent and unified French republican nation, and in part by those promoting alternative visions of the French nation whose mythologies have occasionally made it into the defining images of France. In spite of its diversity and even inconsistencies, a powerful consensus nevertheless emerged from the republican camp, producing a coherent image of modern France. Internally, the French nation was one and indivisible, founded upon the principles of cultural assimilation, acceptance of the core republican values and identification with the 'common' national history derived from the 'common' national experiences. Those coming from outside needed to identify with them in order to be fully French. Externally, France was viewed by its people as a leading nation upon the world scene, with its deep historical roots and profound sense of its civilising and enlightening mission across the globe.

In this final section, we will be examining the question of French identity, seeking to clarify who and what has been considered as genuinely French, and upon which ideas, images, symbols and characteristics their identity has been built. We will explore the links between the coherent identity invented by the republican nation-builders (based on republican universality and designed to promote assimilation) and the more spontaneous and diverse images that emerged, some of which they used in their creative project of nation building, others of which they tried to dismiss, discredit and exclude. It will cover images which have become an important part of the national mythology, a source of identification for the members of the French nation. The unity of attitudes towards what constitutes French identity and the universality of any particular trait, myth or image of the nation are never possible to ascertain completely, and diversity across the population in time and space certainly exists. Nevertheless, some elements of identity are widespread and receive a great deal of public recognition (official and unofficial) and it is these which shall be examined here.

The first chapter will examine those cultural images in their great diversity which are the most common, and which have come to be closely associated with French identity. In each case, the cultural images will be analysed in terms of their significance for the nation as a whole and the degree of unity or consensus around them. In the following chapters, we will examine specific groups whose identity was in some way or another problematic for the French nation, since at least part of their identity was at odds with the core republican values at its heart. The second chapter will deal with the question of religion, covering the difficulties of inventing a national identity which could incorporate different religious groups, particularly given the anticlericalism of vast numbers of republican nation-builders. The final chapter will explore more directly the question of reconciling a supposedly universal identity with differences of gender, ethnic origin and regional diversity.

9

Cultural Representations

Since the publication of Eugen Weber's *Peasants into Frenchmen*, the project of nation building in France has often been conceived and analysed in terms of the impact of modernisation and the degree of cultural assimilation of the population. The original arguments presented rural and backward France taking on and accepting French national identity gradually through the medium of language and culture, brought to them by the roads, railways, republican primary schools and compulsory military service. While the chronology of the process has been questioned, and the 'top-down' model greatly nuanced through the analysis of regional and other forms of bottom-up cultural development, there can be no question that not only the French language itself, but all of the elements of 'high culture' are a great source of French pride and of paramount significance to French national identity. Furthermore, in the context of the democratisation of political life and of the increasing involvement of the masses in the political process, cultural assimilation remained central to the democratic and specifically republican myths of the French nation and to their conception of citizenship. Within the great overarching republican histories discussed in Part I and the national experiences covered in Part II, high French culture has a central role in this process of assimilation, creating the link between the people as French citizens and the State.

But, while high culture, national histories and sophisticated images are important elements of national identities, they are also composed of a myriad of small symbols and images which recall the nation to its members and to others outside. While a handful, such as the flag, are overtly created by the political elite, many arise more or less spontaneously, coming to represent the nation, or at least to be closely associated with the nation as both conscious and unconscious references or representations. Such individual representations of a nation can be found in all areas of culture, from art, literature and cinema through to dress, sport and everyday objects, each contributing to the complex processes involved in the creation of French national cultural identity. This chapter will examine such representations in some detail, their origin, the process which led to them acquiring a symbolic 'national' status, the ability of different groups to manipulate or influence the choice of images and their particular symbolism, as well as the implications of cultural representations for the development and evolution of French national identity.

French Mythologies

Before analysing specific examples, it will be useful to make several observations about the nature and the origin of national cultural representations. Culture in its diverse forms is one of the most significant links between the individual and the nation. It is through cultural practices and representations that the nation seems the most real to its members and from which national identity is derived and articulated in detail on a day-to-day basis.[1] In this particular case, through the recognition and identification with particular cultural forms thought of as 'French', individuals associate themselves in their own minds with the nation as a whole, thereby 'imagining' the national community with themselves as an integral part of it.[2] Since most of the nation is unknown and unfamiliar to any particular individual, that individual imagines the rest of the nation through the cultural representations around her, learning to recognise in them and attribute to them a 'national' meaning, thereby creating a community in the mind held together through culture. As these cultural forms become charged with 'national' connotations, they become 'French' literature, cuisine, art, sport or landscape, and as individuals become familiarised with them and begin to recognise and identify with them with the national undertone in place, so the strength of a national identity increases.

The process whereby cultural objects, practices or their representations acquire 'national' meaning has several dimensions. The first step is familiarisation with the representations. Not all will become foundations of national identity for given individuals, but by their familiarity will be present in the conscious or subconscious, ready to serve as bonds between individuals, common reference points linking them to the greater national identity in particular circumstances. As already suggested, such familiarisation may or may not be the result of deliberate policy through education or propaganda on the part of the national authorities expressly seeking to foster and enhance national identity among a chosen elite or the popular masses of the nation. It is a process in continual evolution. The ways in which culture seems meaningful, and comes to acquire significance through analysis and interpretation is conditioned by a variety of circumstances, not least what has gone before.[3] The most obvious example is national history, gradually constructed and perpetually reinterpreted over the decades such as to resonate with overtones of a particular political flavour, but all of which recall the French nation. Individual representations of the nation, from anniversaries and heroes through to Marianne (the female incarnation of the Republic) and the tricolor flag, are made familiar to the nation through commemoration, repeated representation in statues, street names, on postage stamps and in school lessons in such a way as to encourage an automatic mental link to the abstract nation with each new viewing, constant reminders of what the nation is held to stand for.

The transformation of cultural objects or practices into symbolic representations of the nation is not always the direct result of deliberate actions on the part of the agents of the state, but may be made in a variety of ways. Artistic developments, be they visual, musical, architectural or literary may be billed as typically 'French' to enhance their reputation, or later, when once they have become famous, be associated with the nation through the label 'French classics' as a way of augmenting the nation's artistic prestige. Associations between culture and the nation may originate in advertising, the media, in the production of particular types of goods, where repetition of claims to 'Frenchness' creates symbolic associations. It may also be through the placing, for example, of existing French symbols, or the use of red, white and blue as colours for products which come to be seen as French. Such associations are therefore not always political either, in that cultural representations may be billed as national for artistic or commercial reasons. Thus the control and manipulation of cultural representations of the nation does not always originate among the political elites, but can also arise in a climate of increased nationalisation of the entire cultural sphere of reference.

Thus individuals' links to wider society come to be conceived increasingly through the prism of cultural objects and practices held to be representative of the nation, some of which are deliberately created by the nation-building elite, but many of which originate more spontaneously in the artistic and commercial spheres. The attribution or acquisition of a 'national' signification in every small reminder of everyday cultural life is what Michael Billig has called 'Banal Nationalism'. With increased facility for mass communication, all kinds of cultural representations are nationalised in banal ways – not banal in the sense of unimportant, but only in that their association with the nation is unobtrusive, and neither obvious at first glance nor necessarily noticed at all.[4] In this way, news and weather reports make reference only (or primarily) to France; sports leagues, the reception of radio or television programmes, educational qualifications and diplomas, car licence plates, advertising campaigns, and many supermarket or other retail chains are all specific to France, and exist consciously and subconsciously within national space as continual reminders of the nation. France becomes the frame of reference for everyday life, and permeates elite and popular culture.

The attribution of 'national' meaning to cultural objects and practices and their dissemination as sources of national identity throughout the population can arise in a number of ways. It may be that individuals become familiar with new representations or cultural objects, or learn to participate in cultural practices which are new to them, already charged with national significance from the outset. This is what has been classically called cultural assimilation, be it the learning of the French language, the celebration of 14 July, the recognition of busts of Marianne, reading the 'national' press, the discussion of who is leading in the Tour de France or the purchase of a souvenir Eiffel Tower. Through education or mass communication, new cultural representations charged with 'French' symbolism of varying degrees of subtlety or directness become more predominant, and individuals come to recognise themselves as a part of the national community through them.

On the other hand, pre-existing cultural practices, objects or representations, already familiar, may come to acquire national meaning, symbolising the nation where they had not done before through what can be called cultural appropriation. This is particularly true of local or regional cultural practices, including traditional dress or cuisine, which come to be thought of as typically 'French'. Again this may be due to the conscious efforts of the nation-builders, who for example stressed regional diversity as typically French in school textbooks, in such a way that regional cultural particularity could in fact contribute to French national identity, or through gradual cultural evolution, as with the example of the Basque Beret coming to be seen as typical 'French' peasant headwear.[5]

Given the scope of culture with national, or at least potentially national connotations, and the vast diversity of people who in some way or another consider themselves French, individual representations will vary greatly in their importance within the national community at any given moment in time. Some cultural representations come close to 'universal' recognition, but many are restricted to a particular sub-section of French society; even if everyone is aware of them, the degree of personal identification with each one will vary. In this sense, each particular combination of cultural representations from which individual French national identities are derived will be unique. Among those cultural objects and practices which approximate universal representation of the nation, many examples can be found. The most obvious are those that are drawn from French political and historical culture, actively promoted by the state and its schools, including not only the flag, national holidays and so on, but also political and military heroes, from Napoleon onwards. They were of course introduced in history classes, but it was the widespread visual representations of historical events and people which contributed most significantly to the strength of French history as a source of national identity, particularly as many of these visual representations were produced for artistic or other reasons, rather than as nationalist propaganda.[6] From works of art in galleries through public plaques, monuments and statues, posters, book jackets or on commercial products throughout France, such images create links to 'national' history and form a solid foundation for French identity.

Beyond the obviously political, French identity also resides in such symbols as the Eiffel Tower. Although it can be linked to republican history because of the fact that it was built for the Great Exhibition in Paris in 1889 to commemorate the centenary of the Revolution, the Eiffel Tower nevertheless primarily demonstrates French technological and industrial advancement, and has come to be perhaps the most widely known individual representation of France. Appearing in just about every possible way, even the most sloppy or vaguely allusory reproduction of its distinctive shape causes anyone the world over to think of France. Placed as a logo on any product associates it directly with the French nation. While this may be most often for purposes of international marketing, the French themselves are also acutely aware of the Tower's Frenchness.

A host of other small images of France drawn from daily life have been mythologised over the years through repeated cultural representations. In the mid-1950s, the French philosopher Roland Barthes wrote a series of essays about a handful of such objects or images which had attained what he described as mythical status.[7] Barthes' examples came from several areas of French culture and included 'good wine', the traditional 'steak-frites', the new Citroën and the Tour de France, all of which were held to be 'typically French'. In the summer of 2004, the French magazine the *Nouvel Observateur* published a special issue trying to update Barthes' work to the early twenty-first century, and included a host of other examples of cultural representations which had attained mythical status in contemporary France.[8] Not all of the images were specifically associated with Frenchness, as some were international or indeed universal modern myths that had resonance in France, such as 'fat', 'piercings', reality TV, Harry Potter or Lady Di. Many though were particular to France, and were equivalent to the specifically national myths of Barthes. These included the CAC 40 (the French stock market index), 'Les Bleus' (the national football team), the 35-hour work-week and the 'rentrée littéraire', the tradition of publishing a series of new French novels every September which gets widespread public and media attention. One need not think too hard to come up with a host of further examples of national myths, from camembert cheese or the baguette through to the little moustache and the beret already mentioned.[9]

Probably the greatest single example of French culture which supports French identity is the French language itself. The language of reason and the Enlightenment, the language of love, the language of diplomacy and high society, one of the key attributes of French identity is tied up with speaking the French language (well) and basking in its international glory. Regulated by the Académie Française, that great bastion of style and linguistic correctness, the language itself is held to reflect the national characteristics of rationality and beauty, and the only one in which certain ideas can be expressed. From the report of the abbé Gregoire during the Revolution through every subsequent regime, the spread of the language to the entire population was recognised as of central importance for the French nation and was at the heart of every push towards assimilation, be it of the regions, the lower classes or of immigrants.

Closely tied to the French language, the great literary tradition is also of central importance to French identity. Not only the works themselves, but the sheer number of French writers – poets, playwrights and novelists – form a source of pride and national identity. In the 1942 resistance novel *The Silence of the Sea*, the author has the German officer in the story in great admiration before a bookshelf full of French literature. He begins to list the authors, asking rhetorically which is the greatest, and concluding that with so many to choose from, it is impossible, for 'they jostle each other like the crowd at the entrance to a theatre till you don't know which to let in first.'[10] Even when no longer actually read by the majority of the population, knowledge of the great literary canon still contributes to identity, and the names of authors and their works remain familiar representations of the greatness of the French nation. The fact that many authors were also intellectuals participating in French public life in one way or another merely heightens identification with them.[11] National cultural images are also drawn from within works of literature in the form of characters, from swashbucklers such as the Three Musketeers or Cyrano de Bergerac, through to Jean Valjean, Madame Bovary, le grand Meaulnes or La Petite Fadette. Many of the great classics, especially those of the nineteenth century, were set in historical periods in such a way that they also reinforce the national historical narrative, so important and central for French identity, in addition to their literary merit and contribution to literary cultural identity. Several authors' collected works aimed specifically at presenting their vision of France in all of its richness and detail, such as Honoré de Balzac's *Comédie Humaine*, Emile Zola's *Les Rougon-Macquart* and Marcel Proust's *A la Recherche du Temps Perdu*. Each illustrates the overlap between the fame of the writer, the works and their presentation of French history and society in combination as united representations of the French nation and as sources of French identity.[12]

Along similar lines to literature, French cinema and music also serve as sources of national cultural identity. Much of the repertoire of French cinema draws its inspiration from the national literary canon and builds upon it, but as the cinema industry grew throughout the twentieth century, French film became an important cultural phenomena in its own right. As with literature, the prestige was felt to be good for the nation, and it provided even more stimulating images with which individual members of the French nation could identify. Film stars became icons of Frenchness, the likes of Brigitte Bardot and Catherine Deneuve, of

Figure 8 Catherine Deneuve as Marianne

Jean-Paul Belmondo and Gérard Depardieu representing ideals of French femininity and masculinity respectively. Such stars became famous through their participation in French national cinema, becoming icons of Frenchness, as well as international celebrities, without needing to emigrate to Hollywood in order to do so.[13] The fact that several leading French actresses were used as the models for busts of Marianne, the female incarnation of the republic, demonstrates the power of their images, and the desire of the republican authorities to harness their prestige in the cultural sphere to the service of the republican nation-building agenda (see Figure 8). Notwithstanding interest in American films, French identity also receives a grounding from the distinctiveness of its cinema, styles such as the New Wave or *mode retro* with their quality and particularity enhance the conception of France as an important centre of creativity in cinema.[14] Individual 'auteur' filmmakers, who write and produce their own works, also contribute significantly to this individualism and the creative tradition in French filmmaking. As the home of the Lumière brothers who invented the technique, France can further claim to be the birthplace of cinema, in addition to any pride from later achievements in the films themselves.

The quest to identify, reproduce and popularise specifically French styles in music as representations and sources of Frenchess was significant already in the nineteenth century. Building upon certain past composers or musical styles which could be labelled as 'French' in origin, be they of the more elite opera and classical traditions or from folk music originating in the various regions, a national musical heritage was constructed over many decades.[15] In some cases, as with the right at the turn of the twentieth century, music was overtly used as a 'realm of ideological debate in which [nationalists] could propagate their conception of French cultural identity.'[16]

Music as a source of French identity did not only grow out of politically sponsored initiatives, though. From the traditional folk song, or *chanson populaire*, a solid tradition of popular music grew out of the late nineteenth-century cabaret and continued to evolve throughout the twentieth century into a distinctive tradition of singer-songwriters which became 'a vibrant element of French national identity.'[17] Whether Edith Piaf singing of love, Georges Brassens adapting the literary tradition to a modern idiom, Jacques Brel investigating life and death or Renaud embodying French traditions of political protest and anarchism in song, 'chanson' music and lyrics speak profoundly of France and its cultural, social and indeed political specificity in a form quintessentially French. It is the 'very Frenchness' of this musical tradition, and in particular 'its emphasis on the deployment of sophisticated lyrics in the French language' which both guarantee its popularity within France, and secure it as a cultural form at the very centre of modern French identity.[18] Even outside musical traditions could become adapted into particularly national forms, as Jeffrey H. Jackson has shown for jazz.[19]

In addition to literature, cinema and music, France has long been held as the home of art and creativity in general, inspiring many of the great schools in the visual arts in particular. From the classical and romantic styles through to the Impressionists, Dada or the more abstract variants of the twentieth century, the fact that France is held to be the home of excellence and innovation in painting or sculpture, and French artists the trend-setters of the avant-garde is a great source of pride and cultural identity in France. In some cases of course, it is more than just the style, artist or place of production which is typically French, but the subject matter as well. As with literature, many are drawn from French history or what come to be seen as typically French landscapes and settings, visual art thus contributing both directly and indirectly to evolving conceptions of Frenchness. From the great historical paintings of the Revolutionary and Napoleonic years of Jacques-Louis David and the idyllic 'French' scenes and settings of the Impressionists through to lesser known depictions of some element of national life, visual representations of France and the French have repeatedly been central to conceptions and debates surrounding French identity.[20] Museums and art galleries, through their collection and exhibition of visual representations of the nation, play an important role in selecting and presenting them to its members, acting as 'repositories and embodiments of the nation's collective memory and identity.'[21] Where the state controls the process of selection, attempts can be made to deliberately choose which images receive widespread attention, although given the scale of visual production throughout the period, complete manipulation has always proved difficult.

Although never considered art of the highest quality or merit, perhaps the most obvious example of art helping to invent national identity is through portraiture. True for the depiction of national heroes, but even more so when not of named individuals but of ostensibly 'national' types, such representations have contributed regular and widespread images of 'the French' with which individuals can identify. From the nineteenth-century bourgeois, miner, army officer or peasant through to the businesswoman or waiter of the late twentieth century, regular collections of 'pictures of the French' have been produced.[22] The goal was to portray individual French subjects, 'abstracting them from their context in life (even if referring to it) in such a way as to emphasise their membership of the collection rather than their presence in a real life.'[23] In this way representations of the various social or regional stereotypes were closely linked to the nation, and focus put upon defining French men and women to create and enhance national identity. Outside specific collections, the works of countless individual artists also contribute to the portraiture of what come to be visualisations of national types, such as Jules Breton's rural France.[24]

More perhaps than any of the individual artistic or literary genres themselves, France as the home of the creative arts is one of the most central and enduring images of French cultural identity. Not only are the French themselves highly creative forces in the world of art, but the fact that artists and writers from all over the world come to France for inspiration merely increases national self-importance. This is particularly true of the capital city. Billed as the centre of the artistic world throughout the nineteenth and twentieth centuries, 'gay Paris' not only provides space for writers and artists to work, but the cultural life of the city – in the theatres, galleries and opera houses, on the boulevards, in the cafés, shops and parks – is held to be the richest anywhere. Parisian haute couture has long defined fashion in dress for the rest of the world, through its trademarks, fashion magazines and what could be seen on Parisiennes, representing 'the height of luxury, chic and feminine beauty.'[25] French designers were also the first to have prêt-à-porter collections and thus bring fashion to the masses. France in general and Paris in particular are regularly represented as the centre of the creative artistic and fashionable world, an enduring image of the French nation central to all conceptions of cultural identity. Outside the capital, France is also home to the Côte d'Azur, where the wealthy and beautiful of the world come to relax and to be seen.

Many enduring national cultural representations can also be found outside the realms of 'high' artistic and literary culture, in the realm of everyday life and more popular culture. France is held to be the home of excellent cuisine, with the restaurant emerging as a bastion of this French cultural supremacy, a symbol of French distinctiveness.[26] National culinary traditions and standards are held up not only in restaurants and cafés, but also bakeries, butchers shops and private homes throughout the nation. The most famous French chefs are known by name, and France is the home of excellent cheese, fine wine, and an entire host of 'produits de terroir' – local specialities which gain in terms of marketing from associating themselves with the national tradition of quality eating. Boasting the two-hour lunch break as a way of promoting the French tradition of eating a good, relaxing meal, the French reinforce their national identity every time they sit down at a table.

French identity is also confirmed through national representations in sport. French professional leagues are followed assiduously, as is French success in international events, from European and World championships through to the Olympic Games. Victory as the host nation in the 1998 football World Cup is perhaps the most well-covered, but by no means an isolated event cementing national identity. The fortunes of 'Les Bleus', as their national team is known, are closely followed throughout the nation, and sporting heroes have become significant role models for the young. Not only at the national, but also at the local and regional level, sport has contributed to identity. In Philip Dine's study of rugby football, he contends that it 'played a significant role in the imaginative construction of the contemporary French nation.'[27] France also plays host to international calibre events like Roland Garros (the French tennis Open) and perhaps most importantly the Tour de France. The Tour not only brings the attention of the world to France, but it focuses attention upon the entire national territory.

National cultural representations can also be found in business and scientific realms, and French identity is also drawn from the particularly French business culture often referred to as 'l'exception français'. A highly State-regulated economy, greater job security, established trade unions, shorter working hours and more vacations combined with higher productivity form a part of the 'French economic model' which is consciously maintained and conceived in opposition to what the French think of as the 'Anglo-Saxon' liberal model. When involved in European or global trade and business negotiations, the French exhibit a strong sense of identity derived from their own way of doing things, the distinctiveness of which they are out to preserve. National brands are also common representations of Frenchness, with companies also using national symbols to anchor their products as specifically French, a pairing which reinforces national identity while helping to increase sales. One of the most successful such companies was the French tyre company Michelin, whose marketing strategies both encouraged and profited from French patriotism, associating the company with a series of nationalist causes and making its products icons of Frenchness.[28] In addition to creating consumer goods which are part of the national cultural baggage, overall business success in the modern world itself is also a source of French pride. This is particularly true when combined with scientific or technological advances. Perhaps the largest national icon in the area of technology is the Eiffel Tower which has already been mentioned, but French cars and other consumer goods also contribute, as do discoveries made in France in the area of pure science or technology.

'French Culture' as an Invention

Thus from high art to popular sport, cultural representations contribute significantly to French national identity as the images through which the French see themselves, and the links they perceive between themselves and other members of the nation. Cultural representations have come to define and then regularly reinforce the Frenchness of cultural objects and practices, some of which are created and spread through the population with the national meaning already in place, while others acquire it through association and national appropriation. Through this process of general familiarisation and nationalisation of cultural representations, they enter into the national mythology. Just as the more complex invented national histories discussed in the first section are mythical, and the personal experiences interpreted mythically as national experiences as examined in the second section, so the status of cultural objects as representative or symbolic of the nation is mythical. Not in the sense of falseness, but in that no proof is needed for this close association with the nation, merely repetition with certainty, such that their Frenchness goes without saying. As Roland Barthes put it, myth hides the fabricated quality of the status of cultural things: 'it purifies them, it makes them innocent, it gives them a natural and eternal justification, it gives them a clarity which is not that of an explanation, but that of a statement of fact.'[29] In this way the examples of cultural representations which are considered 'typically French' need never have 'proof' that they are French, it simply goes without saying, and constant repetition is itself enough proof of the truth of the matter. To be French is to identify oneself with French cultural representation, which can be found everywhere, in every area of cultural life.

The fact that national cultural representations are so very central to French identity helps to explain the position of France and the French with respect to the supposed threat of 'Americanisation' and the perception of cultural imperialism coming from across the Atlantic to stamp out French culture, its distinctiveness and the life-blood if its identity. France has a long tradition of 'posing cultural issues in universal terms', [30] turning a Hollywood film, GM crops or a McDonald's restaurant into a threat to the very essence of Frenchness, since they encroach on France's perceived cultural space. The threat seems even more tangible if individual French men or women are at any time seen to be choosing to consume a cultural product which is 'not French'. Because French identity is so strongly rooted in its culture, France has repeatedly sought to have cultural industries exempted from GATT negotiations, preferring to keep some measure of protectionism to ensure that, even if some American culture has penetrated the hexagon, there will always be a protected space for French cultural production.

The role of cultural representations and the process of cultural assimilation and appropriation in the creation of French identity fits in with the republican model and vision of the French nation. Acceptance of enlightened republican principles and the adoption of French cultural traits were held to be important hallmarks of the republican nation, explaining the importance placed upon language and national history, and the belief in the possibility of assimilation into the nation. While the growth and formation of national identity is far more complex than the simple top-down assimilation model often acknowledges, it does demonstrate the significance of historical and cultural identity for the French nation. This identity is also, of course, in constant evolution, as the nation is continually re-invented around the cultural representations of the various groups and individuals it has assimilated through a reverse process of appropriation and re-branding as French of specific cultural features such as local traditions and images. The emergence of certain representations as typically French is the result of a complex process, deliberate actions and spontaneous or coincidental cultural change.

The remaining chapters in this section will deal with the ways in which French identity has been negotiated with several groups who, for a variety of reasons, found themselves on the frontiers of Frenchness, who could be seen as outside the national circle from certain points of view, but who nevertheless managed to find a way to not only acquire French identity themselves, but also to be recognised by others as French. We will first turn away from diverse cultural representations to the specific example of religion, and the complex relationship between religious and national identity in France.

Notes

1 For more on the way in which identity is articulated by culture, see Michael Kelly, 'Introduction: French Cultural Identities', in Jill Forbes and Michael Kelly, eds, *French Cultural Studies: An Introduction* (Oxford: OUP, 1995), pp. 1–7.

2 See Benedict Anderson, *Imagined Communities,* 2nd Ed. (London: Verso, 1991).

3 See Jill Forbes, 'Conclusion: French Cultural Studies in the Future', in Forbes and Kelly, *French Cultural Studies*, p. 295.
4 Michael Billig, *Banal Nationalism* (London: Sage Publications, 1995).
5 For more on the distinction between assimilation and appropriation, see Chapter 11 and Timothy Baycroft, *Culture, Identity and Nationalism: French Flanders in the Nineteenth and Twentieth Centuries* (Woodbridge: The Boydell Press, 2004). On the school textbooks, see Anne-Marie Thiesse, *Ils Apprenaient la France: L'exaltation des régions dans le discours patriotique* (Paris: Editions de la Maison des sciences de l'homme, 1997).
6 For extensive exploration of these questions, see the special issue of *French Historical Studies* devoted to 'French History in the Visual Sphere', 26, 2 (spring 2003), and in particular the introductory article, Daniel J. Sherman and Mary D. Sheriff, 'Convergences: Visualising French History', pp. 173–83.
7 Roland Barthes, *Mythologies*. A. Lavers, trans. (London: Vintage, 2000), pp. 142–3.
8 *Le Nouvel Observateur* hors-série entitled *Mythologies d'aujourd'hui: notre époque est façonnée par des myths* (juillet–août 2004), containing 38 short articles.
9 Collections seeking to collect lists of such cultural objects and symbols include Alex Hughes and Keith Reader, eds, *Encyclopaedia of Contemporary French Culture* (London and New York: Routledge, 1998) and John Ardagh with Colin Jones, *Cultural Atlas of France* (Oxford: Facts on File, 1991).
10 Vercors, *The Silence of the Sea/Le Silence de la mer*. James W. Brown and Lawrence D. Stokes, trans. (Oxford: Berg, 1991), p. 79, first published 1942.
11 See Chapter 5.
12 Beyond the primary works, for Zola, see William Gallois, 'Emile Zola's Forgotten History: *Les Rougon-Macquart*', *French History* 19, 1 (March 2005), pp. 67–90.
13 See Ginette Vincendeau, *Stars and Stardom in French Cinema* (London and New York: Continuum, 2000).
14 For a good overview, see Guy Austin, *Contemporary French Cinema: An Introduction* (Manchester: Manchester University Press, 1996).
15 For a full analysis of the process, see Katherine Ellis, *Interpreting the Musical Past: Early Music in Nineteenth-Century France* (Oxford: OUP, 2005), in particular pp. 147–78.
16 Jane F. Fulcher, *French Cultural Politics & Music from the Dreyfus Affair to the First World War* (Oxford: OUP, 1999), p. 16.
17 Peter Hawkins, *Chanson: The French singer-songwriter from Aristide Bruant to the present day* (Aldershot: Ashgate, 2000).
18 Hawkins, *Chanson*, p. 63.
19 Jeffrey H. Jackson, *Making Jazz French: Music and Modern Life in Interwar Paris* (Durham: Duke University Press, 2003).
20 For a specific discussion of the process, see Richard Thompson, *The Troubled Republic: Visual Culture and Social Debate in France, 1889–1900* (London and New Haven, Yale University Press, 2004).
21 Rebecca J. DeRoo, *The Museum Establishment and Contemporary Art: Politics of Artistic Display in France after 1968* (Cambridge: CUP, 2006), p. 5.
22 For a full analysis, see D. W. S. Gray, 'Pictures of the French,' in Sheila Perry and Maire Cross, eds, *Voices of France: Social, Political and Cultural Identity* (London and Washington: Pinter, 1997), pp. 75–99.
23 Gray, 'Pictures of the French', p. 81.
24 Annette Bourrut-Lacouture, *Jules Breton, Painter of Peasant Life* (New Haven and London: Yale University Press, 2002).

25 See Valerie Steele, *Paris Fashion: A Cultural History,* 2nd Ed. (Oxford: Berg, 1999), p. 274.
26 See Rebecca L. Spang, *The Invention of the Restaurant: Paris and Modern Gastronomic Culture* (Cambridge, Mass.: Harvard University Press, 2001).
27 Philip Dine, *French Rugby Football: A Cultural History* (Oxford: Berg, 2001), p. 4.
28 See the excellent study by Stephen L. Harp, *Marketing Michelin: Advertising and Cultural Identity in Twentieth-Century France* (Baltimore: Johns Hopkins University Press, 2001).
29 Barthes, *Mythologies*, pp. 142–3.
30 Jeremy D. Popkin, *A History of Modern France,* 3rd Ed. (Upper Saddle River, NJ.: Pearson, 2006), p. 312.

10

Religion and the French Republic

'France, oldest daughter of the Church, what have you done with your Baptismal promises?' asked Pope John-Paul II, child of patriotic and Roman Catholic Poland, of the French youth of the mid-1980s. Indeed, it can be argued that for the post-Revolutionary French nation, the question of its ambiguous religious identity has been one of the most difficult to resolve. Alternative presentations of France as the nation of secularism and religious tolerance on the one hand, and the most Catholic of nations on the other give rise to uncomplimentary, if not positively contradictory images, leading to what has become known as 'Les deux Frances' (The two Frances). Indeed the battle between republican secularism, a central value of the Revolution and revolutionary heritage, and the traditional Catholicism of the French elite and peasantry, was an ever-present factor in the social and political conflicts used to define the French nation throughout the modern period. Each of the two perspectives furthermore accords France's religious minorities different places within the larger national identity, and renders their identity and relationship with the nation that much more complicated.

In the following pages we will firstly analyse the evolution of modern France's attitude towards its traditional Catholic identity. We will explore the tensions between the various post-revolutionary French regimes and the Roman Catholic church, their combat for the 'soul' of France as well as their successive attempts at finding compromises. We will particularly look at the significance of the republican ideal of secularism during the build-up to the separation of the church and State in 1905, and to the associated relegation of French Catholicism to the 'private' sphere, in order to analyse the marginalisation of the religious dimension within modern France's quest for its identity. Within the general context of the dechristianisation of post-modern Europe, we will also emphasise the place that the Catholic heritage and experience did nonetheless play, politically, culturally and in the social and personal life of the majority of French men and women. This chapter will finally explore the experiences of some of France's non-Catholic religious minorities (Protestants, Jews and Muslims) and their attempts to secure a place within French national identity.

The Combat for the French Soul

During the *ancien régime*, in spite of numerous episodes of tension between the Papacy and the French crown, there could be no doubts about France's Catholic identity. Catholicism had not only been the religion of the majority of the French population, but it had been the religion of the French State for many centuries. Philosophically, the French absolute monarchy was founded upon the idea of the divine right of kings (inspired by St Paul's epistles) and emotionally it relied heavily on Roman Catholic symbols and images to legitimise its authority. Among many others, Clovis's baptism by St Remi in 496, the Capetian choice of the 'fleur de Lys' (associated with the Virgin Mary) as their emblem and Louis XIII's decision to place the French kingdom publicly under the protection of Mary, all clearly expressed that Christianity, and specifically Catholicism, was the foundation of France's political power.[1] The closeness of the ties led Enlightenment thinkers such as Voltaire to conclude that the Roman Catholic church was too compromised with the ancient order to be saved: it was regarded as 'l'Infâme' and needed to be crushed. But those political reformers knew very well that the theologico-political question was a difficult one, and in spite of their staunch anti-Catholicism, neither Voltaire nor Rousseau ever conceived of a State without any religious grounding. The last chapter of Rousseau's *Social Contract* is entitled 'On civic religion', in which he expresses his respect for the false but socially efficient 'civil religions' of the Greeks and Romans, his contempt for Catholicism, and asserts that society needs a civic religion to teach duty to the citizens, retaining a 'minimum' ethical deism as the social base of his ideal state.

During the early stages of the French Revolution, the church's relationship with the newly established and reform-minded National Assembly quickly turned sour. Through its 'Civil constitution of the clergy' of 1791, the National Assembly attempted to promote a transfer of loyalty of the French clergy towards the new regime, a move which met with great hostility in Rome and was finally condemned by the Papacy. In the following years, a violent movement of de-christianisation, that has been described as the 'most profound social effect' of the Revolution, swept across the country and contributed to the creation of a situation of civil war, in the Vendée in particular.[2] Fearing a counter-revolutionary backlash and inspired by Rousseau's ideas, Robespierre proposed a short-lived new 'civil religion' – the cult of the Supreme Being – while at the same time establishing the free exercise of all religions. Finally, after more than a decade of turmoil, Napoleon secured an agreement with the Papacy in the form of the Concordat in 1802. Through it, he accomplished what the early revolutionaries, inspired by the abbé Gregoire, had failed to achieve: the restoration of the French Catholic church, but under the strict control of the French State.[3] The concluding agreement notwithstanding, the religious conflicts of the revolutionary years, from the 'patriotic curés' to the massacres of priests and nuns in 1792, had left their mark on France's religious identity. Furthermore, Protestants and Jews had experienced a new range of political and civil rights thanks to the Revolution, leaving the relationship between the Catholic church and its 'eldest daughter' inalterably changed.

The 1802 Concordat with the Catholic church lasted until 1905, and this renewed political recognition began with a period of more harmonious relations between the church and the French State. The restoration of the monarchy in 1815 was followed by a relatively successful attempt by the Catholic church at a parallel religious restoration. Gradually, Catholicism regained some of its lost ground although under a new and more emotional form. A new generation of priests influenced by early romanticism had taken the lead in the French church, refusing the old-style Gallic ideals that came to be associated with Classicism, Jansenism and the strict intellectualism of Port Royal in the seventeenth century. They chose their main political allies amongst the conservative and reactionary forces supporting the restoration monarchy (later called legitimists), and even the events of 1830 and 1848 did not change this basic trend of Catholic renaissance. The political and Catholic Restoration is the historical background of Stendhal's novel *Le Rouge et le Noir*, according to which title the heroic time of Napoleon's Empire (symbolised by the red of the imperial army uniforms) had been replaced by the dark age of the clerical power seizure (symbolised by the black of the clerical outfit). Stendhal's descriptions insist on the tensions within Catholicism between the old Jansenists and the new Jesuit power.

Even after the fall of the restoration monarchy, the church's position in relation to the state remained stable and even improved somewhat. In spite of its initially strong anticlerical flavour, the liberal regime of the July Monarchy maintained a relatively peaceful alliance of throne and altar, as anticlericalism gradually declined among the French bourgeoisie as it had declined under the preceding regime among the aristocracy. In 1849, after the Papal temporal power had been confiscated in the turmoil of the Italian revolution, even the newly elected French conservative republican regime, keen to secure the support of the church, sent troops to Rome to help the Pope. Following the coup d'état, as a general rule Napoleon III's Second Empire was also on good terms with the socially conservative and anti-republican Catholic church of its day. It was at this time that the church regained some of its influence in education, when the

Falloux law of 15 March 1850 facilitated the return of clergymen to teach in primary schools, while church representatives were also given seats on the *Conseil Superieur de l'instruction Publique.* It was this apparent compromise by the Imperial power with the church which helped to push Victor Hugo away from the romantic legitimism of his youth to become the prominent voice of republicanism and anticlericalism he became in his later years.

It is thus certainly possible to speak of a Catholic Reconquesta between 1802 and 1870 in France, but that Reconquesta was in fact the work of one particular faction within the French church. The ultramontane and reactionary camp gradually assumed the dominant position, leaving the social and liberal wings of the French Catholic church marginalised and isolated. Attempts at liberalisation from within and reconciliation with a post-Revolutionary France that still identified itself with the Revolution were routinely unsuccessful, prevented by the dominant reactionary camp as well as Rome's refusal to endorse any compromise with modernism or the republic until the 1890s. Even the lyrical illusion of 1848, when the French clergy had seemed to accept the new regime, the village curés dutifully accompanying their parishioners to the urns and, in Paris, some Catholic priests blessing the trees of liberty and speaking in the name of the 'proletaire de Jerusalem', was short lived. By the elections of 1849, it was clear enough that the church was, as a whole, a socially conservative institution led by a politically reactionary elite. The itinerary of Lamennais from his clerical youth, through his liberal years to his solitary old age on the margins of French Catholicism is another example of the difficulties experienced by the early supporters of a reconciliation of the church and the French post-Revolutionary State. The Second Empire saw the reinforcing of the conservative wing within the church, following the lead of the papacy. In 1864, Pius IX (restored with the help of the French army), ignoring the accommodating approach suggested by Paris, published his *Syllabus* condemning modernism and went on six years later to proclaim the dogma of papal infallibility. It was also during these years that Veuillot's powerful, conservative Catholic newspaper *L'Univers* gained a strong sphere of influence, further solidifying the political position of reactionary Catholicism.

Because of the dominance of its reactionary and ultramontane wing and in spite of the newly re-discovered fondness of the French educated public for the liturgical beauties and emotional side of Catholicism (expressed for instance in Chateaubriant's *Genie du Christianisme*), the relative return of the church to the forefront of the political scene after 1815 did not bring with it a full return of Catholicism as a central tenet of French identity.[4] Successive regimes after 1830 presented themselves to be, to a certain extent, the heirs of the Great Revolution, and they were therefore unable or reluctant to put Catholicism at the core of modern France's national identity. The economic liberal elite, as well as the republicans, although having little in common, shared a strongly suspicious attitude towards that reactionary clerical elite often symbolised by the 'Jesuits'. As long as the French church continued to support a return of the legitimist monarchy and maintain its 'foreign' ultramontane allegiance, it could be portrayed by its political adversaries as 'anti-national', and was therefore handicapped in its struggle to promote the idea of a 'Catholic France'. The opening scenes of Victor Hugo's *Les Miserables* (criticised by some of his political allies like George Sand for being too lenient towards the church) express very clearly the crucial issue for the progressive camp: Monseigneur Myriel is a genuinely saintly Catholic priest, but has to acknowledge the truth and kneel in front of the deathbed of a former member of the 1790 National Assembly suspected of regicide. As long as the church remained critical of republicanism and the values of the Revolution, it could not be recognised as integral to the French nation by those on the political left.

While a right-dominated church might have preserved its position within the Second Empire, avoiding further conflict with the state was much less likely in the Third Republic which emerged out of the imperial defeat of 1870. In contrast with the events of 1848, there could be no doubt about the strong anticlericalism of the Paris Commune in 1871. Following its violent and bloody suppression and a five-year period of Royalist and Catholic-lead 'moral order', openly proclaiming repentance for a century of treason to the nation's traditional Catholic and monarchic heritage, the republican camp which finally won the 1876 and 1877 elections was relatively anticlerical, setting the tone for the years that would follow. The clerical party, which had openly supported the restoration of an *ancien régime*-style legitimist restoration with its strong Catholic national identity, had undoubtedly lost, and in such circumstances the days of the 1802 Concordat seemed numbered.

The first republican reforms that attempted to deal with this national religious identity question were the Ferry educational reforms of 1881–2, removing all primary classes from the hands of the clergy in state-funded schools. Little further reform was made for several years, but after the church's very public stance on the side of the anti-Dreyfusards supporting the army High-Command during the Dreyfus Affair, and the subsequent victory of the Radical republicans in the 1898 elections, tension between church and state escalated considerably. Pressure was put upon local priests to follow government instructions, many religious teaching congregations were expelled from the national territory (a lot of them moving to nearby Belgium) by Emile Combes from 1902, and after three further years of crisis between the French government and the Vatican, the legal and constitutional separation of the French State and the Catholic church was declared in 1905, marking the end of the Napoleonic Concordat. The long standing republican ideal of a secular state had become a legal reality, with no official State religion, and faith defined as a purely private affair. Republican secularism affirmed the equal treatment of all religions by the state, but also the total autonomy of the political sphere from any religious issue or institutions. Thus following over one hundred years of tension and gradual political marginalisation, the official exclusion of the Catholic church from the sphere of power had finally been achieved.

The republican camp thus emerged victorious from the principal religious conflict of the nineteenth century, whilst having resolutely refused to consider Catholicism as the core of the nation's identity. At best Catholicism was a religion among others, deserving no special place in French national identity, and at worst the 'Roman' church, led by a foreign Pope with foreign interests in mind which should be regarded as a downright threat to the French nation from within. The church itself, by and large, continually represented an alternative vision of the French nation in opposition to the republican one, perpetuating images of France as the eldest daughter of the church and continuing to include support of the legitimist monarchy and opposition to republicanism and the revolution as part of French Catholic identity. For them, the identity of the true French nation was Catholic, just as its natural leadership was the king, making the republicans simply usurpers both of the State and people. Even though, after the death of the legitimist heir, the relatively fragile liberal and social wings of the Catholic church were pushing for the 'ralliement' of Catholics to the republican regime, supported by the publication of the Papal encyclical *Aux milieux des Sollicitudes* in 1892, the dominant position of Catholics remained hostile to the republic. Following the Dreyfus Affair and the separation in 1905, the reactionary Catholics who had determined Catholic politics throughout the previous century were still the dominant force within the French church, and Catholic acceptance of the positivist and agnostic Republic and of the republican French nation remained only on the fringes.

In spite of the decided republican victory in the political arena, culturally, France was still an old Catholic country where daily life remained rooted in Catholic traditions and symbols. The church bells continued to regulate the rhythm of the daily life of individuals as well as that of the nation. Catholic religious holidays – not only Christmas and Easter, but also Ascension Day, Pentecost, Assumption Day, All Saints' Day as well as a host of local feasts – were maintained by the State and marked out on the calendar.[5] Saint's days continued to receive regular references, the medieval cathedrals spread over the territory were loved by all, and along with more modest village churches, roadside crosses at rural crossroads and on city street corners, as well as the names of many streets themselves remained an essential part of the national landscape and reflected the depth of the French nation's Catholic heritage. Republican rhetoric notwithstanding, most of the French population could see itself as Catholic at the same time as French without any sense of contradiction. The majority of those in rural France in particular remained attached to their Catholic faith and heritage, and continued to understand their French identity as implicitly including Catholicism.[6] In spite of its relative inability to really reach out to the new emerging urban working classes, the church had nevertheless regained a lot of lost ground among the bourgeoisie, the army, women and to a certain extent the intellectual class during the nineteenth century. And, as the dust settled on the law of Separation, it appeared that, in spite of these new political circumstances, a new equilibrium in the church and State relationship could be achieved that would, to a certain extent, acknowledge France's traditional Catholic identity.

The Appeasement of the Religious War

Before enough time had elapsed following the Separation for a new relationship to become solidly established between the church and State, the First World War had shaken the whole of French society and re-cast the position of the Catholic church in France. As early as 1914, the republican State itself had abandoned any ideas of totally excluding the various religious confessions from the public and political life of the wartime nation. On the battlefields or on the home front, their status as moral leaders was quickly recognised and the 'Sacred Union' government spanned every political party, every sphere of the French population and included representatives of the still socially powerful Catholic church. From the initial call to arms and throughout the war, religious motivations and rhetoric were added to nationalist ones to keep the population on the side of the war and motivated to fight. Religious imagery, in particular Joan of Arc, if not positively reproduced, was at least no longer contested as appropriate for the French nation in such a time of war. The church also fulfilled a role in terms of chaplaincy for the French army, and both church and State recognised each other's rights when it came to burying and eulogising over those who had died for the nation. Thus through the First World War, the Catholic church and all major confessions had established more amiable rapports with the republican State, which in return had accepted them as elements not only of some French citizens' private lives but also of the nation's public identity, given the public and necessary support for the war which they had provided. In the decades which followed the war, Catholic presence in government and administrative circles increased slowly but steadily, whilst overt hostility between republicans and Catholics correspondingly declined.[7]

The combined changes brought about by the separation of the church and State, and the partial reconciliation between the Republican nation and French Catholics brought about by the First World War formed the backdrop to altering the balance of influence and internal dynamics of the French Catholic church as well. Over the course of the twentieth century, the relative weight of the different internal wings – liberal, social and reactionary – would alter. The infighting was particularly acute during the 1930s, after which time Catholicism in France could no longer be automatically equated with social and political conservatism, but had moved beyond to new ways of thinking.[8] These changes were far reaching, and had implications for the church's attitudes with respect to the Republic, the papacy and French society, as well as for the vision of the French nation encouraged and promoted by Catholics.

The first significant change was that the reactionary, monarchist and ultramontane version of Catholicism that had dominated the French church during the nineteenth century became gradually marginalised. After having lost the battle for its vision of the French nation, society and political constitution in the years which led up to the separation in 1905, it never again regained the centrality within French Catholicism which it had enjoyed. This faction did not disappear completely from the scene by any means, but most of its attempts at regaining the higher ground would eventually prove calamitous. It enjoyed brief periods of resurgence, for example, during the ideological effervescence and rise of anti-parliamentarianism and fascism during the 1930s, and as a part of the ultra-collaborationist alliance against Bolshevism during the Second World War, but its long-term influence on mainstream public life and national identity remained marginal, even in entirely Catholic circles. Remaining on the fringe of the religious right, the reactionary belief in a French Catholicism at the core of a 'pure' French identity, characterised by antisemitic and racist tendencies, did not disappear altogether from French politics, but could still be found articulated among the support for the traditional extreme right parties, such as Jean-Marie Le Pen's *Front National* or Philippe de Villiers' *Mouvement pour la France* right into the twenty-first century. But even among these groups, references to this form of traditional and essentially mythical French Catholicism have found very little clerical support outside marginal groups such as Monseigneur Lefevre's integrist movement. Furthermore, although the leaders of the *Front National* make a point of celebrating Joan of Arc every year on 1 May, this wing has essentially shed its ultramontanism, turning to a solidly nationalist (and often xenophobic) form of Catholicism. Highly critical of Rome, it was more influenced by Maurras' Catholic atheism that saw the church not as the true bearer of Christ's message of universal redemption but as a powerful rampart against all democratic and individualistic evils, than by their more genuinely religious antecedents.

As the influence of the reactionary wing of Catholicism declined throughout the twentieth century, this left the way open for the social and liberal wings to vie for the dominant position within French Catholic circles. During the nineteenth century, the French Catholic church had already acquired a social wing, increasingly preoccupied with the social and human consequences of the industrial revolution, as well as a liberal wing, which sought to reconcile Catholicism with fundamental democratic values and modernism in general. Remaining relatively marginal within the church alongside the more dominant reactionary group up until the twentieth century, the new circumstances following the separation and the First World War meant that they had a greater chance for development. Over the next few decades, while Catholic liberals would remain marginal within their church, social Catholicism would develop enough to gain a strong political influence not only in France, but throughout much of continental Europe.

In France as elsewhere in Europe, social Catholicism was by no means a rootless apparition in the twentieth century. On the contrary, it had grown from the core of old stock Catholicism, as much as right-wing nationalist Catholicism had. For most of the nineteenth century social Catholicism was outside official organisations, seen in the paternalism of Catholic industrialists or in the works of some of the charitable orders.[9] Developing in the early decades of the Third Republic, the movement was given a great boost following Leo XIII's 1891 encyclical *Rerum Novarum*, stating that it was a duty of all Catholics to help workers. Papal sanctioning led to a more formalised, coherent 'social doctrine' developed for the church, and organised structures began to expand within France, overtly dedicated to a 'social' agenda.[10] In the latter category, examples include the Association for Catholic Youth, formed by Albert de Mun, which had grown to 140,000 members by 1914. *Le Sillon* (The Furrow), founded by Marc Sangnier in 1894, was both an organisation and a publication, spreading Christian democratic ideas throughout France. Although it was disbanded in 1910 for cooperating too closely with those outside of the church (essentially socialists and communists), individuals who had been members went on to form a variety of other organisations with similar agendas in the decades which followed.

The papal support during the 1890s for what had been a minority voice within the French church facilitated the political trajectory from legitimism to Christian democracy. A decade later, as the reactionary right suffered the setback of the separation, even more space was created within French Catholic circles for this form of political, economic and social thinking.[11] Christian Democrats were elected to the Chamber of Deputies, with reasonable levels of success and popularity, sustained over several decades, and helped steer the French Catholic church away from reaction towards this form of social Catholicism. Henri Lorain, Léon Harmel and the abbés democrats, Jules Lemire and Hippolyte Gayraud, are among those who followed this path to political success in the years which followed *Rerum Novarum*. The position of the social Catholics implied loyalty to the republic, acceptance of the separation, and an attempt to adapt the church to modernity and the social realities of industrialisation by finding a particularly Christian or Catholic means of reconciliation. They sought to bring Christian charity to the working classes, supporting fraternity among the workers while at the same time rejecting atheistic, confrontational socialist theories of how to improve the lot of the working-classes. An important dimension of their position was that they continued in some measure to oppose capitalism, at least in terms of its excesses, its overt placing of wealth as the central value and the poverty which came as a result. Thus social Catholicism did not exactly propose a complete reconciliation with the capitalist republic, but sought new tactics to deal with modern problems that worked within the republican system but which preserved what they saw as Catholic values.

Unlike French Protestantism, French Catholicism had never been particularly comfortable with the modern values of individualism or capitalism. With the demise of legitimism, Social Catholicism represented an alternative which was able to propose solutions to the problems of French society without wholly abandoning earlier Catholic social values.[12] There had long been a liberal wing on the periphery of the Catholic church, espousing a more thorough and genuine acceptance of the 'modern' values of individualism and capitalism, seeking to reconcile them with Catholicism. These Catholic liberals remained a small and quite uninfluential group within a church dominated by those who felt that even if the church could accept some modern values, that did not mean it had to accept everything, but could and indeed should resist elements of modernity which went against their vision of Catholic values.

At the same time, this lack of ease with and resistance to individualism and capitalism can partially explain that in spite of repeated condemnations by the Papacy, French Catholics formed numerous 'liaisons' with several modern ideologies sharing its opposition to post-revolutionary, capitalist, bourgeois modernity: fascism, socialism and even occasionally Marxism. During the 1930s, the Communist Party famously followed a policy of 'hands held out' towards French Catholics, and in the 1950s the experiment of the Worker Priests was an attempt by the church to make inroads into the working classes.[13] Even the links that the church made with Marshal Pétain's government during the Occupation can be seen partially in this light, when many leading Catholics among the laity and the clergy were willing to cooperate and support many of the initiatives of the National Revolution which were compatible with social Catholic thinking. These were primarily those in the area of education and the family, and although the church did engage in some public criticism of the government at the time for its participation in the deportation of the Jews to Germany, its support of Pétain nevertheless led to criticism after the war. Less than forty years after the separation, when the church had been severely criticised for making public statements about politics, it was then criticised for not making bold enough public statements about politics when it came to the question of the deportation.

Parts of the Second World War notwithstanding, twentieth-century social Catholicism was ideologically much more in tune with its time's utopias and ideals than its intransigent ultramontane ancestral form had been earlier. Through its political questioning of the excesses of modern capitalism, French social Catholicism has become 'audible' again on the political scene. By the end of the twentieth century, it could even be said that it was welcome there, at least in its moderate social democratic form. In a country which continued to be marked by the law of separation, no official Catholic party was ever formed, but various successful politicians on both the left and right, from Raymond Barre to Jacques Delors, openly acknowledged their debt toward the social Catholic search for a 'third way' between liberal capitalism and bureaucratic communism. This form of Catholic thinking has also greatly contributed to European construction, and more than one anticlerical has bitterly noticed that the flag of the European Union is nothing other than the crown of stars on a blue background that had always symbolised the Virgin Mary for Catholics. Even Charles de Gaulle's or François Mitterrand's tortuous political trajectories need to be assessed with their Catholic backgrounds in mind, and, in spite of the overtly secular nature of the Republic, most French presidents have had public national funerals at Notre-Dame de Paris.[14]

Still within the realm of politics, the shift towards social Catholicism has also given a new public voice to Catholics, particularly priests and members of the clergy, who are fully expected to occupy the public space and express their concern at the fate of asylum seekers or the unemployed or to temper most war-mongering nationalist temptations. Abbé Pierre, who came out and publicly scolded many leading French politicians for their policies towards the poor and homeless, was not only not criticised for being a priest meddling in public affairs, but his constant defence of the homeless led to his being regularly voted the most popular public figure in France (ahead of football and cinema stars) right up to his death in 2006. Through individuals like abbé Pierre, Soeur Emmanuel, or even the Jewish-born archbishop of Paris, Jean-Marie Lustiger, the French clergy has gradually regained a new public image of 'moral conscience' within the French nation. It also acquired a renewed support within the national political and administrative structures: religious leaders were regularly asked to intervene in times of crisis, questioned by the media on social issues and asked to sit on various national committees regarding ethical and sensitive issues. By the end of the twentieth century, the historical rift between republican France and Catholicism had been reformed through the social arena.

On the opposite side of the political spectrum, as official Catholic politics disappeared, anticlericalism and anti-Catholicism correspondingly diminished, and persecution of the Catholic church ceased to be the cement of the left and the means to political support it had been.[15] The fiercely anticlerical Radical party gradually lost its influence on twentieth-century French political life, and in the years leading up to the Second World War, even the French Communist Party, as has already been mentioned, practised a policy of cooperation with Catholics. In such an atmosphere, Catholics were able to make other gains. The separation law of 1905 was never applied in Alsace and Lorraine after they were restored to the national territory in 1918; the medieval, renaissance and classical churches nationalised during the revolutionary period received significant investment from successive republican regimes; and, since 1959, the Catholic educational system became almost fully financed by the State. In 1981, the short lived attempt of the first socialist government of the Fifth Republic to create a unique non-confessional school system was met with such massive protest of Catholic sympathisers (very much in the French national tradition of revolution, strikes and public protests) that François Mitterrand was forced to abandon his plans to end state subsidies to Catholic education. Thus the end of the Concordat and the demise of reactionary Catholic-supported monarchism did not therefore spell an end to Catholic influence in French politics, it simply led to a transformation of the nature of its political influence.

If the separation of church and State in 1905 did not signal an end to Catholic political influence in the long term, as it had been hoped by its proponents, even less did it eliminate Catholicism as a significant component of French national identity. 'Catholic France' by no means disappeared during the twentieth century, but found a place alongside republicanism within national imagery and retained an important place in the nation's social and cultural identities. In its search of its national origins, republicanism, as much as it had been shaped by anticlericalism and anti-Jesuitism, nevertheless gradually incorporated references to France's religious history in its vision of France. At the same time it came to tolerate references to France's Catholic past, its Catholic heroes, feasts, writers and symbols alongside republican ones, accepting them as truly national. The presence of Catholicism in the cultural life of the nation and its identity, in addition to the examples of political protest already cited, can be seen both in the levels of actual practice among the population and in the presence in the intellectual and cultural life of the nation throughout the twentieth century.

In spite of a perception of widespread secularisation from the *Belle époque* onwards, Catholic religious practice continued well beyond the official separation of church and State. Until the late 1970s, the percentage of religious baptisms, weddings and funerals remained stable and only started their decline as a part of the more general western European movement of de-Christianisation of the late twentieth century. Even then, while the significant decrease in Mass attendance may suggest that traditional Catholicism had become a minority religion in France, other signs point towards a resilience of France's Catholic identity in the post-modern world: the rising popularity of Catholic schools in all spheres of the French society into the twenty-first century; the influence of Catholic publishers, particularly in the domain of children's publishing, such as the

Bayard Presse; the popularity of religious figures already mentioned, such as abbé Pierre or Pope John-Paul II; the huge participation in Catholic youth rallies; or the constant, if not increasingly fervent faith of those who have remained within the fold, as demonstrated by the relatively steady, if not increasing level of communicants among those who continued to attend Mass.

The continued presence of Catholic intellectuals in the centre of the cultural life of the nation throughout the twentieth century is further evidence of its place within French cultural identity. Even among the national elites, the rigorous scientific positivism combined with anticlericalism which characterised the patriotism of the first decades of the Third Republic was short lived in its exclusivity. The *Belle époque* saw a tide of prominent intellectuals flirting with if not converting to Catholicism. Often pure products of the new republican educational system and preoccupied with the question of national identity, this group included Ernest Psiachari (who, interestingly, was Renan's grandson), Charles Péguy, and Maurice Barrès. From that time onwards, every intellectual generation has had its Catholic representatives. The pre-war generation was that of Henri Bergson, Jacques Maritain, Georges Bernanos and Paul Claudel. During the Second World War, in spite of the Catholic hierarchy's accommodation with Pétain's collaborationist regime, a Catholic-inspired resistance movement developed, producing important revues such as *Les cahiers du temoignage chrétiens* and *Esprit*, and to which the communist poet Aragon pays his respects in his poem *La Rose et Le Réséda.*[16] More original individual paths still lead to Catholicism, as in the case of the Jewish avant garde poet Max Jacob, fascinated by the legends and tradition of his native Brittany, who would eventually be arrested by the Gestapo and deported. Only its strong Catholic ethos and ideals can coherently explain the evolution of a place like Uriage, that started as a Pétainist elite youth training academy and ended up providing the start for a significant segment of post-war France's political and intellectual life.[17] After the war, in the context of the Cold War and wars of decolonisation, the Catholic voices of Emmanuel Mounier, François Mauriac, Gabriel Marcel and Maxence van der Meersh could still be heard. In the 1950s, the Worker-Priests, in spite of their eventual condemnation by the papacy for their tolerance of openly atheistic communists, showed how far some French Catholics were prepared to adapt to modern lifestyles.[18] In Burgundy, the Protestant Frère Roger created Taizé, an ecumenical Catholic spiritual centre whose popularity has never diminished. By the 1960s, there were even Catholics amongst the ultra left, like Maurice Clavel. Throughout the twentieth century, from the national Catholicism of Maurras or Barrès through to individuals flirting with the Catholic faith and the extreme left, Catholicism remained a living and creative force in the perpetual re-invention of French identity.

Like elsewhere in Europe, however, some ideological elements of orthodox Catholicism remained incompatible with the values of a postmodern democratic State. The church's strong anti-individualism continued to manifest itself in its intransigent positions on 'private' issues like birth control, abortion, sexual freedom, gay rights, family structure and euthanasia. No French politician or political party (not even the Front National) endorsed the church's official discourse on all of these issues, and even if many shared some of the church's concerns about the speed and scope of social change, most of the French population, including the majority of French Catholics, ceased to follow the church's teaching in at least some of these areas by the end of the twentieth century. Thus, as much as Catholicism had regained a legitimate voice on the political scene in numerous areas of social and welfare policy, and as much as its emotional and cultural influence on France's contemporary and historic identity is still powerful, by the end of the twentieth century it had nevertheless lost a significant amount of its influence in the French population's private lives and individual behaviour.

Thus a new religious compromise was achieved during the century which followed the end of the Concordat and the separation of the church and State. The church accepted to withdraw any claim it had for direct political power, or for universal recognition of the essentiality of Catholicism to French identity, but in exchange it has gained more than a new freedom of speech. Having finally moved out of the impasse of mutual suspicion and regular confrontation which had characterised relations between the church and the French Republic during the nineteenth century, through its evolution from legitimism to social democracy (with the help of its fragile liberal wing), French Catholicism was reintegrated into modern France. Its vision of French national identity became more pervasive among the national community and its voice widely respected and listened to on a number of social and political questions.

At the same time, mainstream republican visions of France had also come to accommodate Catholic images, in particular of the links to the land. It has been claimed that François Mitterrand's victory in 1981 had something to do with his choice of including a church tower on his campaign poster representing a typical 'French' rural village (see Figure 5 in Chapter 5). A Socialist presidential candidate actively seeking to link himself in the minds of the voters with one of the most persistent symbols of Catholicism shows how very far the 'two Frances' of the post-revolutionary nineteenth century had become one.[19]

Religious Minorities and the French Identity

While the most widespread religious dimension of French national identity was undoubtedly Catholic, other religious identities have nevertheless also acquired a degree of compatibility with French identity, and extensive religious tolerance has also often emerged as an important characteristic of the secular republican view of the French nation. France has important Protestant, Jewish and Muslim minorities, each of which has suffered periods of persecution, criticism and ostracisation by those opposed to recognising their membership in the French nation. Meanwhile, in their different ways, each group has sought ways to become fully-fledged members of the French national community without at the same time sacrificing their religious integrity.

In some ways, Protestants and Jews had an easier time being considered a part of the republican French nation imagined during the century that followed the French Revolution, since, unlike Catholics, they were not overtly persecuted by the republicans or diabolically associated with the counter-revolution. The Revolution itself had promoted integration of all men into the secular republic, and had accorded rights to minority religions unheard of in *ancien régime* France or indeed in most of Europe at that time. One interpretation, at least, of republican secularism was to promote religious tolerance and freedom, allowing for the integration and assimilation of anyone willing to subscribe to republican values within the French nation. Thus not only was it possible to be fully French and of any religion, but tolerance and religious pluralism were key elements of French identity such as it was invented by republicans from the Revolution onwards. This did not mean that secularism and anticlericalism for some republicans did not imply criticism of all religions, or that persecution, particularly of Jews, was absent, only that an important discourse of inclusion within the national community for different religious groups was present. The possibility of belonging to the French nation was not only articulated by those in the republican elite, but was also overtly sought by many within the religious minorities themselves, who considered themselves to be fully French and who hoped to obtain mutual recognition from other groups within the nation. The remainder of this section will consider the specific experience of three groups in turn – Protestants, Jews and Muslims – before a brief examination of attempts to invent a French nation which could be considered tolerant and multi-faith.

Since the sixteenth century, France was home to a sizable Protestant community, which passed through alternating periods of overt religious conflict with the Catholic majority and relative peace. Protestants could be found among the elite of the *ancien régime*, and strong local Protestant identities developed, mostly in the southwest (Cevennes, Languedoc, Gascogne), but also in eastern France.[20] Like the Catholics and the Republicans, Protestants also developed a vision of the French nation which included its specific references to French history, such as the St Bartholomew's day massacre of Protestants or the proclamation of the Edict of Nantes guaranteeing religious freedom for Protestants and its heroes, such as King Henri IV, the defender of Protestant rights.[21] They interpreted the significance of the 1789 Revolution as guaranteeing them a place within the French nation, and became linked to republicanism as the defender of the rights of minority religions both to practise freely and to be considered bona fide members of the French nation. From the time of the Revolution onwards, by recognising and making common cause with republican values, Protestants were able to achieve successful integration into the French nation. Their integration was so successful that even the political, social and intellectual elites of the nation included individuals from the French Protestant community disproportionate to their numbers.[22] Politically, French Protestants remained associated with the left of the political spectrum and positively identified themselves with republicanism. As a sub-identity within the French nation, Protestantism endured into the twenty-first century, as individuals often continued to be identified by their Protestant heritage, such as Michel Rocard or Lionel Jospin.

Like Protestants, Jews had acquired greater rights and freedoms during the French Revolution, and even more overtly sought a similar, integrated place within the French nation of religious tolerance invented from that time forward. The result of the Revolution was 'emancipation' and although not all Jews had supported the Revolution and its principles, real gains were made in terms of citizenship and equality.[23] The population of Jews in France was largely restricted to the towns, and in particular to Paris (where over 50% lived), with over 40 departments having no resident Jews at all in the nineteenth century.[24] During that century, Jewish organisations were set up in order to promote and aid Jewish integration into French society, while at the same time preserving Judaism. Confirming loyalty to each successive regime, Jewish leaders supported secularism, in the hope that removing religious references in the public sphere would allow them to be free to practise their religion in private.[25] They constructed a narrative version of French history which included Jews, and adapted their religious practice, such that the end of the nineteenth century 'saw a flourishing Jewish community reflect its close association with the country of emancipation in constructing an elaborate ideology of reconciliation and harmony, of faith in progress and universal improvement.'[26] By the beginning of the twentieth century, the Jewish community had found a place within French society, essentially urban French society, and while many did seek to preserve some of their Jewish religious and cultural traditions, for the most part this was only when it did not put their position as fully-fledged members of the French nation at risk.[27] By the mid-twentieth century, members of the French Jewish community had also successfully penetrated the French socio-political elite, the most famous individual perhaps being Leon Blum, the leader of the Socialist party and the Popular Front coalition which won the elections in 1936, making him President of the Council. Occasionally new waves of Jewish immigrants would take a generation or more to adapt to the situation in France, assimilating with differing degrees of ease at each wave. Those who arrived during the 1930s from Eastern Europe suffered greatly at the hands of the French government during the Occupation, and those arriving in France in 1962 following Algerian independence also took some time to adjust. Throughout the period, though, the main objective was integration into the French nation.

Although the republican elite tended by and large to support this position of integration of the Jews, waves of antisemitism did break out on several occasions, leading some to question whether or not Jews could be considered full members of the French nation. From the publication of Edouard Drumont's *La France juive* in 1886, an antisemitic press continued to publish accounts portraying the Jew as an enemy to the French nation that could never be truly integrated. At particular moments, such as the Dreyfus Affair in the late 1890s or the Occupation during the Second World War, this press was more widely read than at other moments and achieved some measure of public sympathy. Such antisemitism notwithstanding, within the republican elite there was always a contingent which believed that integrated Jews were indeed a full part of the nation. Even the Vichy government, which drafted antisemitic legislation and deported Jews to Germany as a part of the Final Solution, distinguished between 'French Jews' and those interwar Jewish immigrants from Eastern Europe who had not yet been assimilated into the national community, recognising at least in part the possibility that Jews could be a part of the French nation.

Thus for both Protestants and Jews, making up a significant minority within the French nation, a degree of assimilation was achieved, such that their communities were considered by themselves and others (if not by everyone) to be fully fledged members of the national community. Although not fulfilling the republican aim of pure individualism which rejected any other form of communautarism, as communities they kept their heads relatively low and were able to forge identities which were fully French, but which sustained religious differences from both Catholicism and republican atheism through their support of the republican secular state with its policies of freedom of religion. In the long term, one could say that each of these religious groups, having passed through several decades of overt persecution or at least marginality, made a kind of arrangement with the republican tradition, recognising the secularism of the republican State in exchange for preserving a place for religion and freedom of religion in the 'private sphere'.

Turning to Islam, France did not see significant waves of immigration into France until the mid-twentieth century, when large numbers of French-speaking Muslims entered the hexagon, primarily from north Africa, such that by the early twenty-first century France was home to five million Muslims. One can debate as to whether the situation differs from that of the other religions already discussed because of a fundamental principle, or simply because of chronology. There are those who argue that the conflicts of the late twentieth and early twenty-first centuries have arisen from the fact that French Muslims did not fully accept the compromise with republican secularism that French Catholics, Protestants and Jews had made in previous centuries, and that there is a fundamental opposition between Islam and the Republic. On the other hand, the real and perceived persecution can be seen as similar to the anticlerical campaign against Catholics which characterised the build-up to the Law of Separation, leading to the view that successful integration is only a matter of time. The 'foulard affair', which denied access to French schools to any girl wearing the Muslim headscarf, is in many ways the republican state flexing its muscles to show that the first loyalty must be to the secular Republic, that religion must not be seen to be interfering with that sphere, and in order to break the hold of any sub-national community on its members, such that all choices are genuinely individual. At the same time, questions have also arisen regarding the financial input into Mosque construction. According to the 1905 Law of Separation, the State is allowed to help religions in their charitable activity, but not their spiritual activity. Nicolas Sarkozy, who was behind the creation of a national Islamic authority (with which he could then negotiate), has also suggested that this law might be changed in order to allow the State to help pay for the construction of Mosques, in order to promote cooperation between the French State and Islamic authorities, and reduce the impact of foreign wealth on Islam within France.[28]

It may be that future compromises will make it as easy to have a French Muslim identity as it is to be a French atheist, Catholic, Protestant or Jew. There are, nevertheless, two distinct differences between Islam and the other religions which have found a compromise with the secular Republic: the legacy of colonialism and the fact that as an immigrant group, they began as outsiders in terms of class and social standing.[29] The historic relationship of French Muslims to the French nation was as a subject, colonised people. Notwithstanding the rhetoric of inclusion which surrounded French imperialism, the reality of the French colonies and the treatment of the 'indigenous populations' in a manner which denied them proper citizenship is a handicap which, while not insurmountable, makes the integration of French Muslims into the national community not simply a question of religion, as their identity is bound to be linked to their historic and cultural status as those who had been formerly colonised.

In conclusion, the republican vision of the French nation was always secular, wavering between religious tolerance in the private sphere and positive hostility towards any religious beliefs, especially where they had an impact upon the political opinions of individual French citizens. In terms of identity, it was hoped that French identity would simply come first, and republicans hoped to prevent communautarism from developing in such a way that the nation would be composed only of assimilated individuals whose identity would be based solely upon their membership in the nation rather than any sub-groups within it. For the Catholic majority, their final acceptance of a secularised state left them free to develop a way to retain their Catholic identity as an integral part of their Frenchness, even gaining some acceptance of the Catholic vision of the history of the French nation. The two Frances had become one France. The Protestant and Jewish religious minorities, pleased with religious tolerance and freedom and accepting of a secularised state, forged a French identity which rendered their Frenchness compatible with their religion. At the same time as individuals were able to assimilate, their sense of a sub-community within the nation did not disappear, however, it was simply not trumpeted loudly, but remained a key part of their individual and group identities. For French Muslims, the task of finding a way to render their religious and national identities compatible has been more difficult, and may simply not yet be complete. Notwithstanding the continued hypocrisy in the conflicts about French Muslim identity, by the late twentieth century, religious tolerance and freedom alongside a loudly proclaimed secular public sphere had become key components of French national identity. In 2003, the deputy Jacques Myard published the proceedings of a colloquium entitled *Secularism at the Heart of the Republic*, which included messages from the then prime minister, Jean-Pierre Raffarin, and Nicolas Sarkozy, future President of the Republic and then Minister of the Interior, along with leading theologians and religious leaders.[30] Such a publication demonstrates the continued resonance of secularism as one of the most fundamental features of French national identity: one that has needed to be regularly repeated, championed and perpetually re-invented right into the twenty-first century.

Notes

1 These images were preserved and enhanced in the great national myth-making age of the nineteenth century. After Philippe de Champaigne in 1737, Ingres, in 1822, triumphantly painted Louis XIII's vow to the Virgin Mary, thereby emphasising the Catholic heritage of the French nation. Given the extent of the symbolism, it is not surprising that a contemporary novel like *The Da Vinci Code* can efficiently play on that religious element in the pre-revolutionary French imagery, and present the French Merovingian dynasty as the authentic blood line of Christ (the real 'Holy Grail').

2 Robert Tombs, *France 1814–1914* (London: Longman, 1996), p. 241.

3 See Robert Gildea, *The Past in French History* (New Haven and London: Yale University Press, 1994), pp. 233–4 for more on Gregoire and the curés patriotes.

4 A young aristocrat critical of Catholicism and of Christianity in general in his 1797 *Essai sur les Revolutions*, Chateaubriant was drawn back to the religion of his childhood after his mother's death when he experienced what he called 'the truth of tears'. In 1802 he published his *Genie du Christianisme* in which he reoriented the Rousseauist and romantic sensibility towards traditional religions.

5 On bells, see Alain Corbin, *Village Bells: Sound and Meaning in the 19th-Century French Countryside,* Martin Thom, trans. (London: Papermac, 1999).
6 There were some regional exceptions.
7 See Maurice Larkin, *Religion, Politics & Preferment in France since 1890: La belle Epoque and its legacy* (Cambridge: CUP, 1995), pp. 147–73. Larkin shows how this trend continued through the Vichy period and beyond the Second World War as well.
8 For a more complete discussion, see René Rémond, *Les crises du catholicisme en France dans les années trente* (Paris: Editions Cana, 1979), and James F. Macmillan, 'France' in Tom Buchanan and Martin Conway, eds, *Political Catholicism in Europe, 1918–1965* (Oxford: Clarendon Press, 1996), pp. 34–68.
9 See J-B. Duroselle, *Les Débuts du Catholicisme social en France (1822–1870)* (Paris: PUF, 1951).
10 For a full history of the movement, see Jean-Marie Mayeur, *Catholicisme social et démocratie chrétienne: Principes romaines, experiences françaises* (Paris: Editions du Cerf, 1986), idem, *Des partis catholiques à la démocratie chrétienne, XIXe–XXe siècle* (Paris, 1980), and François-Georges Dreyfus, *Histoire de la démocratie chrétienne en France de Chateaubriand à Raymond Barre* (Paris: Albin Michel, 1988).
11 In *Les droites en France*, Rene Rémond even goes so far as to say that although they had different origins, Christian Democracy became the modern face of the old stock Legitimist right, as much as Gaullism became that of Bonapartism and Liberalism that of Orleaism.
12 For a discussion of the relationship between Catholicism and modernity, see Marjorie A. Beale, *The Modernist Enterprise: French Elites and the Threat of Modernity 1900–1940* (Stanford: Stanford University Press, 1999), pp. 104–44, and Ralph Gibson, *A Social History of French Catholicism: 1789–1914* (London: Routledge, 1989).
13 The policy was known as the 'politique de la main tendue aux Catholiques'.
14 See Pierre Péan, *Une Jeunesse Française: François Mitterrand 1934–1947* (Paris: LGF Livre de Poche, 1997).
15 See René Rémond, *L'Anticlericalisme en France de 1815 à nos jours* (Paris: Editions Complexe, 1976), p. 270.
16 Louis Aragon, 'La Rose et le Réséda' reprinted in Germaine Brée and George Bernauer, eds, *Defeat and Beyond: An Anthology of French Wartime Writing, 1940–1945* (New York: Pantheon Books, 1970), pp. 202–4
17 John Hellman, *The Knight-Monks of Vichy France: Uriage 1940–1945.* 2nd Edition (McGill-Queen's University Press, 1997).
18 See Stanley Windass, ed., *The Chronicle of the Worker-Priests* (London: Merlin Press, 1966).
19 Regis Debray discusses the links between this well-publicised photograph and the name of the village where de Gaulle choose to retire during his 'crossing of the desert' between 1948 and 1959 – 'Collombey les deux églises'. See Régis Debray, *A demain de Gaulle* (Paris: Gallimard, 1996) and also Philippe Boutry 'Le clocher' and André Vauchez 'La cathedrale' in Pierre Nora, ed., *Les Lieux de Mémoire,* III, pp. 3081–138, Daniel Milo 'Le nom des rues', *Les Lieux de Mémoire* II, pp. 1887–914, and Corbin, *Village Bells.*
20 See R. Fabre, 'Les Protestants' and 'Les communautés Protestantes à la fin des années 1970', in Gérard Cholvy and Yves-Marie Hilaire, eds, *Histoire Religieuses de la France Contemporaine,* Vol. 2 (Paris: Privat, 1989), pp. 36–50 and Vol. 3, pp. 441–4.
21 See Philippe Joutard, 'Le musée du desert: La minorité réformé', Nora, *Les Lieux de Mémoire* II, pp. 2653–77.

22 For a full discussion, see Patrick Cabanel, *Les Protestants et la République* (Paris: Editions Complexe, 2000).
23 Zosa Szajkowski, *Jews and the French Revolutions of 1789, 1830 and 1848* (New York: Ktav publishing house, 1970), p. XLI.
24 Eugen Weber, 'Reflections on the Jews in France', in Frances Malino and Bernard Wasserstein, eds, *The Jews in Modern France* (Hanover: Brandeis University Press, 1985), pp. 9–10.
25 See Phyllis Cohen Albert, *The Modernisation of French Jewry: Consistory and Community in the Nineteenth Century* (Hanover, NH.: Brandeis University Press, 1977), p. 312.
26 Michael R. Marrus, *The Politics of Assimilation: A Study of the French Jewish Community at the time of the Dreyfus Affair* (Oxford: Clarendon, 1971), p. 122. For an example of a narrative history of Jews in France, see Esther Benbassa, *The Jews of France: A History from Antiquity to the Present,* M. B. DeBevoise, trans. (Princeton: Princeton University Press, 1999).
27 Albert, *The Modernisation of French Jewry*, p. 312.
28 At the time of writing this seems unlikely to succeed, as questioning the French model of secularism (laicité) is still extremely controversial.
29 See Chapter 12 for further consideration of this particular problem.
30 Jacques Myard, ed., *La Laicité au Coeur de la République* (Paris: L'Harmattan, 2003).

11

French Identity and Difference

One of the key elements of the republican vision of France was that it was 'one and indivisible' and that membership in the nation was only ever recognised for individuals. The French citizen was 'universal' in this sense, and ought to bear no marks in the public sphere of his or her difference from the others in the national community. Difference should be confined to the private sphere of the home, where individuals and families were free to do as they liked. Two implications arise from this conception of the nation: any individual, through acceptance of republican values and the adoption of French culture, could be assimilated into the nation, and no sub-national group could under any circumstances attain special status, legal or otherwise, which would confer on them any form of special rights or considerations. For this reason, such categories as 'mother tongue' or 'ethnic group' have always been forbidden as questions on the French national census, for fear that this would create awareness of such differences between groups and give rise to potential demands for special treatment. For the case of religion, the previous chapter showed that in terms of identity, in spite of republican aims and rhetoric to the contrary, religious sub-identities did develop and survive in France. The most successful were those that kept a relatively low profile and demanded no special treatment from the rest of the nation other than the freedom to practise their religious beliefs in private. This chapter will explore three further divisions within French society over the two hundred years since the Revolution – gender, race and region – in order to explore the ways in which difference was and was not accommodated within French national identity. It will consider the ways these groups have coped with mainstream desires for them to not think of themselves as groups, and consider the degree of success at reconciling difference with the supposed universality and uniformity of individuals and groups within the French nation.

'Citoyennes'?

Throughout the period when the French nation was beginning to be invented, one identifiable group was always on the national margins: women. For well over a century, the universal citizen described in the opening paragraph was male, and the principal characteristics and identifying features of the French nation were also male. This is particularly true for the republicans, for whom men were citizen-soldiers in a nation born in the battle of Valmy and a republic built upon reason, a decidedly 'masculine' characteristic. Women were excluded from formal citizenship and from the public and political dimensions of national life for a variety of reasons ranging from the traditional view that a woman's place was in the home, through the fear that they were too much under the influence of the church and the fact that they were exempt from military service (a key element of citizenship), to views that they were 'unruly' and irrational, and their impact on the public sphere could only serve to subvert the male reason upon which the Republic was to be built. This did not mean that republicans thought of them as not French, as women did have a prescribed place and role to play within the greater nation, it was merely not in the public sphere. Women could be the muse or the inspiration for the leading men of the republic, they had an important role to play as mothers, raising and properly educating future citizens (as opposed to being citizens themselves), as well as defending morality within French society. In all of these places, though, they were to remain within defined boundaries, dependent upon fathers, husbands and the male political and military collectivity.[1]

It could be argued that not only was the Republic constructed without women, but that it was constructed against them.[2] Although they did use the feminine word 'citoyennes' to address women who supported the Revolution and the Republic, in practice from the time of the Revolution onwards women were systematically excluded from formal membership in the French Republic as citizens. Full rights were formally and legally denied them under the Napoleonic Civil Code, not only in politics but throughout public and even certain elements of private life. Not just the right to vote was withheld, but significant property rights, control over their own money (be it income, dowry or inheritance), and even parental rights over their children were all slow in coming, preserved by fathers and husbands, in some cases right into the twentieth century.[3] In spite of those men and women who defended women as equally deserving of full citizenship (in particular on the extreme left, but nevertheless found throughout the political spectrum to the Catholic right), it took many decades to break through the various objections, in particular during the centre-held Third Republic of the Opportunists and Radicals. Thus although the republican vision of the nation suggested that men and women complemented each other within the French nation, and separate spheres did not mean separate nations, the French Republic was nevertheless a heavily masculine regime from the start. Full citizenship, and therefore full membership in the nation was a male preserve for a century and a half (at least) after the revolution.[4] It was not until 1944, amid the turmoil of war and liberation that France finally adopted universal suffrage, and women officially and legally took their place as equal citizens in the republican State.

Women may have been excluded from the national political community formally between 1789 and 1944, but that did not stop many from engaging in public activity and political activism. Historically, women's public involvement had been channelled through the Catholic church and its female religious orders as nuns, teachers and nurses. Excluded from the republic, they could nevertheless find a place within the church where they had a recognised public role to fulfil. By the nineteenth century, though, on top of the ever increasing popularity of these orders, women also participated in an entire range of political organisations outside of the church, ranging from those overtly dedicated to securing greater rights for women through to a host of other lobby groups, politically motivated and philanthropic aid organisations, trade unions (official and unofficial), as well as political parties across the spectrum, although more prominently on the left. Women activists were important in each of the Revolutions, the Paris Commune, as well as most significant strikes and protests.[5] Ironically, perhaps the most difficult types of organisation to found, drive forwards and gain acceptance within the French Republic were those aimed primarily at achieving women's citizenship and full political rights, due to the nature of the individually defined relationship between the population and the nation. It was true in France, as elsewhere in the world, that diversity in terms of religion, social background, education and opinion created such differences among women within the same nation that finding common grounds for cooperation in a single organisation was often difficult at the best of times. The individualism and rejection of groups within the nation that characterised republican France, however, added a greater challenge to women seeking to defend their rights. As Joan Wallach Scott has pointed out, feminists seeking full citizenship in France had to cope with the paradox of needing to constitute a separate group as women in order to be accepted by men as a part of common humanity as individuals.[6] In the words of Susan K. Foley, they needed to invoke difference in order to deny difference.[7]

The paradox of needing to form a group in order to be considered as individuals was only one of the obstacles to be overcome before women could achieve full recognition as citizens of France. These obstacles varied according to the constituency blocking or slowing down the process, and included: the perceived links between women and the Catholic church (for the anticlerical left); the traditional opposition to women in the public sphere (for the socially conservative throughout the political sphere); the discourse of women as irrational or unruly and therefore a liability to a

Republic founded upon reason; the gendered implications of the 'citizen-soldier' as the pillar of republicanism, thereby excluding women;[8] and the fact that many groups in favour of female political inclusion in principle nevertheless had higher priorities, whether bringing about the working-class revolution for the socialists, or restoring the monarchy for those on the right in favour of female suffrage. Even among feminists, there were those who prioritised rights for property or divorce above those of full citizenship, as well as those who approached feminist claims positively, but from a perspective of separate spheres.[9]

One can add that through a century of massive and regular political upheaval, any change whose full ramifications were unclear was feared, as it might bring about another full-scale revolution, the fall of a particular regime or an undesirable and irreversible transformation of French society. Not only was the political impact of women's rights a question mark, but so was the effect change might have upon families, couples and all manner of personal relationships. Siân Reynolds argues that in the development of French nationhood, through textbooks as well as mainstream national and republican histories of France, one of the givens, the unquestioned basic assumptions was 'the unchanging nature of French women.'[10] Any hint that they were changing into something new and modern needed to be avoided, for who could tell where it would lead, and what unforeseen negative consequences it might have for the future well-being of the French nation. This combination of extra fear of change and the paradox of needing to form a group to be recognised as individuals in the particularly French way, alongside the particular and vehement objection of the anticlerical Radical republicans to women's suffrage, helps to explain why the extension of full citizenship rights to include women and the adoption of universal suffrage was put off for so much longer in France than in most of its European neighbours. Even towards the close of the Second World War, it seemed more a question of not being able to resist the pressure any longer, than of eagerness to make the leap to universal suffrage.[11] Given the context of the liberation and the end of the war, the event also received much less publicity and fanfare than it merited, and is still often considered in historical accounts as a kind of afterthought.

The systematic exclusion of women from citizenship in the Republic, coupled with the republican vision that the French nation and the French Republic should be considered as synonymous, has implications for the national identity of French women. Many women could and did identify themselves with Catholic France, as opposed to republican France. As the republican vision of the nation gained wider acceptance and the Republic became the victorious political regime, this alternative would be unsustainable in the long term for those women who sought inclusion and a way to make a public contribution to French society. Those seeking a way to be French, republican and female without contradiction, but with recognised rights of citizenship, had first to find a way to escape the potential conflict between group identity as women and that of individual membership in the wider nation already discussed.

This paradoxical situation led the French feminist movement to develop in a more individualistic manner than those which developed in Great Britain or the United States – more even than class, religious or political differences can explain. When looking back at the history of women's integration into the French nation, one can observe a tendency to downplay collective activist organisations and to commemorate individuals rather than 'groups' of feminists fighting for women's rights. Thus women such as Flora Tristan, Louise Michel or Simone de Beauvoir became famous for their political activity and public voice, yet there is no real equivalent in French national mythology to the 'suffragettes'. Often fighting for women's rights alongside other rights, these heroines' feminism may even be given a lower profile than their other activism (as trade unionists, communards or intellectuals, to take the three examples already stated) as a way to ensure that their profile was even higher, while at the same time fitting in with the French republican idea that everyone ought to be thought of as an individual, not as a member of a sub-group within the nation. Thus these women could be seen as 'genuine' national figures striving for the progress of the entire French nation and humanity, not just for women. At the same time of course, this made the struggle for women's rights that much harder as this dimension of their activism was often downplayed. In the same way, much of the writing of French women's history, and the re-writing of women into the global narrative of the French nation has had to be done by non-French scholars, as those French historians of women have needed to be careful, so as not to be excluded from French academic circles as 'particularists' whose work has little bearing on mainstream and 'important' history.[12] This is not to say that French women's history is not a thriving and innovative field, just that it has occasionally been frowned upon by the historical establishment immersed in republican individualism that consider it as breaking with tradition.

A second difference between French feminism and its Anglo-Saxon equivalents which can also be traced back to republican individualism is the relatively smaller place given to overt opposition to men. Since the goal of French feminists was to be recognised as individual citizens on par with men, within the same national structure and framework, and to be found alongside the men, there was less of a tendency to declare men as the enemy. It was the unfairness of the system which needed to be counteracted, and the means for women to enjoy the same rights and freedoms as men which was sought, meanwhile preserving their qualities as women. Within republican spheres, French feminism used 'republican motherhood' as one of its primary platforms, calling for greater legal and political rights for women in a way which would not represent a threat to established social and family structures. Drawing upon the perception of women as having special moral qualities, and 'acceptance of woman's

Figure 9 Joan of Arc

special role as mother and homemaker ... was the unanimous feminist position from 1848' among republican circles.[13] In the same way, birth control was nowhere near as significant for French feminists, who did not always see the way to liberation through restriction of motherhood, but through public recognition of its greater value.[14] In general, French feminists were far less interested in developing a feminist 'counter-culture' with which to identify than their British and American counterparts, and the notion of being a 'feminine' feminist was continually viewed as important.[15] To be a 'French woman' was about inclusion in the revolutionary republican national culture and identity as citizens, while at the same time preserving female moral and maternal qualities; openly to declare rivalry and opposition to men, when the goal was to join them, was not always felt to be the most productive means to achieve equality. Thus the fact that within republican thinking, French nationality implied denial of any significant sub-group goes some way to explaining the nature of French feminism and its particularities.

Women's formal exclusion from the Republic as citizens until 1944 did not mean that there were not female images associated with national identity. The most significant is Marianne, the female incarnation of the Republic who traditionally appears in the Phrygian cap of the Revolution, always beautiful, and in a variety of states of dress and undress, according to the circumstances and taste of the moment. Portrayed in statues at the Mairie in every French village as a means to unite the nation, illustrated in all forms of art from paintings through to postage stamps, used on French coins and in caricature to represent France, Marianne is a pervasive symbol of the French Republic and nation. Although individual French women were still kept out of the public sphere, with Marianne as a symbol, 'France', the nation and Republic, could be imagined as a woman, could be adored, venerated and put on a pedestal, held as worthy to fight and to die for. A second female symbol of the French nation is Joan of Arc, a single figure in whom the various strands of French nationalism could agree was worthy of commemoration (Figure 9). On the one hand, as a Catholic virgin and martyr, she was attractive for the Catholic nation-builders. On the other hand, her cult became much more widespread across the nation under the Third Republic, when her patriotism faced with the English enemy was proclaimed exemplary, even by republicans. Representations of Joan in armour on horseback became much more widespread, particularly in military circles. Naval vessels and military buildings were named after her, and troops subjected to patriotic propaganda featuring her. Thus Joan of Arc was promoted as an embodiment of the French nation, a female symbol of military victory, Frenchness and sacrifice for the good of the nation which could unite republicans and Catholics alike in patriotic thought. Although a real historical figure, not a made up embodiment of the nation like Marianne, Joan of Arc and her deeds were sufficiently removed from the normal and the present to pose no real threat to the masculine-dominated republic. Furthermore, the fact that she was known as 'Jeanne la Pucelle', celebrating her status as a virgin, meant that she was entirely in the public sphere. She did not cross the established divide between private and public, which she would have done had she also been a mother, for example. In this way she was less threatening to the established republican order, since she was in a sense de-sexed, or at least gave up her femininity for the nation.

If we turn to the period after France adopted universal suffrage and women were considered full citizens of the Republic, the difficulties in reconciling female difference and national identity did not completely disappear. Firstly, equality in terms of laws and citizenship did not, of course, automatically translate into equality in practice in the public sphere, be it in the workplace, elected politics or public discourses. The public face and image of the 'French citizen' remained largely male, and mid-twentieth century feminists, called the 'first wave', were still focused upon overcoming the inherent gender hierarchy within French society where women were considered inferior. Simone de Beauvoir and others sought a situation where female qualities were not held as inferior, and women not relegated to the place of the 'second sex'.[16] Equality of rights and citizenship needed to be followed by an equal valorisation and treatment of women in practice, be it in the public sphere or in the way gendered language was used and defined.

After May 1968, a 'second wave' of feminism developed in France which was 'characterised by a turn away from a valorisation of Equality and a move towards the affirmation of Difference.'[17] Only one element among several strands of feminism in the late twentieth century, it can be argued that this second wave was in many ways invented by American feminists who focused exclusively upon those feminisms in France who were concerned with difference.[18] Even so, continuities can be found between second wave feminisms affirming difference and earlier French feminisms in that the articulated difference is not hostile, but about the positive affirmation of female qualities, as a group and for individuals. When one looks at women in France, even in the years following the sexual liberation of the 1960s, femininity and motherhood are still valued by feminists and by French women as a whole. Thus political figures such as Segolène Royal can use both femininity and motherhood as plusses in their political campaigning, contrasting sharply with the 'iron lady' image of Margaret Thatcher, or those of Angela Merkel or Hillary Clinton, who need to show themselves to be as tough as men. In this way, drawing upon sexiness, seductive powers or even motherhood is not humiliating for French women, even when in the public sphere, but a positive affirmation of femininity.

Alongside the sexual liberation of the mid-twentieth century emerged the widespread fascination with the image of the seductive and sexy woman popularised through French cinema. Numerous French films have had the nature of woman as their primary subject, giving rise to the enduring image, particularly outside France, of the 'French woman'. Examples range from *Et Dieu Créa la Femme* (Roger Vadim, 1956) and *L'homme qui aimait les femmes* (François Truffaut, 1977) to *8 femmes* (François Ozon, 2002). Stars such as Brigitte Bardot symbolised both the newly liberated and provocative younger generation of French women, as well as a valorisation of seductive femininity. Even Gérard Depardieu considered that one of the primary elements which made him a star was a certain feminine quality in him. While not traditional exactly, the femininity of the sexy woman is still defined according to the relationship to and difference from men, as motherhood had been before. As with motherhood, the preservation of this very feminine image further distinguishes France from Britain and America.

Consistent with the view that men and women represent different qualities of the nation, but very much against the republican tradition of never officially recognising any group within the nation, the end of the twentieth century saw wide ranging debates about quotas for women in elected positions and public institutions leading to the debates about parity. During the mid-1990s, an entire range of proposals emerged suggesting ways to bring the numbers of women candidates and representatives into line with

Figure 10 A French woman protesting at the National Assembly in Paris, February 2004 (the word on the wall means 'law')

those of men. These ranged from requiring political parties to present an equal number of men and women candidates to proportional financing of political parities according to the numbers of women they presented.[19] The idea was sufficiently popular among the French public that almost every political party made public statements along the lines that greater numbers of women representatives was a desirable goal for France. Debate intensified, however, as to whether or not a parity law was the most appropriate and justifiable means to achieve it, raising numerous questions of principle, including references to the traditional nature of French sovereignty and republican universalism to which parity can appear in contradiction.[20] In response to the Constitutional Reform Bill of 1998, opponents of parity such as the feminist historian Elisabeth Badinter argued that markers of identity such as sex, age, colour and physical ability should be irrelevant to an individual's public life, therefore putting parity into the Constitution would contradict the fundamental principle of abstract universalism.[21] The bill, insisting on parity and putting the onus on the political parties to present equal numbers of men and women candidates was passed at the end of 1999, but the debate will remain open regarding whether it will reconcile sexual difference with the universal French citizen in the long term.[22] Many problems remain for coming to terms with sexual difference in the single nation. In response to the conflict over Islamic headscarves (foulards), many French feminists continue to see the hijab as a symbol of female oppression reminiscent of earlier times, rather than as an affirmation of cultural difference for a religious community. In 2004, during the debate over a law which would ban ostentatious religious symbols (i.e. the foulard) from certain public places, such as schools and government offices, French women were divided between their support for republican secularism and desire to 'liberate' Muslim French women from oppression, on the one hand, and a desire to allow freedom of cultural expression and religious tolerance, on the other (Figure 10).

Inventing a vision of the French republican nation and a corresponding national identity which allows for some measure of individual difference between the sexes without either compromising unity or removing the central image of the 'universal' citizen who (in public space) ought to bear no marks of his or her difference has been, and remains a challenge. Resistance to bringing women into the public sphere in France, and to recognising them as a constituent group within the nation has been significant in the two hundred years since the Revolution, and while 'the exclusion of women from politics is not specific to France, the centrality of the construct of republican universalism and the resistance to the representation of social categories is.'[23] The inclusion of parity for women into the Constitution of the Fifth Republic has potential implications for other groups who can be said to be 'different' and who could also make a claim to representation or rights within the universal French republican nation. The next category of difference we will consider is race.

The French Melting Pot

As mentioned in the introduction to this section, ethnicity has never been a recognised category for classification or differentiation in France. As with gender, in the name of republican universalism and the absolute equality of every individual French citizen before the law, different ethnic groups can make no claims and have no right to representation as a group within the French Republic. With the case of immigrants seeking to become full members of French society, the French model of assimilation would have them integrated as individuals within the republican nation, with no mediating bodies to represent them officially before the French state. Many French republican leaders have considered the successes of the republican model of assimilation as a great source of pride, and point to the lack of sectarianism throughout French history as a direct consequence of this way of thinking, and an important marker of French identity and French difference from the Anglo-Saxon world in particular. This section will first examine the question of assimilation of immigrant ethnic groups across the two hundred years since the Revolution, looking at the ways in which citizenship was acquired, and how membership in the nation was (and was not) extended. It will then turn to representations of the nation to see how, in the imagery of the nation such as it was invented throughout the nineteenth and twentieth centuries, the multi-ethnic component appears.

The French model of assimilation is a conscious and prominent element of nation building in France and a marker of French pride and identity. That individuals of diverse origins could become truly French through the acquisition of French language and culture and the acceptance of the republican values of the Revolution (such as liberty, equality, fraternity, democracy and secularism) has become a fundamental characteristic of the French nation. If one considers the two models of ethnic composition of societies – the melting pot and the mosaic – France must be placed solidly in the camp of the melting pot. Gérard Noiriel, in his book *Le Creuset Français,* has gone so far as to describe France as the ultimate melting pot, far more successful at moulding individuals of diverse origins into a single national body with a common core of key values and cultural characteristics than the United States, the archetypical model of the melting pot society.[24] While this discourse also applied to the regions (see below), when describing the process for immigrants, the individuals would not take more than two generations to become fully French. For the second generation, birth in France guaranteed French citizenship (*jus solis*), and passage through the French school system guaranteed the acquisition of the French language and a knowledge of national history and geography which would serve as the foundations for exercising citizenship within national political institutions. The men would then do their military service, and their induction into the nation would be complete. Upward social mobility would be possible for these later generations, although only one short step up at a time.[25] This society of assimilated individuals can be contrasted with that in Great Britain, where groups of immigrants are permitted and encouraged to maintain the cultural traditions of their home culture, and government services are provided in a variety of languages such that cultural communities flourish, or with Canada, which boasts of the cultural 'mosaic' that is Canadian society, supported by a national ministry of multiculturalism. Republican France sought from quite early on overtly to create a nation in which no such divisions would exist, with a single national culture that was open and accessible to all who were willing to adopt it, if not immediately, at least by the second or third generation. While the State was willing to allow associations of immigrant groups (regulated by the law of 1901), they were to ensure facility of integration, rather than the perpetuation of their own customs.[26]

France has been a country of high immigration throughout the period since the Revolution and for much of the nineteenth and twentieth centuries the French model of assimilation appeared to work extremely well. Although originally developing a system whereby children of immigrants remained foreign, successive French regimes sought to nationalise the children of immigrants born in France as a way of ensuring that they did French military service.[27] This was sometimes conditional on having been in France for at least two generations, but represents a clear objective on the part of the state to integrate children of immigrants as quickly as possible, once they had passed through the French school system and adopted French culture, as a way of strengthening the nation (even if they were more reluctant with respect to the original immigrants themselves). This objective did not diminish with the passing of time, but was reaffirmed and strengthened by successive republican governments beyond the First World War.[28] The vast majority of the immigration during this period was from bordering regions – Italians, Belgians, Spaniards and Portuguese, with a gradual increase in numbers from eastern Europe, Poles in particular. While one can indeed identify 'ethnic' differences between these migrants and 'the French', they were for the most part both white and Catholic, with few Protestants and very few from outside Europe, although there were quite a few Jews.

The further afield the place of origin of a particular group of immigrants was and the less their culture resembled French culture, the more likely to provoke a long lasting negative reaction it was. During the nineteenth and early twentieth centuries, only the Jewish community was culturally very much removed from this mainstream southern European Catholic background and was perceived as trying to preserve its specific traditions and religious heritage. Here, as we saw in the last chapter, in spite of a clear willingness on the part of the Jewish immigrants to assimilate French society, they had a harder time than the others and suffered from periodic outbursts of antisemitism and declarations that Jews could not be truly 'French', that even after many generations they could never be assimilated into the French nation. Such antisemitism could be found across the French political elite, within Catholic, monarchist, republican and socialist circles, and was developed into a consistent political discourse which grew and receded according to the circumstances. Outbursts of antisemitic feeling tended to happen at moments of crisis or high unemployment when the simplest outlet was to blame those immigrants exhibiting the cultural traits the most strange and 'foreign' to the French. The most obvious example began in the 1930s, when Jewish immigrants were coming in greater numbers from eastern Europe, and escalated during the Occupation when it was held that they could not become or be considered truly French because they were ethnic Jews. This particular rise in antisemitism culminated in the Jewish statutes of Marshal Pétain's Occupation government, and the French participation in the deportation of Jews to German concentration camps.

Nonetheless, even at the height of the republican nationalist discourse of inclusion during the nineteenth century, there was still an ethnic dimension to the French nation and nationalist discourses. Although there were relatively few references to 'the French race', ethnic nationalist thinking was not confined to the reactionary right, but could also be found among the developing imagery of the republicans, who referred to the 'French people' and regularly contrasted them with foreign peoples or races.[29] References in history textbooks to 'our ancestors the Gauls', while primarily aimed at demonstrating the longevity of France, nevertheless also helped to invent a history of common descent, linking modern France not only with the geographical territory of ancient Gaul, but also as an ethnic group with a myth of common origin and shared blood. Furthermore, as pseudo-scientific racist theories developed in the post-Darwinian period, when biological dimensions were added to numerous social and political theories, specific physical features were attributed to Jews. These features, it was argued, were what prevented them from being truly 'French'. Such biological racism augmented the perception that the Jewish community was ethnically distinct from the French nation, a position which found resonance in many different circles within France.

By the mid-twentieth century, the situation was rendered more complicated by the fact that much of the new immigration came from outside Europe, was non-white and more culturally different from mainstream French national culture than earlier waves of immigration had been. After the economic crisis of the 1970s, and subsequently high levels of unemployment in France, a renewed anti-immigration discourse grew which led to the electoral progress of Jean-Marie Le Pen's National Front. Discrimination increased in frequency, and a perception grew that the high numbers of immigrants were not only contributing to high levels of unemployment, but also posed a threat to French national identity.[30] In his analysis of immigration in France, Alec G. Hargreaves contends that suggesting it is cultural differences which render immigrants unable to assimilate is a way of blaming the immigrants themselves, and is indeed symptomatic of an economic crisis, for the 'steady rise of non-Europeans in migratory inflows during the post-war period did not prevent the French from expressing growing acceptance of these immigrants as long as there was rising economic prosperity and a favourable labour market.'[31] After the crisis began, however, immigrants were held to be not satisfactorily integrating into the national community, and thereby undermining it. Whether this was because they were unwilling to adapt, or simply that the cultural differences were too great to be overcome, the republican assimilationist model, it was felt, was no longer going to work, and French national identity was going to suffer from 'foreign' influences. Debates also developed as to the cause of this failure among those who considered non-assimilation as a threat: was it due to a weakness in the republican model to start with or a transformation in the nature of the immigrants arriving in France at the time?

This wave of immigration was further complicated by the fact that many of the immigrants were coming from France's former colonies, which had no parallel for earlier generations of immigrants. Having already been subject to many decades of classification as 'indigenous' and denied full citizenship rights during the colonial period on the grounds that they could not be assimilated, it was that much more difficult for the French to accept them in later years as potentially assimilable immigrants with a real possibility for full citizenship, even after the normal passing of a few generations. Such thinking applied particularly to those coming from Algeria. Not only were they the largest group in numbers, but the tension which had surrounded the Algerian War had left great bitterness in France, contributing to feelings of suspicion among the French towards these immigrants in particular, viewing them as unassimilable and potentially threatening to French national identity and the economic well-being of the country. Similarly, the legacy of broken promises with regards to citizenship and opportunity of the colonial period left those immigrants from Algeria and other colonies with parallel suspicion towards the French who spoke of possibilities for integration and assimilation, both regarding its possibility and desirability. Thus both French society and the immigrants of the later period approached the question of national integration with a greater degree of mutual suspicion and wariness than had been the case for earlier generations of immigrants. De facto racism on the ground in the aftermath of an economic crisis could only serve to exacerbate this problem, leaving French society confronting the paradox of wanting immigrants to assimilate on the one hand, but not in fact allowing them the means to do so on the other.

The late twentieth-century crisis of the republican model of assimilation has indeed some parallels to its earlier crises, but differs slightly. Commentaries regarding cultural differences rendering assimilation impossible do recognise a structural similarity between the antisemitism of the earlier period and the racism of the later phase. In both circumstances, popular ground level persecution, fear and discrimination at the individual level was complemented by an elite political programme seeking popular support by drawing upon ethnic prejudice, sustained by an academic and intellectual discourse justifying the position.[32] Once the legacy of colonial hierarchies was combined with perceived racial differences and the fact that Muslim immigration was non-Catholic (indeed non-Christian), a single group was formed which was both racially and religiously 'other', as earlier Jewish immigration had been viewed, but which also had to contend with the complicated legacy of cultural interaction from the colonial period before having even arrived in France.

The hesitancy towards France born of the colonial experience made the new immigrants themselves more wary of promises and less willing to seek integration than the Jewish community had been in earlier years. The school system – the great institution promoting republican integration – also no longer worked in exactly the same way. Mass education by the end of the twentieth century was designed to keep most children and youths in school or college as long as possible, and combined with high levels of youth unemployment, it has been unable to help children of immigrants integrate into national society as easily as it did during times of economic prosperity, nor has it created sufficient numbers of highly educated individuals to become symbolic representatives of the immigrant communities among the elite of the nation. The refusal to envisage any kind of 'positive discrimination', absolutely incompatible with republican individualism, limits the possibilities even further. The original goals of mixing together on the primary school benches the youth of the nation from all backgrounds also no longer works well in a system where entire schools service only immigrant communities in the *banlieues*. Finally, it can be observed that even after more than one generation in France, the non-white immigrants of the twentieth century are not as integrated as those children or grandchildren of previous waves of immigration have been. It is of course impossible for non-white immigrants to achieve the republican ideal of bearing no visible marks of their difference when in the public sphere, but even so, the process has slowed down.

Explanations for the differences are many and varied, and depend in part upon the political position and objectives of the person providing it. Perhaps indeed this slowness of integration represents a failure of the republican model, as detractors claim, or alternatively that the culture of more recent immigrants blocks assimilation. Alternatively, France may simply be in the throes of a cyclical crisis such as it has gone through before, and it is only a matter of time and economic recovery before the problem will right itself. Extra generations may be required because of the seemly unending economic crisis of high unemployment, or it may be that in an era of mass communication and easy travel, contact with homelands are maintained longer, and for this reason integration will simply take an extra generation or two. Meanwhile, children of immigrants may not always be patient enough to be willing to wait several generations for social promotion, or to go through the slow, traditional one-step upwards at a time of earlier immigrants. The wearing of the hijab, for instance, although a symbol of female oppression in some contexts, can also be viewed as a way for a younger generation to claim, hold onto and positively assert cultural difference. It could also be that French society can only bend so far, and that non-white immigrants are simply resisted because of racism. In any case, French society at the end of the twentieth or the beginning of the twenty-first century has been unwilling to recognise ethnic or racial difference officially as a category, or create special arrangements or concessions for ethnic minorities as it very begrudgingly has for women. Although there are calls for some form of affirmative action as a way to solve the problem, the traditional argument that the French republican nation is indivisible, and that such differences cannot and should not be recognised or they will undermine equality of opportunity, continue to be the dominant position.[33] It looks like the debate surrounding national identity and the French assimilationist melting pot will continue to be alive for some time to come.

Turning away from the actual process of integrating and assimilating immigrants into the nation, it is worth taking a brief look at the ethnic and racial component of representations of the French nation. French national consciousness accords little place to the vast numbers of immigrants which constituted a huge part of the body of the nation throughout the post-Revolutionary period. Unlike the United States, which accords pride of place in its national story to the fact that it was built by tough immigrants who carved a civilisation out of the wilderness, France does not have a myth of being built or even strengthened by immigration. By contrast to the US, the pride is in the French culture, and insofar as immigrants helped to make France great, it was only because they were so quickly assimilated into a French society which was already superior by virtue of the values of the Revolution and the cultural achievements which it represented. The French nation was thus not invented as the product of waves of immigration, but as something born within the hexagon of the Revolution, to which others from outside might join, but who do not fundamentally add anything to it.

Occasionally descriptions of the experience of immigrants in France might be discussed or represented, but always as an aside or a parenthesis to the national story rather than an integral part of it. Once immigrants, or more likely their descendents, have become properly assimilated, they will have become part of the mainstream of the nation and their story will be the same as the others', their immigrant origins simply disappearing, at least from the viewpoint of the main narrative of the French nation.[34] This apparently seamless absorption into the national story and the accompanying disappearance of immigrant origins is mostly true for those descendents of immigrants of white origin. Alternatively, the term 'immigré' has come to mean anyone who is not white, no matter how many generations their families have been in France or how long they have had French nationality: a label which cannot be shed.[35] Thus those non-whites, even after several generations of education and work in France, have found themselves barred by skin colour from the kind of assimilation that French republicans prided themselves on achieving for immigrants from all over Europe. The theoretical equality of opportunity enshrined in the constitution and at the heart of the republican discourse has not been good enough, but no way has been found to change that without contravening the universal values upon which the nation has been founded.

Part of the difficulty in assimilating non-white immigrants into the national story comes from the nature of images representing the French nation. Racial difference has only made rare appearances, and was never sustained in such a way as to encourage the feeling that all individuals really are equal in the nation or that anyone can belong. Such representations of diverse ethnicity and race in France have often appeared in a manner which strengthened racial divides, reinforced stereotypes of racial difference and promoted the colonial discourse of segregation, rather than republican discourse of inclusion. From advertising and music through to comic books, film and literature, racial difference continues to be represented as 'other', if not in whole than in part, creating an extremely complex notion of racial hierarchies and difference.[36] This may be in part because it would be promoting a 'difference' within public representations, so long resisted by republican nation-builders, even though it goes against the same discourse of assimilation at another level. One very recent attempt to create a multi-racial image of the French nation was the 'Black, Blanc, Beur' description of the French national football team during the 1998 World Cup campaign when France was crowned world champions at home, paralleling the 'Bleu, Blanc, Rouge' of the national flag. A multi-racial image of the nation unified and victorious is very much the kind of representation which has been absent from the process of inventing images for France throughout most of the modern period, and even here the team attracted comments from critics that it was not 'truly French' (although the victory helped to quiet such voices). President Nicolas Sarkozy's first government in 2007, which included three young women from ethnic minorities, is another example of an attempt to invent a multi-ethnic French identity. His doing so, however, has provoked criticism that he is following American tradition rather than French, and critics have therefore labelled him Sarkozy 'l'américain'. His decision to create a ministry of immigration and national identity also provoked a ferocious reaction from the political and intellectual elite that this contravened the great French tradition of republican universalism, and would destroy one of the pillars of French identity.

By the early twenty-first century the suggestion that France might envisage some form of multiculturalism, that immigrants should be allowed if not encouraged to retain some of their cultural practices even as they integrate into French society has thus been opened for discussion. For the most part, the reactions were negative, the republican tradition of individual universalism and accompanying refusal to officially recognise differences or distinctions based on race or ethnicity within the French nation remains powerful among the French people and the political elite. Even though discourses of rejection of racial or cultural discrimination (via tolerance of differences) have begun to be employed in France, many still feel that they are inappropriate to the circumstances, too American, and no reason to reject the great national tradition of French universalism. Thus even into the twenty-first century, French identity has retained a strong element of rejection of difference within the indivisible republican nation.

Regions and Local Identity

Like race and gender, regional difference has until recently not always been tolerated beyond a certain point by French republican nation builders. Although still subject to the universal republican nationalist discourse of assimilation, regionalist movements have certainly always been viewed with suspicion by republicans, especially if there is even a hint of separatism (or decentralisation) about them. Regional cultural diversity, on the other hand, has been, if not always promoted, then at least accorded a recognised place within the French nation and national imagery. Thus for the regions, a small concession was accorded to the notion of unity with diversity in a single nation. It was clear, however, that diversity never implied 'difference', and there was certainly never any question of individuals or groups getting special treatment, rights or concessions according to their region of origin. Regions and the individuals living in them, like immigrants, were expected to acquire the minimum of French national culture and republican values and thereby assimilate into national society.

Republican national identity rested upon ensuring that the primary loyalty was to the nation, and politically, this translated into centralisation. During the 1789 Revolution, in an attempt to break the aristocratic power base in the provinces of the *ancien régime*, the revolutionary government created the departments – administrative divisions which had little or no historical or emotional resonance, as they were not associated with anyone's past or identity (see Figure 1). It was feared that the monarchists could use provincial support to restore the monarchy, so the best way to prevent it was through tight control from the capital using departmental administrators who were representatives of the central state. Furthermore, from the earliest days they also envisaged teaching the entire population the French language. Knowledge of French would draw them out of the narrow influence of those who could potentially use the provincial languages to mobilise the population (the clergy and old nobility) by giving them access to the 'rational' thinking and writing that could only be done in French, and ensure their access and participation in national culture. In short, using the now classic phrase of Eugen Weber, they would turn the 'Peasants into Frenchmen', or assimilate them into the national culture in the same way just discussed for immigrants.[37]

The republican model of assimilation has been judged to have been even more successful in the case of the regions than it had been for immigrants, although many recent case studies have suggested that the process was far more complex, and that the regions and regional populations made a far more active contribution than Weber suggested. Regional and local elites, as well as the population, saw it as being in their own interest to integrate the nation, but nevertheless adapted a national identity in their own image.[38] Thus instead of a nicely packaged identity coming from the centre to the periphery, each periphery imagined and invented a national centre which related to their own experience, as often as not with the concurrence of the national authorities. Regionalist movements and discourses developed in many places, but most often with the overt, outwardly trumpeted intention of not undermining the French state, but complementing it through the promotion of 'French' regional characteristics. Sometimes they were interested in decentralisation, but were repeatedly having to assure the authorities that they were not separatists, posed no threat to the nation, and in many cases were dedicated republicans, not reproducing a kind of reactionary regionalism.[39] Perhaps the most obvious example of the inter-mingling of regional and national is the use of school textbooks in the golden age of French nationalism during the Third Republic. As Anne-Marie Thiesse has shown, Republican textbooks varied from region to region and drew heavily on local imagery in their representation of the French nation.[40] The most famous individual book of the age was Bruno's (Augustine Tuillerie) *Le Tour de la France par Deux Enfants*, which championed regional diversity as a positive characteristic of the French nation.[41] It taught every child about the various regions and not only where their own region was relative to the rest, but how important its contribution was to the diversity of France. The underlying message was that if you loved your village, this showed that you loved your nation, and any local or regional ties could thus be drawn or appropriated into strengthening national identity.[42] Local and regional cultural practices could continue, whilst both undermining regionalism as a political force and positively contributing to French national identity.

Thus a certain degree of difference could be tolerated at the level of local folkloric customs, since they could be subsumed and appropriated as a part of French national cultural identity. Local variants in cuisine, dress, customs, architecture or dialect, as well as village festivals showed richness and variety in the nation, but did not seriously undermine the great national cultural values of language, high culture and the revolutionary tradition, since those cultural characteristics associated with the regions were essentially not those of high or educated literate culture. Anyone from the regions hoping to join the elite would need to accept, adopt and identify with French national culture as it has been described in Chapter 9. As discussed in Chapter 2, the very process of integration of the regions and their populations into the nation is an important episode in the history of the nation. The provinces and provincials became colourful variants in national identity, but often appear somewhat comic in national representations because of their rustic or backward qualities. Among great works of French literature, themes such as regional rivalry within France or the poor, uneducated provincial arriving in the capital figure often. Some also romanticise the countryside, presenting the simple life with nostalgia alongside humour. Authors such as Marcel Pagnol, whose books and the films made from them, depict and romanticise the French nation of the countryside, symbolising a rural France which has become an important dimension of French identity.

By the mid-twentieth century regional difference and variety had also become important for local economies trying to tap into the tourist market. Colourful local traditions attract tourists who will also purchase local produce, especially if it is 'typical' of the region. The resurgence of regionalist movements in several areas of France can in part be attributed to the support which regional economic promotion has been receiving. Particularly following the move towards greater decentralisation and the creation of regional assemblies under François Mitterrand, the promotion of regions and regional distinctiveness took off considerably, but rarely at the expense of national identity. After all, regional cultural differences conferred no special rights or privileges on a region or its inhabitants, so republican universalism remained intact as a principle governing the French nation.

Two particular cases merit discussion where debates surrounding differences of individual regions did touch on questions of special treatment: Alsace-Lorraine and Corsica. After the return of the two departments of Alsace and the Moselle region of Lorraine to France in 1919 following almost fifty years of annexation to Germany, several legal distinctions were identified, in particular to do with religion. The three departments had not been part of France in 1905 when the church and State were separated, meaning that the Concordat was still in legal effect there. The first move of the French State, in accordance with the principle of the indivisible republic and no special treatment, was to extend the separation law to include Alsace and Lorraine. This move was met with such hostility among the population in the regions, however, that the government was forced to back down and allow the three departments special status within the French Republic regarding the status of religion. The second example is Corsica, where separatists engaged in terrorist activities in order to obtain independence from France during the last few decades of the twentieth century. At one point, a debate was raised in France as to whether or not Corsica ought to be simply given special status, with some sort of power devolution to the island which would keep it within the Republic but allow it a greater deal of independence in order to reduce the separatist pressure. Objections to the idea were numerous, and mostly on the grounds of the one and indivisible Republic which could not and should not recognise any difference between groups of citizens.

An interesting aside is the case of Algeria. Although discussed in Chapter 8 as a French colony, it can also have a place here, for at one point it was thought that Algeria, unlike the other French colonies, was on track to become a part of the main French territory. It had been divided into three departments, and although subject to several special kinds of laws, was subject to hopes that it would be brought into line with the rest of France as soon as practicable. Todd Shepard has argued that Algeria's eventual independence does not change the fact that in the years leading up to the Algerian War, a significant part of the French elite considered it as genuinely French, and that this independence needs to be viewed not as the inevitable result of colonisation, but as failed nation-building.[43] Following the convulsive decades of decolonisation, this is what happened to the colonies which remained attached to France (the DOM-TOM): they were made departments and in theory treated equally with all other French territory. In practice, some distinctions remained, for example civil servants posted there are still credited in salary terms as having a post which is 'abroad'. Given the relatively low population in the DOM-TOM though, the national equilibrium was not upset by such minor concessions to difference.

The case of the regions is one example of how far difference can be admitted within French identity. The republican ideal of the universal citizen bearing no marks of his or her difference becomes a little blurred when it comes to the regions, although any suggestion of special rights always engendered debate and disagreement, even if in the end difference prevailed. The fact that the cultural differences were tolerated as a kind of rustic element of their culture, for the rural and quaint, also meant that difference could be conceived as not really threatening to high French culture.

Conclusion

French nation-builders sought to invent a nation with a single identity, one which was culturally homogenous, admitted no sub-groups or categories of citizenship, but would instead be made up of universal citizens all equal to one another. This section has examined various specific groups with cultural identities which in some way or another posed a problem for the universal French republican identity. While the universalist, assimilationist values did work in many cases, not every group could be integrated as quickly or indeed as easily as others: religious, ethnic and regional minorities, as well as women, each in their own way sought to negotiate ways to be integrated into the French nation without completely losing their specific identities. It is clear from this analysis that the universalist model of undivided French identity is an ideal for which republicans strove, rather than an objective description of the reality of the French nation and French society across two hundred years. Difference persisted, in spite of being 'ideologically inadmissible'.[44] Officially, France in the early twenty-first century still refuses to recognise 'difference' or the rights of groups, clinging tenaciously to the French model of assimilation, universality and equal opportunity. The exception is the parity law for women in politics, successfully passed because women were not perceived in some quarters as different. Representations of the nation by the end of the twentieth century had come to include references to some sorts of difference within the national identity.

The nation could be perceived as accommodating gender differences, taking pride in regional diversity, accepting of the odd reference to religion, but still struggling somewhat with racial differences as being representative of 'true, eternal France'. It may be that the Republic has become sufficiently established in France that it can sustain and withstand cultural differences within its population, and that one of the fundamental characteristics of French republican national identity – cultural and ethnic universalism and lack of recognised differences – will be phased out, but it looks like not going without a fight.

Notes

1 Susan K. Foley, *Women in France since 1789: The Meanings of Difference* (Basingstoke: Palgrave, 2004), pp. 140–4.
2 As do, for example, Siân Reynolds, 'Marianne's Citizens? Women, universal suffrage and the republic in France', in Siân Reynolds, ed., *Women, State and Revolution: Gender and politics in Europe since 1789* (Brighton: Harvester, 1986), p. 110, and Joan B. Landes, *Women and the Public Sphere in the Age of the French Revolution* (Ithaca and London: Cornell University Press, 1988), p. 171.
3 Sylvia Schafer, *Children in Moral Danger and the Problem of Government in Third Republic France* (Princeton: Princeton University Press, 1997).
4 See Siân Reynolds, *France Between the Wars: Gender and Politics* (London and New York: Routledge, 1996), pp. 208–9.
5 Patricia Hilden, *Working Women and Socialist Politics in France 1880–1914: A Regional Study* (Oxford: Clarendon Press, 1986).
6 Joan Wallach Scott, *Only Paradoxes to Offer: French Feminists and the Rights of Man* (Cambridge MA.: Harvard University Press, 1996). For an alternative view, see Anne Verjus, *Le cens de la famille: Les femmes et la vote, 1789–1848* (Paris: Belin, 2002).
7 Foley, *Women in France*, p. 293.
8 See Chapter 6.
9 Landes, *Women and the Public Sphere*, p. 172.
10 Siân Reynolds, 'Albertine's Bicycle, or: Women and French Identity during the *Belle Epoque*', *Literature and History* 10, 1 (2002), p. 38. See also Mary Louise Roberts, *Disruptive Acts: The New Woman in Fin-de-Siècle France* (Chicago and London: University of Chicago Press, 2002).
11 Reynolds, *France Between the Wars*. For more on the quest for the vote, see Paul Smith, *Feminism and the Third Republic: Women's Political and Civil Rights in France 1918–1945* (Oxford: Clarendon Press, 1996), and James F. McMillan, *France and Women 1789–1914: Gender, society and politics* (London: Routledge, 2000).
12 See Karen Offen, 'French Women's History: Retrospect (1789–1940) and Prospect', *French Historical Studies* 26, 4 (Fall 2003), pp. 727–67.
13 See Claire Goldberg Moses, *French Feminism in the Nineteenth Century* (Albany: State University of New York Press, 1984), pp. 204–5.
14 This is particularly true given regular French anxieties about declining birth rates and the subsequent weakening of France. See Moses, *French Feminism*, pp. 232–3.
15 See for example Andrea Masker, '"Mademoiselle Aria Ly Wants Blood!" The

Debate over Female Honour in Belle Epoque France', *French Historical Studies* 29, 4 (Autumn 2006), pp. 638–40, where she discusses the reaction to Ly's challenge to a fellow newspaperman to a duel.

16 Simone de Beauvoir, *The Second Sex* (London: Vintage, 1997), originally published 1953.

17 Lisa Walsh, 'Introduction', in Kelly Oliver and Lisa Walsh, eds, *Contemporary French Feminism: Oxford Readings in Feminism* (Oxford: OUP, 2004), p. 2.

18 Christine Delphi, 'The Invention of French Feminism: An Essential Move', *Yale French Studies* 87 (2001), quoted in Ibid, pp. 6–7.

19 For more detail, see Gill Allwood and Khursheed Wadia, *Women and Politics in France 1958–2000* (London and New York: Routledge, 2000), pp. 192–212.

20 Ibid, pp. 215–18.

21 Quoted in Ibid, p. 209.

22 Foley, *Women in France*, p. 297 argues that it does.

23 Allwood and Wadia, *Women and Politics in France*, p. 229.

24 Gérard Noiriel, *The French Melting Pot: Immigration, Citizenship, and National Identity*. Geoffroy de Laforcade, trans. (Minneapolis: University of Minnesota Press, 1996). French title: *Le Creuset Français.*

25 For an example of the way it takes several generations, see Philippe Rygiel, *Destins immigrés: Cher, 1920–1980, trajectories d'immigrés d'Europe* (Besançon: Annales littéraires de l'Université de Franche Comte, 2001).

26 On the positive contributions of associations, see Nadia Kiwan, 'Managing Marginalisation: Young French-North Africans and Local Associations,' *Modern & Contemporary France* 13, 4 (November 2005), pp. 465–81; on the perceived threats of associations to France and the attempts to regulate them, see Claire Andrieu, Gilles Le Béguec and Danilelle Tartakowsky, eds, *Associations et champ politique: La loi de 1901 à l'épreuve du siècle* (Paris: Publication de la Sorbonne, 2001).

27 See Patrick Weil, *Qu'est-ce qu'un Français? Histoire de la nationalité française* (Paris: Grasset, 2002), pp. 37–61.

28 Paul Lawrence, 'Naturalisation, Ethnicity and National Identity in France between the Wars', *Immigrants and Minorities* 20, 3 (November 2001), pp. 1–24.

29 For a full discussion; see Timothy Baycroft, 'Ethnicity and the Revolutionary Tradition', in Timothy Baycroft and Mark Hewitson, eds, *What is Nation? Europe 1789–1914* (Oxford: OUP, 2006), pp. 28–41.

30 See J. Freedman, *Immigration and Insecurity in France* (Aldershot: Ashgate, 2004).

31 Alec G. Hargreaves, *Multi-Ethnic France: Immigration, Politics, Culture and Society*, 2nd Ed. (New York and London: Routledge, 2007), p. 147. For a full discussion of immigration and identity, see pp. 140–64 and Peggy Anne Phillips, *Republican France: Divided Loyalties* (Westport: Greenwood Press, 1993).

32 See Gerard Noiriel, *Immigration, antisemitisme et racisme en France (XIXe–XXe siècle): Discours publics, humiliations privées* (Paris: Fayard, 2007) for more on the development of political discourses of racism and antisemitism.

33 For an example of the call for affirmative action, outlining the debates involved, see Alain Renaut, *Egalité et discriminations: Un essai de philosophie politique appliquée a couleur des idées* (Paris: Seuil, 2007).

34 See, for example, S. Ireland and J-P. Proulx, eds, *Immigrant Narratives in Contemporary France* (Westport: Greenwood Press, 2001), and Mireille Rosello, *Postcolonial Hospitality: The Immigrant as Guest* (Stanford: Stanford University Press, 2001).

35 Jane Freedman and Carrie Tarr, 'Introduction', in Jane Freedman and Carrie Tarr, eds, *Women, Immigration and Identities in France* (Oxford: Berg, 2000), p. 2.
36 Quite a few recent works have begun to describe such complex representations of race in France across the centuries. See, for example, the excellent collection edited by Sue Peabody and Tyler Stovall, *The Colour of Liberty: Histories of Race in France* (Durham and London: Duke University Press, 2003), and in particular with reference to the topic discussed here, Dana S. Hale, 'French Images of Race on Product Trademarks during the Third Republic', pp. 131–46 and Leora Auslander and Thomas C. Holt, 'Sambo in Paris: Race and Racism in the Iconography of the Everyday', pp. 147–84. See also Mark McKinney, 'The Representation of Ethnic Minority Women in Comic Books', in Freedman and Tarr, *Women, Immigration and Identities*, pp. 85–102, Brett A. Berliner, *Ambivalent Desire: The Exotic Black Other in Jazz Age France* (Amherst and Boston: University of Massachusetts Press, 2002) and James A. Winders, 'Mobility and Cultural Identity: African Music and Musicians in Late-Twentieth-Century Paris', *French Historical Studies* 29, 3 (summer 2006), pp. 483–508.
37 See Chapter 5 for a full discussion of Weber's thesis.
38 For examples of regional studies, see Timothy Baycroft, *Culture, Identity and Nationalism: French Flanders in the Nineteenth and Twentieth Centuries* (The Royal Historical Society Studies in History Series. The Boydell Press, 2004); Caroline Ford, *Creating the Nation in Provincial France: Religion and Political Identity in Brittany* (Princeton: Princeton University Press, 1993); Peter Sahlins, *Boundaries. The Making of France and Spain in the Pyrenees* (Berkeley: University of California Press, 1989); and James R. Lehning, *Peasant and French: Cultural Contact in Rural France During the Nineteenth Century.* (Cambridge: CUP, 1995).
39 Anne-Marie Thiesse, 'Les deux identités de la France', *Modern & Contemporary France* 9, 1 (2001), pp. 9–18. In this article, Thiesse refers not to the traditional two Frances of church and republic, but to the two Frances of nation and region. For more on regionalism and its relationship to the republican nation, see Julian Wright, *The Regionalist Movement in France 1890–1914: Jean Charles-Brun and French Political Thought* (Oxford: OUP, 2003), and Stéphane Gerson, *The Pride of Place: Local Memories and Political Culture in Nineteenth-Century France* (Ithaca & London: Cornell University Press, 2003).
40 Anne-Marie Thiesse, *Ils Apprenaient la France: L'exaltation des régions dans le discours patriotique* (Paris: Editions de la Maison des sciences de l'homme, 1997).
41 See John Strachan, 'Romance, Religion and the Republic: Bruno's *Le Tour de la France par Deux Enfants*', *French History* 18, 1 (2004), pp. 96–118.
42 For more on the difference between assimilation and appropriation, see Baycroft, *Culture, Identity and Nationalism.*
43 Todd Shepard, *The Invention of Decolonisation: The Algerian War and the remaking of France* (Ithaca and London: Cornell University Press, 2006). See also Chapter 8.
44 Jill Forbes, 'Conclusion: French Cultural Studies in the Future', in Jill Forbes and Michael Kelly, eds, *French Cultural Studies: An Introduction* (Oxford: OUP, 1995), p. 293.

Conclusion

As this text has shown through an examination of national history, national experience and national identity, inventing the French nation has been a complex process of attaching symbolic significance to an entire host of cultural traits and practices, historical places, events, people and institutions. Over the two hundred plus years since the French Revolution of 1789, many 'Frances' have been invented, sometimes becoming widely recognised and the subject of general consensus, whilst at other times dwindling into obscurity or even rejected outright. French national images, ideas and myths have been in a state of perpetual reinterpretation and renewal, arising directly from the political context which has seen deep rivalry during quests for power within the French State. The gradual dominance of the republican vision of the French nation has meant that it was republican myths, symbols and images which predominate, integrating many others along the way. Much of the nation was mythologised through the deliberate, conscious policies of nation-building on the part of (mostly faceless) political elites, but always bound and influenced by the constraints of spontaneous reactions from the population.

The French nation has a long list of characteristics to define and identify it for its members. From the home of the Revolution with a long and glorious history, through its enlightened values and deep artistic and literary culture to its tolerance, revolutionary spirit, individualist republican universalism and a host of small cultural practices, the national mythology is extensive. In the period following the Second World War, many of the earlier conflicts surrounding the interpretation of the Revolution diminished in their contemporary relevance, only to be replaced by other debates over the nation's history and defining attributes. Belief in French 'exceptionalism' remained one of the most significant elements of French nationhood throughout the entire period under study – a specificity derived from historical and cultural interpretation, developed and intensified across the years with reference to all types of political, economic, social and cultural aspects of life. The existence of a French republican 'model' for organising society, as well as integrating and assimilating those outside or on the margins of the nation, is one of the most deeply held, enduring elements of French national identity. This model is the lens through which France's relationship to other nations, to its colonies, as well as to its own immigrants and minority groups has continually been understood right into the twenty-first century.

In the closing decades of the twentieth century and the early years of the twenty-first, both the creation of the European Union and the onslaught of globalisation have been perceived as potential threats to, if not the French nation itself, at least this special French way of doing things. De Gaulle was primarily opposed to British entry into the European Economic Community on the grounds that without them, it would be easier for France to dominate the agenda and set the model for how the Community, and later the Union, would function. With the enlargement of the Union, this threat became greater, and is certainly an important factor in the French rejection by referendum of the European Constitution. Similarly, globalisation, American economic and cultural imperialism and new waves of immigration are each in their own way perceived to be encroaching on the French way of doing things. In spite of the worries of nationalists, neither globalisation nor the strengthening of the European Union seem to be diminishing the emotional power or daily reality of the French nation in the twenty-first century. Perhaps de Gaulle was right when he said that 'la France ne passera pas' (France will not pass away).

Selected Further Reading

Agulhon, Maurice, *The French Republic 1879–1992*. Oxford: Basil Blackwell, 1993.

Aldrich, Robert, *Greater France: A History of French Overseas Expansion*. Basingstoke: Macmillan, 1996.

Alexander, Martin S., ed., *French History Since Napoleon*. London: Arnold, 1999.

Baker, Keith Michael, *Inventing the French Revolution: Essays on French Political Culture in the Eighteenth Century*. Cambridge: Cambridge University Press, 1990.

Baycroft, Timothy, *Culture, Identity and Nationalism: French Flanders in the Nineteenth and Twentieth Centuries*. Royal Historical Society New Studies in History. London: The Boydell Press, 2004.

Beale, Marjorie A., *The Modernist Enterprise: French Elites and the Threat of Modernity 1900–1940*. Stanford: Stanford University Press, 1999.

Beaune, Colette, *The Birth of an Ideology: Myths and Symbols of Nation in Late-Medieval France*. Trans. Susan Ross Huston. Berkeley: University of California Press, 1991.

Bell, David A., *The Cult of the Nation in France: Inventing Nationalism 1680–1800*. Cambridge MA: Harvard University Press, 2001.

Bernard, Philippe and Henri Dubief, *The Decline of the Third Republic*. Cambridge: Cambridge University Press, 1985.

Betts, Raymond F., *France and Decolonisation 1900–1960*. Basingstoke: Macmillan, 1991.

Blatt, Joel, ed., *The French Defeat of 1940: Reassessments*. Oxford: Berghahn, 1998.

Burrin, Philippe, *Living with Defeat: France under the German Occupation 1940–1944*. Trans. Janet Lloyd. London: Arnold, 1996.

Chafer, Tony and Amanda Sackur, eds, *Promoting the Colonial Idea: Propaganda and Visions of Empire in France*. Basingstoke: Palgrave, 2002.

Collingham, H. A. C., with R. S. Alexander, *The July Monarchy: A Political History of France 1830–1848*. London and New York: Longman, 1988.

Datta, Venita, *Birth of a National Icon: The Literary Avant-Garde and the Origins of the Intellectual in France*. Albany: State University of New York Press, 1999.

Drake, David, *Intellectuals and Politics in Post-War France*. Palgrave, 2002.

Evans, Martin, ed., *Empire and Culture: The French Experience, 1830–1940*. Basingstoke: Palgrave, 2004.

Fishman, Sarah, Laura Lee Downs, Ioannis Sinanoglou, Leonard V. Smith and Robert Zaretsky, eds, *France at War: Vichy and the Historians*. Oxford: Berg, 2000.

Flood, Christopher and Nick Hewlett, eds, *Currents in Contemporary French Intellectual Life*. Basingstoke: Macmillan, 2000.

Flynn, Gregory, ed., *Remaking the Hexagon: The New France in the New Europe*. Boulder, CA: Westview Press, 1995.

Foley, Susan K., *Women in France since 1789: The Meanings of Difference*. Basingstoke: Palgrave, 2004.

Ford, Caroline, *Creating the Nation in Provincial France: Religion and Political Identity in Brittany*. Princeton: Princeton University Press, 1993.

Freedman, Jane and Carrie Tarr, eds, *Women, Immigration and Identities in France*. Oxford: Berg, 2000.

Gerson, Stéphane, *The Pride of Place: Local Memories and Political Culture in Nineteenth-Century France*. Ithaca and London: Cornell University Press, 2003.

Gibson, Ralph, *A Social History of French Catholicism: 1789–1914*. London: Routledge, 1989.

Gildea, Robert, *France 1870–1914*, 2nd ed. Longman, 1996.

Gildea, Robert, *The Past in French History*. New Haven and London: Yale University Press, 1994.

Gluckstein, Donny, *The Paris Commune: A Revolution in Democracy*. London: Bookmarks, 2006.

Godin, Emmanuel and Tony Chafer, eds, *The French Exception*. New York and Oxford: Berghahn, 2005.

Golsan, Richard J., *Vichy's Afterlife: History and Counterhistory in Postwar France*. Lincoln and London: University of Nebraska Press, 2000.

Gosnell, Jonathan K., *The Politics of Frenchness in Colonial Algeria 1930–1954*. Rochester: University of Rochester Press, 2002.

Hargreaves, Alec G., *Multi-Ethnic France: Immigration, Politics, Culture and Society,* 2nd ed. New York and London: Routledge, 2007.

Harp, Stephen, *Learning to be Loyal: Primary Schooling as Nation Building in Alsace and Lorraine, 1850–1940*. DeKalb, Northern Illinois University Press, 1998.

Harrison, Carol E., *The Bourgeois Citizen in Nineteenth-Century France: Gender, Sociability and the Uses of Emulation*. Oxford: Oxford University Press, 1999.

Hazareesingh, Sudhir, *From Subject to Citizen: The Second Empire and the Emergence of Modern French Democracy*. Princeton: Princeton University Press, 1998.

Hazareesingh, Sudhir, *The Legend of Napoleon*. London: Granta, 2004.

Hewitt, Nicholas, ed., *The Cambridge Companion to Modern French Culture*. Cambridge: Cambridge University Press, 2003.

Hunt, Lynn, *Politics, Culture and Class in the French Revolution*. London: Methuen, 1986.

Jackson, Julian, *France: The Dark Years 1940–1944*. Oxford: Oxford University Press, 2001.

Jackson, Julian, *The Fall of France: The Nazi Invasion of 1940*. Oxford: Oxford University Press, 2003.

Jackson, Julian, *The Popular Front in France: Defending Democracy 1934–38*. Cambridge: Cambridge University Press, 1985.

Jenkins, Brian, *Nationalism in France: Class and Nation since 1789*. London and New York: Routledge, 1990.

Johnson, Martin P., *The Dreyfus Affair: Honour and Politics in the Belle Epoque*, Basingstoke: Macmillan, 1999.

Jones, Colin, *The Great Nation: France from Louis XIV to Napoleon.* London: Penguin, 2002.

Kedward, Rod, *La Vie en Bleu: France and the French since 1900.* London: Allen Lane, 2005.

Keegan, John, *The Battle for History: Re-Fighting World War Two.* London: Hutchinson, 1995.

Keiger, J. F. V., *France and the World since 1870.* London: Arnold, 2001.

Kidd, William and Siân Reynolds, eds, *Contemporary French Cultural Studies.* London: Arnold, 2000.

Koreman, Megan, *The Expectation of Justice: France 1944–1946.* Durham and London: Duke University Press, 1999.

Lacorne, Denis, Jacques Rupnik and Marie-France Toinet, eds, *The Rise and Fall of Anti-Americanism: A Century of French Perception.* Trans. G. Turner. Basingstoke: Macmillan, 1990.

Lacouture, Jean, *L'histoire de France en 100 tableaux.* Italie: Hazon, 1996.

Larkin, Maurice, *France since the Popular Front: Government and People 1936–1996.* Oxford: Clarendon, 1997.

Lebovics, Herman, *Bringing the Empire Back Home: France in the Global Age.* Durham and London: Duke University Press, 2004.

Macmillan, James F., *France and Women 1789–1914: Gender, Society and Politics.* London: Routledge, 2000.

Macmillan, James F., *Twentieth-Century France: Politics and Society 1898–1991.* London: Arnold, 1992.

Magraw, Roger, *France 1800–1914: A Social History.* Harlow: Longman, 2002.

Mayeur, J.-M. and M. Rebérioux, *The Third Republic from its Origins to the Great War 1871–1914.* Cambridge: Cambridge University Press, 1984.

Maza, Sarah, *The Myth of the French Bourgeoisie: An Essay on the Social Imaginary 1750–1850.* Cambridge, MA: Harvard University Press, 2003.

Miller, Paul B., *From Revolutionaries to Citizens: Antimilitarism in France 1870–1914.* Durham and London: Duke University Press, 2002.

Moran, Daniel and Arthur Waldron, eds, *The People in Arms: Military Myth and National Mobilisation since the French Revolution.* Cambridge: Cambridge University Press, 2003.

Mouré, Kenneth and Martin S. Alexander, eds, *Crisis and Renewal in France, 1918–1962*. New York and Oxford: Berghahn, 2002.

Mousnier, Roland, *Social Heirarchies: 1450 to the Present*. Trans. Peter Evans. London: Croom Helm, 1973.

Noiriel, Gérard, *The French Melting Pot: Immigration, Citizenship, and National Identity*. Trans. Geoffroy de Laforcade. Minneapolis: University of Minnesota Press, 1996.

Nora, Pierre, ed., *Les Lieux de Mémoire*, 3 vols. Paris: Quarto-Gallimard, 1997. Translated as *Realms of Memory*, 3 vols. Trans. Arthur Goldhammer. New York: Columbia University Press, 1996–1998.

Nossiter, Adam, *The Algeria Hotel: France, Memory and the Second World War*. London: Methuen, 2001.

Peabody, Sue and Tyler Stovall, eds, *The Colour of Liberty: Histories of Race in France*. Durham and London: Duke University Press, 2003.

Plessis, Alain, *The Rise and Fall of the Second Empire 1852–1871*. Cambridge: Cambridge University Press, 1985.

Phillips, Peggy Anne, *Republican France: Divided Loyalties*. Westport: Greenwood Press, 1993.

Popkin, Jeremy D., *A History of Modern France*, 3rd ed. Upper Saddle River: Pearson, 2006.

Price, Roger, *Napoleon III and the Second Empire*. London: Routledge, 1997.

Prost, Antoine, *Republican Identities in War and Peace: Representations of France in the 19th and 20th Centuries*. Trans. Jay Winter with Helen McPhail. Oxford: Berg, 2002.

Rearick, Charles, *Pleasures of the Belle Epoque: Entertainment and Festivity in Turn of the Century France*. London: Yale University Press, 1985.

Rémond, René, *The Right Wing in France From 1815 to de Gaulle*, 2nd ed. Trans. J. M. Laux. Philadelphia: University of Pennsylvania Press, 1969.

Reynolds, Siân, *France Between the Wars: Gender and Politics*. London and New York: Routledge, 1996.

Ross, Kristin, *Fast Cars, Clean Bodies: Decolonisation and the Reordering of French Culture*. Cambridge, MA: The MIT Press, 1995.

Ross, Kristin, *May '68 and its Afterlives*. Chicago and London: University of Chicago Press, 2002.

Rousso, Henry, *The Haunting Past: History, Memory and Justice in Contemporary France*. Trans. Ralph Schoolcraft. Philadelphia: University of Pennsylvania Press, 2002.

Rousso, Henry, *The Vichy Syndrome: History and Memory in France since 1944*. Trans. Arthur Goldhammer. Cambridge, MA: Harvard University Press, 1991.

Scott, Joan Wallach, *Only Paradoxes to Offer: French Feminists and the Rights of Man*. Cambridge, MA.: Harvard University Press, 1996.

Seidman, Michael, *The Imaginary Revolution: Parisian Students and Workers in 1968*. New York and Oxford: Berghahn, 2004.

Shafer, David A., *The Paris Commune*. Basingstoke: Palgrave, 2005.

Shepard, Todd, *The Invention of Decolonisation: The Algerian War and the Remaking of France*. Ithaca and London: Cornell University Press, 2006.

Smith, W. H. C., *Second Empire and Commune: France 1848–71*, Harlow: Longman, 1996.

Sowerwine, Charles, *France since 1870: Culture, Politics and Society*. Basingstoke: Palgrave, 2001.

Sternhall, Zeev, *Neither Right nor Left: Fascist Ideology in France*. Princeton: Princeton University Press, 1996.

Sweeney, Regina M., *Singing Our Way to Victory: French Cultural Politics and Music during the Great War*. Middletown: Wesleyan University Press, 2001.

Tombs, Robert, *France 1814–1914*. Longman, 1996.

Tombs, Robert, ed., *Nationhood and Nationalism in France From Boulangism to the Great War 1889–1918*. London: Harper Collins, 1991.

Tombs, Robert, *The Paris Commune, 1871*. London: Longman, 1999.

Ungar, Steven and Tom Conley, eds., *Identity Papers: Contested Nationhood in Twentieth-Century France*. Minneapolis: University of Minnesota Press, 1996.

Vinen, Richard, *France 1935–1970*, Basingstoke: Macmillan, 1996.

Weber, Eugen, *France: Fin-de-siècle*. Cambridge, MA: Belknap Press, 1986.

Weber, Eugen, *The Hollow Years: France in the 1930s*. London: Sinclair-Stevenson, 1995.

Weber, Eugen, *Peasants Into Frenchmen: The Modernisation of Rural France 1870–1914*. Stanford: Stanford University Press, 1976.

Zeldin, Theodore, *France 1848–1945*, 5 vols. Oxford: Oxford University Press, 1979–81.

Index